Concordance

During the height of the civil rights movement, Blacks were among the most liberal Americans. Since the 1970s, however, as Blacks have turned from activism to formal politics and gained increasing representation in national, state, and local government, they have moved closer to the political center.

In this new, updated edition, Katherine Tate studies the ways in which the nation's most prominent group of Black legislators has developed politically. Organized in 1971, the Congressional Black Caucus (CBC) set out to increase the influence of Black legislators. Indeed, over the past four decades, they have made progress toward the goal of becoming recognized players within Congress. And yet, Tate argues, their incorporation is transforming their policy preferences. Specifically, since the Clinton Administration, CBC members—the majority of whom are Democrats—have been less willing to oppose openly congressional party leaders and both Republican and Democratic presidents. Tate documents this transformation with a statistical analysis of black roll-call votes, using the important Poole-Rosenthal scores from 1977 to 2019. While growing partisanship has affected Congress as a whole, not just minority caucuses, Tate warns incorporation may mute the independent voice of Black political leaders.

Katherine Tate is Professor of Political Science at Brown University.

THE POLITICS OF RACE AND ETHNICITY

Series Editors Rodney E. Hero, Arizona State University
Katherine Tate, Brown University

Politics of Race and Ethnicity is premised on the view that understanding race and ethnicity is integral to a fuller, more complete understanding of the American political system. The goal is to provide the scholarly community at all levels with accessible texts that will introduce them to, and stimulate their thinking on, fundamental questions in this field. We are interested in books that creatively examine the meaning of American democracy for racial and ethnic groups and, conversely, what racial and ethnic groups mean and have meant for American democracy.

Concordance

---

*Black Lawmaking in
the U.S. Congress
from Carter to Obama*

New Edition,
With New Preface and Afterword

Katherine Tate

University of Michigan Press
Ann Arbor

New edition with a new preface and afterword published 2020

For questions or permissions, please contact um.press.perms@umich.edu

Published in the United States of America by the
University of Michigan Press
Printed and bound by CPI Group (UK) Ltd, Croydon, CR0 4YY

First published August 2020

A CIP catalog record for this book is available from the British Library.

Library of Congress Cataloging-in-Publication Data applied for.

New edition, with new preface and afterword:

ISBN 978-0-472-03834-3 (pbk.)
ISBN 978-0-472-12809-9 (ebook)

Cover: Congressional Black Caucus Annual Legislative Conference Veterans
Braintrust (2017), courtesy American Federation of Government Employees
(AFGE) (CC BY 2.0).

Preface and Acknowledgments

I witnessed much of the politics I describe in this book growing up in Elkhart, Indiana. Elkhart was a typical blue-collar city that once boasted of a musical instrument factory but whose main factories now build recreational vehicles (RVs) or parts in the manufactured housing market or convert vans for business or luxury, personal use. The city is known as the "RV Capital of the World." I had a driver's license as a high school student and experienced the long lines for gas during the Carter presidency. One family friend, an African American blue-collar worker, shocked us when he abruptly said he was voting for Ronald Reagan, the Republican, in the 1980 presidential election. I left the region after college and graduate school. While seeking the votes of workers in an industry heavily dependent upon the performance of the economy, President Obama made two campaign stops to Elkhart. South Bend, right next door to Elkhart, is the home of Mayor Pete Buttigieg, an early candidate for the 2020 Democratic presidential nomination.

I want to thank the two anonymous reviewers and Professor Jane Mansbridge at Harvard for their constructive reading of the book manuscript. The data collection was partially funded by grants from the Dirksen Congressional Foundation and the University of California, Irvine's Center for the Study of Democracy, then directed by Professor Russell Dalton. The claims made in this book are my own, but I also want to thank political scientists Keith Poole and Howard Rosenthal for making their important NOMINATE data, used throughout this book, publicly available. The recent data reviewed in the new afterword to this paperback edition was compiled by an undergraduate research assistant, Mary Arend, with her work funded by Brown University's Presidential Scholars Program. This program, which recruits low- and middle-income students to research early in their undergraduate experience, is managed by Professor Emily Oster. Last but not least, I thank Elizabeth Demers, Senior Acquisitions Editor, for the reissuing this book in paperback and the University of Michigan Press staff for their work on the production of this book.

Contents

Digital materials related to this title can be found on the Fulcrum platform via the following citable URL: https://doi.org/10.3998/mpub.3923464

CHAPTER I

Black Policymakers and a Theory of Concordance

Concordance: a state or condition of agreement or harmony

With the election of Barack Obama as the first African American president of the United States in 2008, and with Democrats as majorities in both houses in the 111th Congress, African Americans achieved their highest levels of membership in the dominant governing coalition to date—a phenomenon known as "minority political incorporation" (Browning, Marshall, and Tabb 1984). By 2009, there were 41 Black members of the U.S. Congress, including one U.S. senator and the nonvoting delegate for the District of Columbia.

This book tells the story of the evolution of those Black members from outsiders to the system and radical critics of it to the position of insiders, with more mainstream political views. Radical policies are those that lie outside of the Left-Right continuum, because they are extreme, or because they defy conventional understandings of what constitute government rights and benefits. The book shows how this evolution from radicalism to mainstream liberalism stemmed from two parallel trajectories. On the one side, the Black politicians became more moderate in their views and took on more central leadership positions in the Democratic Party. On the other side, the Democratic Party itself became more liberal on racial issues and adopted a number of policy stances that benefited Black citizens. I call this process "concordance." The result is that Black lawmakers at the national level are more likely to vote with the Democratic majority than they ever have in the past, a process that generates both material and symbolic benefits for Black Americans. At the same time, the task of radical critique must now fall, by and large, to extragovernmental movements and organizations.

The Congressional Black Caucus (CBC), whose evolution is the subject of this book, has been the subject of considerable controversy. One view holds that, given the institutional features of the U.S. government, its bicameral congress, two-party system, and majoritarian features, Black legislators are likely to play primarily a symbolic role in government. As a small numerical minority, they lack the power to change anything significant in Washington. Their racial agendas are often politically unpopular and the laws they support are often too liberal for the public, so they are unlikely to gain majority support on their central issues. Moreover, as legislators who have a strong ideologically driven agenda, they are loath to engage in compromise, a necessary ingredient in national policymaking. For all these reasons, Black lawmakers are likely to make their mark primarily as radical voices in an institution dominated by conservative interests. Because they are so committed to their ideologies, they are not likely to become active policymakers.

The second view points out that Black lawmakers often blend their radicalism with political compromise to craft legislation. The articulation of Black racial interests and the broadening of a national agenda to include those interests are vital parts of their bargaining strategy, but the Black members of Congress do not stay with words alone. They vote as a bloc often to leverage their influence over policy outputs in government. Most of them also acknowledge that compromise is a political necessity in their roles as liberal activists. The balance is sometimes tricky. Ronald V. Dellums, for example, wrote in his congressional memoir: "Obviously, compromise is almost always inevitable in the legislative process." Nevertheless, he added, "I took the position that it would always be important that progressives refrain from yielding to the temptation to strike these deals prematurely" (2000, 70). Black members often bloc vote in opposition and later compromise as part of their bargaining efforts. In this way, they are active policymakers in the U.S. Congress, taking on a role far larger than the mere articulation of Black policy interests.

In this book I argue that the Congressional Black Caucus has evolved from the first position to the second. Past researchers on the legislative effectiveness of Blacks have promoted both views. One important study contends that the Congressional Black Caucus was unable to deliver genuine policy change for Blacks. Robert Singh (1998) argues that because of the members of the Caucus had few votes, the Democrats rarely needed them. Further, he adds, the CBC was too ideologically rigid to bargain with leadership effectively: "The CBC possessed fewer than thirty members from 1971 to 1992. Such numbers would have proven a formidable bloc in the Senate but constituted a relatively minor portion of the House. Even so, a bloc of twenty or so legislators could constitute a force in the House, provided that it could bargain effectively. In the CBC's case, however, its ideological immoderation and ambitious objectives undermined and consistently limited its influence" (Singh 1998, 153). By contrast, David Canon (1995), writing at about the same time, argues that the CBC was influential as a cohesive set of bloc voters in the House, and that CBC members' voting behavior saved legislation that Democrats cared about in some floor votes.

Since these studies, Black House legislators have become more moderate and less cohesive than they once were, especially with the addition of many new Black members from the South elected in 1992 (Canon 1999; Champagne and Rieselbach 1995; see Whitby 2007 for a review). Yet even in the early years of more radical ideology and bloc voting Black legislators were able to win landmark legislation in spite of conservative opposition—including the 1982 extension of the Voting Rights Act, the 1983 Martin Luther King holiday, U.S. sanctions against South Africa, and the 1991 Civil Rights Act. On the other hand, they aggressively pursued but won only a very weak version of the Humphrey-Hawkins jobs creation legislation in 1978. They lost their efforts to reshape the crime bill and welfare reform bill under President Clinton. More recently, Black legislators backed and helped pass President Obama's landmark health reform bill and won a law reducing drug sentencing disparities but have not succeeded in other efforts, such as major prison reform.

In this book, I analyze a measure calculated from the roll-call votes of Congressional Black Caucus members that shows how liberal or conservative they are on economic policies and government spending programs from 1977 to 2010. Like other congressional caucuses, membership is voluntary, leadership is elected, organizational sanctions are limited, and members are free to vote their own interest. Members cannot speak for the caucus unless authorized but they are free to do and say anything publicly and on the House floor. All Black members of Congress have an invitation to join, but a few have elected not to participate for reasons of ideology and partisanship, such as former member J. C. Watts (R-OK) and Tim Scott (R-SC), now a senator.

I find that members of the Congressional Black Caucus have to some degree become more moderate, compared to the majority, on these policies. I also examine the floor votes of Black members in the House from the 1977 to 2010 to see how often they voted with the majority of House members on major legislation, and find that they are now voting more often with the majority.

I also specifically examine the role of Black legislators in congressional budgetary politics. Congress adopts a federal budget to set the spending priorities of this nation. Since 1981, the CBC has put forward an "alternative budget" that has reflected their priorities as Black legislators representing the interests of Black Americans. In garnering votes for the alternative budget the CBC has managed to maintain exceptional solidarity over the decades. The votes of the members of the Caucus for their budget have been unanimous in some years and in other years have seen the defection of only one member. Bill Gray (D-PA), for example, served as chair of the House Budget Committee from 1985 to 1988. Because he could not see himself as voting against his own committee, he simply voted "present" on the CBC budget in those years. Sanford Bishop (D-GA) saw himself as a "moderate" and thus twice failed to support the CBC's budget alternative shortly after the Republican takeover of the House of Representatives in 1995. He has, however, since supported the CBC budget under the George W. Bush and the Obama administrations. Finally, Artur Davis (D-AL) voted "present" in 2009 on the CBC alternative budget when, as a representative, he was also running for governor of his state and did not want to appear too radical in that race.

Despite this relative homogeneity in support for the alternative budget, however, small but important divisions have cropped up among CBC members in their votes for two other alternative budgets in the House, put forward respectively by the fiscally conservative Democrats ("Blue Dogs") and the Progressive Caucus of Democrats under both Bush and Obama. These divisions reflect the major changes I report in Black legislative behavior over the thirty-three year period I cover. The move from more radically Left positions to more moderate ones and the move to vote more frequently with the House majority when their party is in power has occurred independently of the change in membership brought about by the election of new Black moderates from the South, such as Mike Espy (D-MS) and Artur Davis (D-AL). My analysis finds no support for the claim that the decline in Black liberal ideology in the House occurred only through the steady chipping away of the size of Black majorities in Black-led districts through redistricting.

Black legislative behavior, I theorize, has changed as a result of their political incorporation. Their gradual incorporation in the system has made Black legislative leaders less radical and more pragmatic. They are less likely to challenge party and Democratic presidential leadership through ideological debate. They are also less likely to vote as a united liberal faction on the floor against party and presidential leadership. Yet incorporation is a two-sided, dynamic process. As Blacks have entered into politics to change the policies of this nation, they have themselves undergone change as legislators. At the same time, minority political incorporation has helped make the Democratic Party more liberal. Through this process of mutual adaptation, or concordance, Black House members have shifted their politics closer to the mainstream as their numbers have increased and as they have advanced in party and legislative leadership roles. At the same time, through their numerical increase and their leadership roles they have had an increasing influence on the Democratic Party. In general, we may expect concordance, in which minorities and their party move closer together, in periods of minority political incorporation. That incorporation in turn facilitates party unity even in periods of divided government. Thus, the two major findings of this book are congruent. First, the CBC has become less radical because of incorporation. Second, there is greater rapprochement, or "concordance," between Black legislators and the Democratic Party in national politics.

This analysis of Black legislative behavior relies not only on Black House members' votes on legislation from 1977 to 2010 but also on their level of support for six presidents and for the Democratic Party, as well as their willingness to vote with the House majority over time, using data from the *Congressional Quarterly Almanac*. The analysis also assesses major newspaper coverage of the Congressional Black Caucus during this period.

The theory of concordance presents a new, theoretical account of the dynamic relationship between minority incorporation and legislative behavior. Conceptualized as a two-sided process, incorporation begins with challenges to the system to win favorable outcomes by members of the minority group, and then leads to the modification of minority legislative behavior as minorities gain power and adapt to the system.

Political Incorporation Theories, Empowerment, and Blacks in the U.S. Congress

Whenever the numbers of a minority group in elective office increase those minorities are likely to gain more influence over policy. Minority political incorporation, defined as minorities having membership in the dominant governing coalition (chiefly in city councils, county boards or commissions, or legislatures having Democratic majorities), has been shown to be strongly linked to policy responsiveness. One award-winning study of ten cities, for example, shows that cities with elected minorities who were part of the Democratic establishment adopted citizen police review boards and hired more minority municipal employees (Browning, Marshall, and Tabb 1984). Many other studies have shown that descriptive representation (the extent to which ethnic minorities or women are present in government) and incorporation (their influence in government) promote minority policy responsiveness (Meier and Stewart 1991; Meier et al. 2005; Haynie 2001; Ochs 2011; Preuhs 2006, 2007; see also Eisinger 1982). Minority political incorporation should therefore lead to the translation of political power into greater economic and social gains for minority groups, for example, in reducing racial and ethnic disparities in health, housing, crime, education, wealth, and poverty. Minority incorporation, thus, leads to minority empowerment.

Despite impressive data showing policy gains for minorities through minority office-holding and incorporation, however, Black empowerment theories have attracted a small set of critics. Minority officeholders cannot greatly transform the lives of minority citizens by, for example, eliminating racial and ethnic disparities. The political process by design is inherently too conservative for minority groups to achieve great change through their politics. The dominant group will almost always "use the political system to maintain and enhance their power and status" (Hero 1992, 204). A legacy of the formal and informal exclusion of Blacks and Latinos from politics also continues to constrain their influence (Hero 1992). White majorities often oppose minority redistributive policy demands by framing such policies as inconsistent with American values (Kinder and Sanders 1996). On the city level, the fiscal limits of local governments cannot support redistributive policies (Peterson 1981). Political processes are often dominated by conservative business interests, which minority mayors must accommodate (Stone 1989). Thus, while minority incorporation has produced some policy changes in cities, urban fiscal policies have not been altered following minority incorporation (Pelissero, Holian, and Tomaka 2000).

Institutional Barriers

The criticism that minority empowerment is limited by procedural and electoral processes applies with even greater force to the U.S. Congress. In general, there are three broad arguments about the limited policy outcomes for racial and ethnic minorities in the U.S. Congress. The U.S.

governmental system was designed to quell radical influences through the separation of powers. As a consequence, Blacks as a radical ideological minority cannot wield much influence. In addition, in any majority-rule polity, political minorities cannot by definition win through majority rule. Indeed, a 12 percent minority may be outvoted on every one of its important issues. For this reason, many scholars consider permanent minorities a failure in the democratic process (see Safford's 1995 discussion of John C. Calhoun and Lani Guinier; see also Walzer 1970). The U.S. system of single-member plurality "winner take all" districts exacerbates the problem, creating situations where minorities can end up without even the proportion in the legislature that they have in the population. Many scholars have proposed solutions such as proportional representation (as in some U.S. cities) or cumulative voting (as in Illinois for several years) to give minorities fairer representation (e.g., Guinier 1994), but such changes in the national electoral system are unlikely.

As for the presidency, some scholars believe that American Black legislators are particularly disadvantaged by a presidential system as opposed to a parliamentary one (Singh 1998). Although presidents play an important role in policymaking, they cannot dissolve Congress to strengthen their leadership as they could do in a parliamentary system. Instead, American presidents must work with the party in control. Even when their party is in the majority, the political agendas of African American legislators can be ignored. Franklin Delano Roosevelt, for example, refused to give his support to any of the antilynching legislation proposed in Congress during his presidency, even as Blacks became an important part of the Democratic Party's constituency and that party was firmly in control of Congress.

Although modern presidents have become more powerful legislative actors than the framers of the U.S. Congress intended (Beckmann 2010), they are nevertheless more reactive than proactive. Even today, minorities cannot count on American presidents to provide important leadership in race relations. Wilbur C. Rich's (2007) study of the American presidency and race relations contends that presidents represent the state more than they reflect the pressure politics of the nation; in representing the state, American presidents have played a major role in defending mechanisms that maintain the racial status quo. The civil rights movement was successful in plunging several presidents into racial turmoil, leading to passage of landmark civil rights legislation and new civil rights agencies, but today presidents protect themselves from minority criticism by appointing Blacks and other minorities to high-profile jobs, which, Rich writes, "gives blacks a feeling of incorporation into the [Democratic] party" (2007, 247).

The Republicans copy these tactics, bringing high-profile Black leaders to the White House. For Rich, these appointments represent gestures more than real empowerment.

The particular bicameral system adopted in the U.S. is particularly conservative. The Senate is one of the most undemocratic features of the American political system. It was designed to be a slow-moving, politically moderate chamber meant to cool the "hot tea" served by the faster and more politically responsive House. Although some contend that the two chambers are not very different in style, the Senate's supermajoritarian features constrain the politics of those on ideological extremes (Binder 2003; Brady and Volden 2006). It is well known that before 1965, civil rights legislation was blocked by the filibuster in the Senate. In 1975, the Senate reduced the number of votes necessary for cloture from two-thirds to three-fifths, but despite (and some say because of) this change, the new partisan warfare that has emerged in Congress has led senators to engage in even more obstructive tactics since the 1970s (Schickler 2001; Sinclair 2006). Minority legislation is greatly disadvantaged in this environment. In addition, only a handful of Blacks have served in the nation's upper chamber. The allocation of two seats to each state has given minorities significantly less political representation than Whites (Lee and Oppenheimer 1999).

Historically, slave-owning interests seeking the continued subjugation of Blacks greatly influenced the original design of America's political system. The counting of slaves as three-fifths of a person for creating seats in the House of Representatives and delegates in the Electoral College for a long time bluntly augmented the power of slave owners in the U.S. government. According to historian Garry Wills (2003), the three-fifths rule gave the South one-third more seats than their free population warranted. Ten of the fifteen American presidents before the Civil War were slave owners. Other provisions in the original U.S. Constitution protected the slave trade and slaves as property in free states (Tate, Lyles, and Barker 2007). For many years power reserved to the states under the U.S. Constitution's Tenth Amendment was used against minorities seeking civil and voting rights protections from the federal government under the Fourteenth Amendment. Other scholars contend that federalism has harmed the interests of Blacks especially (Miller 2008).

The times have changed, haven't they? On civil rights, studies report that southern U.S. senators have grown more liberal as a consequence of Black political mobilization since the 1960s (Hood, Kidd, and Morris 1999, 2001). Southern House members are also more liberal than a generation ago (Whitby and Gilliam 1991). However, the Senate remains particularly resistant to change. One recent study found that Black representation in the state's electorate generally had no influence on the voting behavior of U.S. senators from 1988 to 2004. Another recent study based on 2000 and 2004 data found that Whites are more likely than Blacks and Latinos to have their interests represented in the U.S. Congress (Griffin and Newman 2008).

Many scholars have established that Black constituents receive better policy outcomes when Black legislators represent them (Grose 2011; Canon 1999; Minta 2011; Tate 2003; Whitby 1997). Yet Blacks remain a small minority of the population of the United States as a whole, and many features of the presidency, the Senate, and the Constitution place further obstacles in the way of Black influence in the policymaking process. African American legislators have found it difficult to win support for their political concerns, whether they compromise or not.

Party Politics

The two-party system, built by the U.S. winner-take-all electoral system, also has negative consequences for the policy representation of African American interests. Paul Frymer (1999) contends that racial issues have been suppressed by both parties who compete for the median *White* voter. He writes that the Democratic Party, which has consistently represented Blacks since President Lyndon Johnson's 1964 election, has periods of "intense inner turmoil" over electoral defeats, which he attributes to its advocacy of Black concerns (1999, 44).

Some contend that Frymer's arguments are less compelling in light of Barack Obama's 2008 election, making him head of the national Democratic Party. The party has become more responsive to Black voters, in short. There is empirical evidence to support this claim. Centrist Democrats have increasingly supported their party's liberal policy efforts, but the liberalization of the Democratic Party should not be confused with *racial* liberalism. The question of whether the party has made moderate policies more acceptable to Blacks through minority leadership or has aggressively pursued more liberal ones merits further discussion. President Clinton's bipartisan agenda was more successful than his liberal one under divided government. So the Democratic Party continues to evade rather than respond to the racial concerns of Blacks in order to appease moderate White voters. In spite of the new and stronger presence of liberal Blacks in the party, Democrats still court the center vote. Thus, while the Democrats may be a more liberal party than it once was, it will still refuse to support a *racial agenda* pursued by African Americans in spite of its new racial diversity. President Obama has still given conservative speeches chastising Blacks for failing to take greater responsibility for their group's problems. Critics charge that his administration has failed to make the economic empowerment of African Americans a national priority. Thus, radical ideas must be expressed in the nongovernmental realm, since mainstream parties will not do so.

The Problem of Racism

Lani Guinier (1994) contends that when racial divisions are strong, White majorities shun minority legislators and their agendas. "When [Adam Clayton] Powell was sworn in [in 1945]," writes historian Maurine Christopher, "Mississippi's John Rankin refused to sit beside him" (1971, 198). Rankin was one of the southern members of Congress who still referred to Blacks as "niggers" in floor speeches (Hamilton 1991). Powell was only one of two Black members of Congress at the time. When he arrived, the congressional press room, barbershop, and dining rooms were all segregated. Later, when federal law finally ended segregation in public facilities in 1964, racially biased distribution of policymaking authority in Congress continued the tradition. In the Democratic Party, the "committee on committees" has a central role in making committee assignments, routinely denying over 40 percent of freshman their desired assignments. Black lawmakers seem to have had even less power than others in this process. Shirley Chisholm (D-NY) was assigned initially to the Committee on Agriculture even over her protest that there were "no trees in Brooklyn" (1998, 79–80). She was then placed on Veterans Affairs. Ron Dellums (D-CA) argued with conservative White leadership for a place on the Armed Services Committee in 1974. While Charles Rangel and Harold Ford Sr. were placed on the House's powerful Ways and Means Committee in the mid-1970s, two other Blacks were denied places on the House Budget Committee in the 1980s. One study established that, as late as 1996, Black Democratic members of House generally held fewer seats on prestigious committees than White Democrats. Even Black freshmen Democrats received fewer prestigious assignments than White freshman Democrats (Tate 2003, 75–79; see also Canon 1999).

Minority females seem to face double discrimination. Mary Hawkesworth (2003) finds that minority female legislators were slighted and systematically shut out of the House deliberations over welfare reform legislation during the 103rd and 104th Congress. While White members circulated stereotypes about welfare recipients (Hawkesworth 2003, 545), all of the women of color, including Republican Ileana Ros-Lehtinen, voted against welfare reform in the 104th Congress (Garcia Bedolla, Tate, and Wong 2005). The nation's first Black female Senator, Carol Moseley Braun (D-IL), recalled an incident during her first year in office where racially conservative Senator Jesse Helms (R-NC) started to sing lines from "Dixie" to her in the elevator. He told Senator Orrin Hatch (R-UT), who was also present, that he was going to sing the lines until Moseley Braun started to cry (Lee 1993).

Many of these incidents are relatively recent. The Senate forced Republican Majority Leader Trent Lott to resign in 2002 after he made a statement, at a celebration for Senator Strom Thurmond, wishing that Thurmond's pro-segregationist party had won the 1948 presidential election. Thurmond had switched parties over civil rights and never basically recanted his early political views favoring segregation. Lott himself had a record of racial conservatism, having voted against making Martin Luther King's birthday a national holiday, for example, as a congressman from Mississippi. The newspapers reported with less public heat Democratic Majority Leader Harry Reid's comments about Senator Barack Obama during the 2008 presidential campaign that he was "light-skinned," "with no Negro dialect, unless he wanted to have one." Why Reid chose to use the "antiquated term Negro," writes McIlwain and Caliendo, "is anyone's guess" (2011, 220), but it might have served as a soft reminder by Senator Reid to his audience about how times have changed for Blacks.

Blacks face not only the sometimes subtle denigration of their leaders but also whatever lingering racism remains among the American public. Surveys show great declines in expressed racism but continuing forms of more subtle racism, as in, for example, the belief that Blacks have a lesser commitment to the work ethic (Kinder and Sears 1981; Tesler and Sears 2010; Bobo 1983). Conservatives have denounced the articulation of a race-conscious agenda as "reverse racism" and have sought to dismantle Black political gains through a countermovement that includes themes of American exceptionalism (a belief in the inherent correctness of past and current American policies), neoconservatism (broad claims that U.S. social policies have failed), and morality politics (the claim that liberal—but not conservative—social engineering by the government is always wrong) (Walters 2003).

Even liberal presidents trim their sails on racial subjects. Although President Clinton created a presidential commission in 1997 to advance a national dialogue on America's racial problems, he also, in order to win passage of his 1994 crime bill, refused to support the CBC's efforts to make race statistics a part of the sentencing phase. Furthermore, neither President Bush nor President Obama wanted the United States to participate in the 2004 and 2009 United Nations conferences on racism since the conference considered or approved resolutions that included language also denouncing Israel as racist.

Incorporation: A Two-Sided Process

The institutional constraints, two-party politics, and lingering racism just described explain why Black legislators cannot be expected to deliver many significant policies that develop from a pro-Black ideological agenda. What can they do, then? We know from other studies that minorities can win some responsive policies from the government when the minority legislators join the dominant governing coalitions. This study, however, shows that minority political incorporation is a two-sided process, with both the legislators and the dominant party undergoing change.

On the one side, primarily through replacement and accommodation, Black legislators in the House of Representatives have become more moderate. Black citizens may be disappointed in the results that they get from the expanding numbers of Black political leaders because the institutions in which they work shape the behavior of these political elites just as institutions shape the behavior of all elites. Parties offer inducements to members in exchange for support for collective goals (Aldrich 2011; Cox and McCubbins 2007). Although minority members may have pursued unconventional methods to win their elections, once elected they are likely to adopt the goals of their larger collective. Thus, a dialectic emerges between new elites and established institutions.

Martin Shefter (1994) describes in this way a similar dialectical process in the history of political incorporation in American cities. The most radical Black leaders in New York City lacked ties to the regular party organizations, and the party itself attempted to purge its most radical leaders. In 1956, for example, Congressman Adam Clayton Powell, a Democrat from New York, took the radical stand of endorsing Republican president Dwight Eisenhower for a second term in 1956 on the grounds that the Democratic Party's record on civil rights was too weak (Shefter 1994, 229). The Democratic Party, in response, sought to limit Powell's influence by promoting challenges to him in primary elections. (Ultimately the U.S. Congress took the issue out of the party's hands by voting to expel Powell in 1967 on charges of corruption. Two years later, he won a U.S. Supreme Court ruling that his expulsion was unconstitutional, and returned to Congress, though stripped of his seniority. In 1970, Charles B. Rangel, who had the backing of many powerful people in the party, defeated Powell in the Democratic primary.)

By contrast, the relatively moderate Black leaders tend to be closely linked with their parties, as was William Dawson, the racially moderate Chicago member of Congress who served concurrently in the House with Powell. David T. Canon finds some evidence that racial moderates are more likely to serve in party leadership positions than Black ideological radicals, whom he calls traditionalists (1999, 187). Black legislators have also become more moderate over time because of personal factors, such as generational membership, religion, and military service (Rocca, Sanchez and Nikora 2009). Data from the 101st to 108th Congresses show convincingly that in the House older Blacks are further on the traditional left than younger Blacks.

Some replacement of radicals may occur through elections. About half of Black House incumbents are challenged in their primaries (Tate 2003, 58). Some case study data suggest that moderate Blacks will go farther in the Democratic Party than traditionally more radical candidates. For example, two Black moderate political leaders who challenged traditionally radical Black House representatives in their primaries and won then went on swiftly later, with Democratic Party backing, to run for the U.S. Senate. In Georgia the media attacked Cynthia McKinney, who was elected in the surge of new Black House members in 1992, as too radical to represent the Whites in her district because of her trenchant opposition to the Bush administration. In 2002 Denise L. Majette, an African American state judge, challenged McKinney and defeated her in the Democratic primary. Majette then chose to run for the U.S. Senate in 2004 after serving one term in the House. She lost her senate bid. McKinney won back her seat in the 2004 open-seat contest, but lost the next election to Hank Johnson, a Black county elected official with less racially oriented views.

The most famous case is of Barack Obama, who failed, while a state legislator, to unseat U.S. House representative Bobby L. Rush, who in addition to his Student Nonviolent Coordinating Committee membership boasts in his congressional biography of being a 1968 cofounder of the Illinois Black Panther Party. Rush was recently reelected in 2008 to the 111th Congress. Obama, however, then successfully ran for the U.S. Senate in 2004. The ability to mount a U.S. Senate bid requires millions of dollars as well as significant party support. It also requires a majority of voters in an electorate that is never majority Black. Thus, new Black elected leaders with their eyes on advancement to the Senate will more than likely be closer ideologically to the Democratic Party in policy leadership than to traditional Black elected officials because they will be thinking of the political opportunities later to run in a statewide election.

Current incorporation theories often fail to acknowledge these differences in strategic visions, the effects on candidate selection of the opportunity structure, and the effects of the arsenal of rules and procedures that parties use to increase their power in governing bodies. The U.S. Congress has complex rules, procedures, and norms. Recent reforms of the rules and procedures, and the ensuing changes in norms have increased the influence of parties in the House (Rohde 1991; Sinclair 1983). Parties provide committee assignments for members and select leaders, such as committee chairs, who support their goals. They also provide opportunities, goods, and exchanges such as logrolls that otherwise are not available (Smith 2007). Presidents, as heads of the national party, also use their authority to influence members of Congress (Beckmann 2010). This exercise of power affects members' behavior, as it is intended to do.

For all the structural reasons just listed, incorporation in the political system should, over time, produce growing political moderation among minority legislators. Because American political parties operate under a winner-take-all election system, they will aim at the median voter unless their more extreme donors and party activists intervene. This aim at the median voter usually serves as a moderating force, undermining any radical policy agenda. New groups also find that they need to accommodate the policy interests of the dominant governing party coalition in order to advance and become more effective legislators. As they advance in the political system, they enter centralized leadership roles where the collective fate of the party is as important as Blacks' efforts to increase their share of seats. Even when an opposition party is in power, as with the Republican ascendancy following the defeat of President Jimmy Carter, Black lawmakers found they had to increase their support for more conservative policies because only such policies could pass.

Writing in the aftermath of the Socialist Party's decisive support of German imperialism, Robert Michels (1999) insisted that political parties have both oligarchical and conservative tendencies. Over time, they will generally sacrifice their radicalism to advance political objectives in the real world. Their leaders will also seek more powerful leadership roles and turn toward professionalism in order to improve the direction of their organization's affairs. So too in the United States where even relatively radical

Blacks were able to advance within the Democratic Party and as they did so they became more moderate. What Michels did not realize, however, was that the entry of these formerly radical leaders can itself change the party over time. In the case of the United States, as more Black representatives entered its leadership ranks, the Democratic Party became more liberal. In turn, these changes made radical Black lawmakers less likely to dissent and more likely to support both the Democratic presidential leadership and the House voting majority. The two trends were thus mutually reinforcing.

In short, incorporation is a dynamic, contested process between radicals and moderates. First, minorities are likely to use their newly acquired power and authority to implement policies in ways that radically challenge leadership. They are representing relatively disenfranchised groups who respond to radical ideas and see themselves as challenging the status quo. These new minorities see themselves as outsiders seeking inclusion to make radical changes. However, these newcomers are influenced by the political process as much as they seek to influence outcomes. As theorized by Browning, Marshall, and Tabb (1984), Black leaders will have increasingly influential roles in Democratic policymaking as their numbers expand, but their effectiveness will always be limited by the institutional constraints of the political system. Black lawmakers will never be able to win radical outcomes without the backing of extraelectoral forces, such as protest, legal rulings, and world events. Unlike Browning, Marshall, and Tabb, I argue that Black lawmakers will tend to become less radical as they gain more power.

The CBC and a Theory of Concordance

Until now, much of the literature on Black members of Congress has taken a somewhat static approach, sometimes presenting these legislators as simply radical and ineffective, sometimes as strong players in the game of American politics. This analysis offers a more dynamic understanding of the political behavior of Black legislators. It shows how Black legislators have incentives to become less radical, in the sense of being less likely to challenge party and Democratic presidential leadership through racially ideological debate and voting against the party majority.

Part of this change comes through accommodation to the voters in a district. The majority of voters today are White, and at any given time they are likely to see radical racial ideology and the policies that flow from it as inconsistent with mainstream American values. Even civil rights protection for Blacks was historically considered too radical because it required new, "unconstitutional" authority from the federal government. (Williams 2003; Katznelson 2005). Today, civil rights protection is less controversial, but special programs for Blacks are still considered radical, and sometimes both unconstitutional and "unfair."

On the larger liberal-conservative dimension, most Black people benefit much more from larger liberal policies that increase employment, raise the minimum wage and earned income tax credits, and provide health, schooling, and childcare for the poor, but the liberal social policies that benefit minorities are also *racially* contested. To gain majorities among White voters, Black lawmakers must avoid focusing on the racial consequences of either liberal or conservative social policies. They will often find that they can win support for Black liberal interests only if they limit their overt quest for racial goals. As they link the fortunes of Black citizens more and more with a larger liberal agenda, Black lawmakers are forced to move away from radical tactics, in particular the tactic of voting as a united racial faction in defiance of party and presidential leadership.

The theory of concordance advanced here explains how the political environment has changed in Washington for Black legislators. The first half of the theory argues that Black lawmakers have become more moderate, and I have data to show this transformation of Black legislative behavior here. The second half of the theory argues that Black political incorporation has made the Democratic Party more responsive to Black interests; this empirical study is earmarked for another book. The party has liberalized, but congressional scholars to date have not credited minority incorporation as the major reason for this. Here I theorize that it is part of the reason why the Democratic Party has liberalized.

The claim that Black legislators have become more moderate is controversial. Kerry Haynie (2005) finds no support for this claim. His analysis, however, is based on interest group ideological ratings, which are calculated using a fraction of roll-call votes and are not scaled reliably over time. In this study, I use a measure developed by Keith T. Poole and Howard Rosenthal that is calibrated precisely to measure change over time in legislative behavior.[1]

Figures 1, 2, and 3 provide evidence for concordance. Figure 1 shows the ideological scores of the CBC and the Democratic Party from 1977 to 2008. There is a clear trend toward convergence. These ideological scores for the 95th Congress to the 111th Congress are taken from Poole and Rosenthal's coding of legislative behavior for all congressional sessions. On the basis of the universe of roll-call votes, they calculate scores that identify how similar legislators are in how they vote. For the postwar Congress, what they call the "first dimension" represents Left-Right voting patterns on bread-and-butter issues. The "second dimension," which includes civil rights, also includes many other noncongruent issues (Poole and Rosenthal 2007; McCarty, Poole, and Rosenthal 2006). It has become less predictive since the 1980s and is not analyzed here.[2] On the first dimension, congressional voting behavior has become increasingly stratified on pure Left-Right grounds (Poole and Rosenthal 2007).

On the first dimension of bread-and-butter issues (such as increased taxes for the rich or greater support for Medicaid), the scores for members of the Congressional Black Caucus have been strongly liberal since its inception. With negative numbers indicating liberalism, in 1977 the average CBC score was –.56, while for all the members of the Democratic Party in the legislature it was –.29. Over time, the CBC average score has become slightly less liberal on this dimension, averaging –.46 in 2008, while the Democratic Party became somewhat more liberal, averaging –.34 in 2008 (see figure 1). These converging moves meant that the ideological gap between the CBC and the Democratic Party narrowed from .27 to .12 in these thirty-one years. The trends for both Blacks and House Democrats (minus Blacks) are statistically significant (see appendix B for the raw data and calculations of statistical significance for these trends shown in this chapter).

Figure 2 shows the party unity scores among Black Democrats and the Democratic House Caucus from 1977 to 2010. Both Black Democrats and others in the Democratic House Caucus now strongly support the Democratic Party's policy agenda. Figure 2 reveals, in contrast to figure 1, that Black party unity scores have always been somewhat higher than scores for the Democratic House caucus as a whole. Black unity scores range from a low of 74 in 1978 to a high of 99 in 2008. Here, it is the Democratic House caucus that has come closer to the Black average, as unity scores for this group range from a low of 63 in 1978 to a high of 92 in 2007 and 2008. This pattern is not simply linear, however. Black scores entered the 90s for the first time in 1993, then dropped to the high 80s for the rest of the Clinton administration, only to return to the 90s in 1999, just one year before Republican George W. Bush won the disputed 2000 presidential election. Black's party unity scores remained in the 90s throughout Bush's presidency. The Democratic House caucus did not achieve party unity scores in the 90s until 2007, the year that restored Democratic control in the House. Thus, exceptionally high Black party unity was realized during the Bush presidency, while it took Democratic Party rule in the

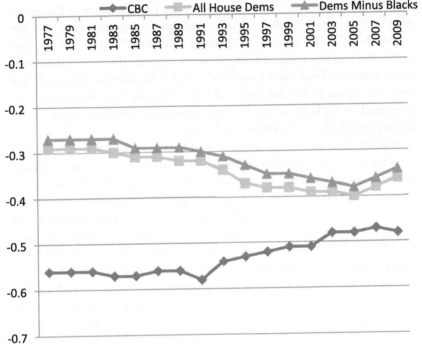

Fig. 1. Ideological scores for the CBC and the House Democratic Caucus.
(Data from NOMINATE scores, first dimension, and as calculated for CBC
House legislators.)

House to obtain record-high levels of party unity for all of its members. The increases in party unity for Blacks (where I can analyze the data) over time are statistically significant. As Black legislators have become more numerous and more powerful, they have clearly responded to the incentives favoring party unity.

Figure 3 shows that Black House Democrats and the Democratic House Caucus also have grown more alike in the percentage of time they support or oppose legislation backed by the president. The data from 1977 to 2010 indicate that in light of the stronger party discipline, especially under recent Republican presidents, Black voting patterns have now become quite close to those of members of the Democratic House Caucus. Under President Ronald Reagan, Democrats as a group were more likely than Blacks to back the president's policy priorities, but Democrats in general became less supportive of George W. Bush in the 2000s. In short, polarization has made Democratic legislators generally converge on the position of Blacks.

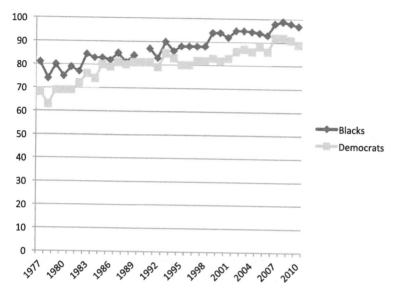

Fig. 2. Party unity scores for CBC House Democrats and the Democratic House Caucus

Party unity has reduced Democratic support for the policy agendas of Republican presidents (see Fleisher and Bond 2000), which had never earned high support from Black legislators. (The data also show that toward the end of the Clinton administration Black legislators backed the president more strongly than the party as a whole.) These large increases in party unity have reduced political friction between Blacks and other Democrats under Republican presidents since Reagan.

Finally, Black participation in House majority votes has increased over time. *House majority participation* is a new measure, introduced here, that shows how often members vote with the House majority on key bills each year. This analysis uses the *Congressional Quarterly Almanac* definition of key bills as pertaining to legislation involving a national controversy, presidential politics, or a great impact on the lives of Americans. The *CQ Almanac* identifies about a dozen key bills each year. Figure 4 shows House majority participation scores for the CBC and the Democratic House Caucus from 1977 to 2010.

Three points can be made from these data. First, figure 4 shows that over time the CBC scores have mirrored those of Democratic Party legislators as a whole closely. When the Democratic agenda does well in general, with most Democratic members voting with the House major-

Gap

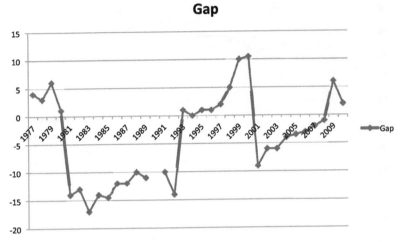

Fig. 3. The gap between CBC House Democrats and the Democratic House Caucus in legislative support for the president

ity, members of the CBC are also more likely to vote with that majority. Secondly, majority participation scores for the CBC and both of the two parties have increased over time, presumably because of increasing party discipline in both parties. When Blacks were challenging the president and the party during Carter's term, both Blacks and the Democrats became less effective. Later, the CBC scores increased significantly from an average of 53 percent of the time in which they voted with the House majority (score of .53) to 69 percent of the time (.69) under Clinton when the Democrats still had their House majority. This pattern probably made both Blacks and the Democrats more effective.

A third point is that a more polarizing partisan dynamic has greatly affected the policy character of major House legislation. House party members have become more aggressive in controlling the policy agendas of the House. In 1993 and 1994, the Democrats under Clinton were able to pass legislation that largely reflected their policy agenda. Then, after Republicans captured the House majority in 1995, Democrats voted for legislation that the House majority favored (or blocked) only 41 percent of the time. Before, under Carter, both parties (and the CBC) voted with the House majority a little more than 50 percent of the time. Now it is more a winner-take-all scenario with partisan control of the House more critical than which party controls the presidency. The majority party leader's essential role is getting party factions to unite to pass bills (Cox and McCub-

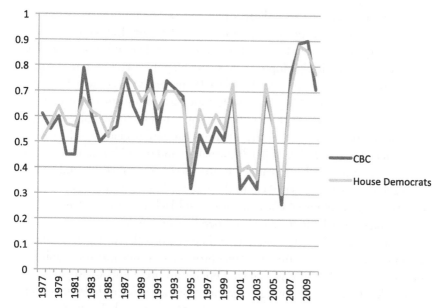

Fig. 4. Percentage of time the CBC and House Democrats vote with the House majority to pass/reject key bills. Each year, *Congressional Quarterly Almanac* lists about a dozen key bills that the House voted on that represent "a matter of great controversy," "a matter of presidential or political power," and "a matter of potentially great impact on the nation and lives of Americans."

bins 2007, 228–330; Mayhew 1966). There is a polarized policy environment currently in Washington; moderate leadership in the House, in fact, has essentially disappeared (Mann and Ornstein 2012).

The data as shown in figure 4 complicate the account of how political incorporation has transformed the legislative behavior of Blacks in Congress. The general trend of party polarization and the politics emanating from divided government leading to a winner-take-all policy dynamic may be the ultimate causes of these changes in the CBC. Nevertheless, I believe that incorporation as a concurrent trend is still there. Ideological changes through incorporation, shown in figure 1's Poole and Rosenthal scores, have taken place among Black legislators that make it easier for them to support policy leadership by the political party and president.

The multivariate analysis in chapter 7, this book's concluding chapter, reveals the sources of these changes in Black legislative behavior favoring moderation. Specifically, Black support for the president's policy initiatives and Black support for the House majority's key votes reduce their radicalism. Yet the analysis also indicates that the Democratic Party is not the direct source of growing Black legislative moderation. Rather, the Democratic Party both elevated some of the party's most liberal Blacks to leadership positions and itself adopted a more liberal policymaking stance. These two factors have made it easier for Black lawmakers to become better team players in the system. They are now less inclined to pressure their party or the president to support their radical group interests using collective tactics. In addition, the analysis makes clear that cohort change—the loss of the civil rights generation of Black lawmakers and the addition of moderate Blacks from the South—has added to the growing ideological moderation of Black Democratic lawmakers in the House. The analysis does not indicate that the shrinking of Black majorities in Black-led districts has directly caused Black legislators to vote less liberally over time.

Finally, the multivariate analysis in chapter 7 reveals that the Republican ascendancy in Washington after 1994 provoked various forms of capitulation from Black lawmakers. Under Republican presidents or Republican-controlled Houses, the voting behavior of Black Democratic lawmakers is significantly more conservative than under Democratic-led government.

The CBC's Diminished Radicalism

In addition to these measures drawn from voting behavior, we can also find evidence that the CBC has grown less radical from its press coverage. The Congressional Black Caucus was formed in 1971 as an effort to increase Black legislative influence in the U.S. Congress. The thirteen founding members of the CBC were Shirley Chisholm, George Collins, William Clay, John Conyers, Charles Diggs, Ron Dellums, Walter Fauntroy, Gus Hawkins, Ralph Metcalfe, Parren Mitchell, Robert Nix, Charles Rangel, and Louis Stokes. Conyers and Rangel, original CBC founders, were still serving in the 112th and 113th Congresses. The seniority that each of them amassed in their long tenures led to significant leadership positions. Conyers served in the 111th Congress as chair of the House Judiciary Committee and Rangel as chair of the powerful Ways and Means Committee (a position he had to leave because of ethics allegations). Conyers, as chapter 2 establishes, was an exceptionally ardent critic of President Carter, and he remains left-of-center today in policy tone, criticizing the party and President Obama in a radio show in 2009 for failing to support a single-payer proposal (one where the government provides for everyone's health insurance) in the health care debate (Seelye 2009). Although he has now built a strong record of backing the party on floor votes as well, Conyers remains somewhat of an exception to the trends reported in this book.

Caucuses in the House and Senate are formed as an effort to influence the legislative process beyond what regular participation in Congress offers (Hammond 1998; Miler 2011). The CBC was organized in 1971, while the legacy of the civil rights movement was still strong, to strengthen the policy efforts of Black legislators. Founding member William L. Clay describes the early years of the CBC as one that began with a direct policy challenge to President Richard Nixon, boycotting his State of the Union address because he had refused to meet with the group. Chapter 2 details how the old CBC then challenged President Carter, a president from their own party.

In contrast to the 1970s, when the Congressional Black Caucus took strong stands against the Democratic Party and also against the presidents, members of the CBC have become over time more heavily integrated into the party itself. Bill Gray's elevation to the powerful position of the chair of the House Budget Committee in 1985 began the transformation of the CBC's political style (Singh 1998). The *Congressional Quarterly Almanac*, which began reporting party leadership positions in 1985, shows that from this year on the number of Blacks in party leadership positions, including as regional or assistant whips or on policy committee posts, steadily rose. In 1985, seven Blacks held party leadership posts, with Charles B. Rangel having the most powerful position as a deputy whip. Among the old guard, Parren Mitchell had become an at-large whip (with William Gray), Harold Ford was a regional whip, Cardiss Collins was on the policy committee, and William L. Clay was on the party's campaign committee. By 1986, the number of CBC members in Democratic Party leadership posts had increased to nine. By 1993, 11 Blacks were serving in party leadership positions, and John Lewis had become one of the party's four chief deputy whips. By 1995, 17 Blacks, all CBC members, were serving in party leadership positions. By the 110th Congress (2007–09), Jim Clyburn (D-SC) held the House's third-ranking leadership position as majority whip, responsible for the formulation of Democratic Party policy and its passage. In the 111th Congress (2009–11), along with Clyburn as majority whip, G. K. Butterfield, John Lewis, and Maxine Waters were three of the nine chief deputy whips, selected by Speaker Nancy Pelosi in consultation with Clyburn, both of whom were elected by the Democratic Caucus. Lewis had been a whip since 1991, when he was appointed to maintain CBC representation in response to Bill Gray's resignation from the House to head the United Negro College Fund.

The advancement of Blacks in the House has had spillover effects even on such small matters as the hiring of staff, since as chairs Black members in Congress are more likely to hire minority staffers than are White committee chairs (Lorber 2009). More substantively, these positions of power on committees give Black members the capacity to exercise considerable influence on policy and on oversight (Minta 2011). With greater access to power, Black members have more reasons to support the party's policy agenda in the legislative process. With greater access to power, moreover, Black party leaders now have many incentives not to oppose party positions. Lower-ranking Black members have, in turn, many incentives not to oppose Black party and legislative leaders. Champagne and Rieselbach note that "some, perhaps most, black legislators may find it difficult to oppose legislation written in committees that blacks chair or on which blacks have exerted substantial influence" (1995, 151).

Legislators to a great degree are competitive, rational actors (see, e.g., Shepsle and Weingast 1995). They are, therefore, generally loyal to committees, and rarely challenge the policymaking authority of those committees. This loyalty is strengthened when one becomes chair of a committee. As mentioned earlier, after being made chair of the House Budget Committee, Gray famously voted "present" on the CBC alternative budget amendments, breaking the CBC's hoped-for unanimity. John Conyers (D-MI) was also forced to abandon a pledge to investigate the grounds to impeach President Bush in order to be appointed chair of the Judiciary Committee (Smith 2009, 18).

In his memoir, Charles Rangel explains how he faced a choice between loyalty to a Black agenda and accommodation to the committee on which he served. In 1974, at the end of only his second term in office, Rangel had just won a place on the prestigious and powerful House Ways and Means Committee. He wanted to advance further by seeking a position in the Democratic House leadership structure, but the chair of Ways and Means, Dan Rostenkowski, told him bluntly that unless he backed the Committee's agenda, he would never recommend him for leadership posts. Rangel pointed out to Rostenkowski that it was unfair to stand in the way of his further leadership, especially since he was the Committee's first Black member and had amassed significant seniority. Rangel reports this exchange in his memoirs:

"Rosty," I said, "you can't do that."

"That's the way it's done, Charlie," he replied.

"But Rosty, I'm black. I can't explain to anybody why as a senior member I was not recommended."

"You're not playing the race card on me, are you?" he asked. "Yes I am," I said. "I'm the first black on this committee. How am I going to explain that I was supposed to surrender my vote to you no matter what?" (2007, 177)

All members of Congress face significant pressure by party leaders and committee chairs to "surrender their votes" to the agenda of the committee. In addition, however, legislators support parties because they identify with their team (Lee 2009). They are motivated not only by their ideology but also by their bonds to their political party. Thus, party and committee work can reduce Black policy radicalism.

Expansion in numbers has also made the CBC less radical. Brought into the House in large numbers in 1992, southern Black lawmakers have shown themselves more moderate than northern ones. Black southern legislators were more supportive than Black northern legislators of President Clinton's bipartisan policy efforts, including his deficit-reduction budget resolutions. Under the Bush presidency, six Black members of Congress, all from the South, voted twice, in 2004 and 2006, for President Bush's constitutional amendment banning same-sex marriage. Some of these legislators have voted this way because of their political ambitions. In their districts, which are majority White, they must court the moderate White vote. In 2010, Artur Davis (D-AL) twice voted against President Obama's health care legislation, and was the only Black member of Congress to do so, as part of his campaign to win a statewide race in his politically conservative state of Alabama.

A final factor depressing the political radicalism of the CBC is the new, more partisan atmosphere in the U.S. Congress. This new context has two features. First, periods of divided government, in which one party holds the presidency and the other the Congress, have become more commonplace since 1952 (Fiorina 1992). Phases of divided government included two years of Truman under a Republican Congress in 1947–48; and then a succession of Republican presidents (Eisenhower, Nixon, Gerald Ford, Reagan, and George H. W. Bush) under Democratic-controlled Congresses (Mayhew 1991). President Clinton experienced a term of divided government when the 1994 national elections threw majority control of the Congress to the Republican Party. Republican president George W. Bush experienced divided government when the 2006 elections produced a Democratic majority, with a Democratic House Speaker and Senate majority leader. When a Democratic president faces a Republican congress, Black Democrats are more likely to support their president. They are particularly likely to vote for the president's policy initiatives, even when they must compromise their ideological stands to do so. When Democrats control both the Congress and the presidency, as in the Carter administration, Black legislators feel freer to threaten gridlock, a standard move in Congress (Brady and Volden 2006), in order to get leverage for their agenda. When a Republican president faces a Democratic Congress, a set of complex incentives come into play. As in the Reagan era (particularly in budgetary politics), a Republican president can offer incentives, both ideological and patronage, to conservative and moderate Democrats in return for support for Republican policies. These moves tend to isolate Black lawmakers. Increasingly, to gain positions in the House, however, some Black lawmakers may support some bipartisan policies backed by Republican presidents. Others may support such policies in order to craft reputations as bipartisan national leaders. For many such reasons, the data show that after Reagan had left office, Black lawmakers became less radical and more moderate under Republican control.

In addition to divided government, party polarization has also greatly affected the CBC's legislative strategy. As the parties intensify their competition and take policy positions further and further apart, the legislators in Congress are deferring more and more to their parties in their votes. The parties are working harder to offer inducements to legislators who might on one or another issue vote for a policy promoted by the other party (Rohde 1991). In this situation, the CBC as a minority group is less likely to win policies opposed by a majority of Democrats, and the Democratic Party will not introduce bills they cannot pass. This increased polarization in the House is one major explanation of the pattern in figure 2, establishing that Black members as well as Democrats overall have become dramatically more supportive of their party's policy initiatives since 1977. Today, Black House Democrats support their party's legislative priorities over 90 percent of the time. Importantly, the Democratic Party took over some nonracial issues that Black radicals deeply care about, including forcing on President Bush a timetable for withdrawing from the U.S.-Iraq War.

Why did partisanship increase in Congress? Party polarization has many sources. First, when President Johnson signed the Civil Rights Act in 1964, he predicted accurately that the socially conservative but somewhat racist electorate in the South would over time now desert the Democratic Party, and the two parties would sort themselves out more congruently along ideological lines (Lowry and Shipan 2002). This greater congruence explains why the policies of the major parties have polarized, making it more difficult to reach agreement on legislation both can support (Brunell, Grofman, and Merrill 2010). Legislative rule changes have also made the parties more important in the policymaking process, giving them more authority over the individual votes of their members (Sinclair 2006). The electorate may also have polarized, voting for more partisan representatives (McCarthy, Poole, and Rosenthal 2006). Some have suggested that redistricting caused the parties to polarize in Washington, but little empirical evidence exists for this claim (McCarty, Poole, and Rosenthal 2009). Finally, party discipline is dynamic. When one party becomes more unified, the other party may have to do the same in self-defense (Lebo, McGlynn, and Koger 2007).

In addition to these sources of polarization, the growth and elevation of Black lawmakers has itself contributed to the liberalization of the Democratic Party. The increasing ideological congruence within the party that has come with polarization has reduced political tensions between Blacks and others in the party. Because Black Democratic members of Congress are all liberal on the main bread-and-butter issues that divide the parties, Blacks feel no longer left out when the party simply counts on their support. Moreover, the party can no longer formulate an agenda that depends on cross-over Republican votes, so it requires every Black legislator's vote. In the spirit of this new solidarity with the party, the CBC is less poised to challenge it ideologically. Ironically, any new source of Black party dissent is poised to come, not from Black progressives, but from Black moderates who seek votes from more conservative Whites through bipartisan policymaking.

In the U.S. Congress, Black support of the Democratic presidential leadership and House majorities yields a greater participation in legislative victories. The incorporation of African Americans in Congress has been crucial to many important liberal victories. Although a majority of Congress continues to reject many race-specific policies promoted by the CBC, the Black legislators are more likely to win on broad policies that they favor, such as higher minimum wages, government spending to stimulate the economy, and children's health care programs.

The decline in Black radicalism among Black legislators evidenced in this book has important implications in our theoretical understanding of African American politics and the American political system. Adolph Reed Jr. (1986) has argued that Black elected officials represent their Black constituents better than do the less accountable Black protest leaders. Others counter that radicalism, now seen primarily outside the electoral realm, is necessary for a strong defense against a political and social system that perpetuates racial inequality. The evolution of the CBC, from aggressively articulating a Black policy agenda to adopting a more moderate stance and becoming stalwart supports of the Democratic Party, suggests that pressures for radical change must now come from extraelectoral activism.

Structure of the Book

The book is organized into eight chapters. The second chapter begins with an examination of the CBC during the Carter administration. Black lawmakers in that period possessed an ambitious legislative agenda to tackle Black unemployment and ultimately poverty through job creation programs. As previous scholars have noted, the CBC's ideological stance made it difficult for Black members to compromise with moderate Democratic president Jimmy Carter. Because they were able credibly to threaten to produce gridlock in Congress, they were able to experience some power in this situation. For his part, Carter was responding to what he correctly perceived as a rightward turn in the American electorate, but was, nevertheless, defeated after serving a single term.

Chapter 3 explores the stance of Black lawmakers during the Republican presidencies of Ronald Reagan and George H.W. Bush. This was a period of important discord between Blacks and the Democratic Party. The cooperation of many members of the Democratic Party with the Reagan presidency helped fuel the presidential bids of Black civil rights activist Jesse Jackson in 1984 and 1988. Black legislators gave extremely little support to President Reagan's policy agenda in these years. Indeed, the divide between them and the rest of the Democratic Party in the House in Reagan's first term was greater than in any other measured year. Eventually, however, House Democrats' support for Reagan's policies waned during the beginning of his second term, so the gap between the Democratic majority and Black legislators began to close.

Black influence in Congress was less during the Reagan-Bush years than under President Carter because they could no longer credibly threaten gridlock if their policy interests were not satisfactorily met. Yet even in these years they won important victories, including the Martin Luther King holiday and the 1982 extension of the Voting Rights Act, which the Democratic Party solidly backed. With partisanship increasing in this period, the Democratic caucus supported President George H. W. Bush less than it had President Reagan, bringing the party as a whole closer to the policy interests of Black Democrats in the House. The party was not fully united, however, and some divisions began to emerge even among Black lawmakers as some no longer continued the traditional opposition to regressive tax cuts.

Chapter 4 examines the growth of cooperation between Blacks and the Democratic president Bill Clinton during the 1990s. Several factors explain why Blacks' level of support for Clinton was higher than that for President Carter in the 1970s, even though Clinton too was a moderate on the Democratic spectrum. First, Black numbers in the House had increased dramatically to a total of 39 (including DC's nonvoting delegate) as a result of the new majority-Black districts created in the 1990s, many in the South. The elections of 1992 also brought Carol Moseley Braun to the U.S. Senate as the nation's first Black female and first Black Democrat to serve in that body. The new regional diversity brought about by greater numbers of Black members from the South combined with a greater presence of Blacks in party leadership posts enhanced Black rates of cooperation with the president and their party. Presiding over a good economy and drawing on his background in Southern culture, Clinton was also very persuasive with Black leaders and popular with Black voters. In Clinton's second term, when the Republicans gained control of the U.S. House of Representatives in 1994 and stripped all Democrats, including the Black legislators, of the legislative power they had accumulated through seniority, those Democrats, Blacks included, had a different incentive for moderation. As members of the minority party, they now could pass little legislation for their constituencies without the support of the GOP majority.

Chapter 5 examines the role of Black lawmakers during a period of united GOP control under George W. Bush's presidency. In this period, although in a weak political position, Black lawmakers nevertheless achieved a significant victory with the reauthorization of the 1965 Voting Rights Act in 2006. Congressman John Lewis (D-GA) testified on the floor about his direct participation in the violent struggle for voting rights in the South as a young civil rights activist. In general, party polarization continued to increase, as the Democratic Party itself became more liberal. There was growing concordance, and Black lawmakers saw less to argue about within their party. At the same time, ironically, ideological diversity increased in the Black ranks, as several southern Black lawmakers took moderate roles and voted against their colleagues. Sanford Bishop and Harold Ford Jr. voted for some of the policies pushed by President Bush, including some of the Republican tax proposals and the financial industry bailout. They may have seen these proposals as benefitting their constituents, or they may have wanted to build a moderate policy record in order to advance to higher office and national leadership posts in Washington. This chapter examines the various reasons why Black lawmakers did not radicalize against Bush-Republican policies as they did under Reagan.

Chapter 6 studies the role of Black legislators under the Obama presidency. As the nation's first African American president, Obama has taken stances best characterized as pragmatic rather than ideological, especially in regard to racial issues. In his first year in office, Obama was successful in getting Congress to pass many of his policies. The *Congressional Quarterly Almanac*, coding presidential successes since 1953, reports that Obama's presidential success score in 2009 surpassed the record high that President Johnson set in 1965. Johnson had to overcome a Democratic caucus strongly divided on the issue of race, while Obama benefitted from a more strongly united Democratic majority in Congress. The Democratic compromise over health care legislation, crafted under the Obama administration, deeply disappointed many liberal Democrats, included some Black lawmakers whose earlier history had once been one of ideological purity over political pragmatism. Black members of Congress still have participated massively in Obama's legislative victories, even more than in Clinton's. Their participation in these victories, which were also significant compromises, reduced the scores on liberalism scores for Black lawmakers, as did the support of some CBC members for Obama's agreement to conservative bipartisan economic and tax policies.

Chapter 7 presents statistical evidence showing that Black ideological scores have shifted toward the center primarily due to the greater role that Blacks now play in the policymaking process in Congress. Greater support for a Democratic White House and for the Democratic House majority's policy goals has reduced the liberalism of Black lawmakers. Republican control of the House has also reduced the liberalism of Black House members.

Finally, in chapter 8, I discuss the emerging debate about Black political leadership in Washington. On the one hand, some argue that any decline in Black radicalism is bad for Blacks. The Black community is likely to suffer because the generation that successfully mounted the broad challenge to American apartheid in this country is now retired or deceased, and younger Black lawmakers are more moderate. Civil rights activist Julian Bond, chairman of the NAACP, once remarked that "segregation taught us all to think alike" (Ifill 2009, 18). He took retirement in 2010. Thus, the CBC is in retreat.

By contrast, others argue that the political incorporation of Black lawmakers helps Blacks politically through, chiefly, the liberalization of the Democratic Party. Blacks' roles in the party and as leaders in Congress represent the best way for Blacks to win strong representation for their collective interests. The CBC may no longer be a vehicle for radical change in the status of African Americans, but it plays a continuing and important political role nevertheless. The baton of radical change must then be passed to the nonelectoral arena of social movements, protest groups, and progressive organizations.

CHAPTER 2

President Carter and the Old CBC

I have a very interesting relationship with the Black Caucus. Sometimes we have been in harmony, sometimes I am not in complete agreement.

—President Jimmy Carter[1]

Black legislators argued that they didn't get what they wanted from the Carter administration, and some weren't sorry to see him go. Carter was the first Democrat to occupy the White House since Lyndon B. Johnson. While Johnson endured the political turmoil caused by Blacks over their demands for civil rights and responded with major civil rights and voting rights legislation, Blacks were experiencing very tough times economically in the late 1970s. Black lawmakers wanted an equally aggressive response, such as full employment and a rebuilding of America's cities. Furthermore, there were alarming trends belying the racial progress that had been achieved during the civil rights movement. Out-of-wedlock births in the Black community had increased, moving more Black families into poverty. Black members in the House had formed a group in 1969, but Black lawmakers felt that there was an illusion of Black political power. Racial gerrymandering in the country still was used to keep Blacks out of elective office. It took several decades of voting rights lawsuits and a strengthening of federal voting rights law in 1982 before there was a serious expansion of Black political power (Davidson and Grofman 1994). The legality of busing for school integration had been tested in the 1970s. Now affirmative action was being litigated.

Carter, meanwhile, was a moderate Democrat, one who believed that America was headed in a conservative direction. He, in fact, lost his reelection bid to a staunch conservative Republican, Ronald Reagan, in 1980. In retrospect, the Carter presidency was caught in the middle of an economic upheaval. Inflation was a major problem that dogged his administration—gas prices just shot up—as was the Iranian hostage crisis, which remained unresolved until after President Reagan took office.

The data showing this combativeness from Black lawmakers in the Carter administration are seen in the CBC opposition to Carter's budgets and their low presidential support measures. Black House members, all Democrats during this time, went along with the House majority on major legislation from 45 to 61 percent of the time. This chapter discusses first budgetary politics and the CBC under Carter, then the measures of presidential support, party unity, and House majority support as calculated by the author using *CQ Almanac* statistics from 1977 to 1980. The major policy battles in the Carter administration are described in more detail. The CBC held a tight, ideological posture during these years.

Black Political Concerns during the Carter Presidency

The trouble between Black lawmakers and President Carter began on the first day of his administration. The CBC strongly opposed his appointment of Griffin B. Bell to attorney general. Blacks were disturbed by southerners like Bell with histories in the South's segregationist past. In addition to Bell, the president had nominated Irby Turner Jr. to the board of the Corporation for Public Broadcasting. Irby was a Mississippian who had been a member of the Citizens' Council, a prosegregation organization (Bruno 1977). Bell's own opinion about the matter appeared too sanguine. He told a reporter that if "all candidates for federal office were judged by their racial stands of 30 years ago . . . 'everybody in the South would be barred from office.'" He initially refused to resign from two Atlanta social clubs that had no Black or Jewish members (Alpern, Shannon, and Doyle 1977). Furthermore, during his Senate confirmation hearings Bell called himself a moderate. Carter himself had made headlines in 1976 and caused Black consternation when he used the words "ethnic purity" in a statement that he would not tamper with American neighborhoods during his campaign for president. The U.S. attorney general was at the front line of civil rights and voting rights enforcement. Black legislators had already experienced years of what they called enforcement delays from the Nixon-Ford administrations.

Bell was as good as his word; he was a moderate. The Justice Department's legal brief in the *Bakke* case sought the middle ground by stating that race can be used to overcome past discrimination, but that quotas such as the one used in the *Bakke* case are unconstitutional, and deprive Whites of their civil rights. The CBC, along with Black civil rights leaders such as Coretta King, Vernon Jordan Jr., and Benjamin Hooks, lobbied the White House for changes to the brief, as ending affirmative action programs for minorities would cause a serious civil rights setback for Blacks (Peterson 1977). Bell turned the task of preparing the brief on *Bakke* to two Black liberals—Wade McCree and Drew Days. In the end, elite support for the radical Black position that quotas represented a very legitimate response to the nation's long, formal exclusion of Blacks in education and employment faded.

Racial conservatives sought to dominate during the Carter administration. In 1979, the *Washington Post* reported that the Carter administration was attempting to end minority set-asides for government business (Pine and Seaberry 1979). Only after heavy criticism from Black lawmakers and civil rights groups did the Carter administration restore provisions of its new multilateral trade pact that maintained minority set-asides for small and minority-owned companies. Black lawmakers in Washington aggressively criticized, nagged, and goaded Carter: "'Mr. President, when you are wrong, I will criticize you'," Rep. Parren Mitchell reportedly told Jimmy Carter directly (Trescott 1977b). As head of the CBC, Mitchell also said in 1977 that "there's a new mood in America that's anti-black." He was characterized in the article as perpetually angry—watching *Roots*, the acclaimed television series about Alex Haley's slave ancestors, for example, made Mitchell angry. He told the reporter that he wanted to lash out at White people after watching *Roots* (Trescott 1977b).

As stated earlier, Black unemployment, too, was at a crisis level. Notably bad were figures for teenage Black employment rates. William J. Wilson's *The Truly Disadvantaged* (1987) published figures of Black male unemployment rates in 1960 versus 1980. In the Northeast, 59.1 percent of Black males aged 20–24 were employed in 1960; that figure fell to 48.1 percent by 1980. In the South, only 29.2 percent of Black males 16 to 19 held jobs in 1980. Wilson contends that there were reasons other than racial discrimination that caused such high levels of unemployment for young Black males, and they included their concentration in the central cities where unskilled jobs had grown scarce. Figure 5 presents unemployment figures by race compiled by the Bureau of Labor Statistics from 1975 to 2010.[2] As one can see, Black unemployment levels increased dramatically in 1975 to 14.8 percent only to decline slightly in 1978 and 1979. Black unemployment

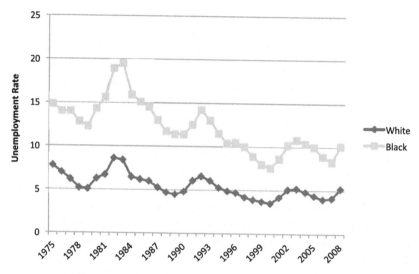

Fig. 5. Unemployment rate by race. (Data from Current Population Survey statistics.)

remained high during the 1980s, to drop slowly during the 1990s and early 2000s. It spiked again in 2002, and then, after falling, rose again during the great recession of 2008–9, and has remained high. The worst racial gap in unemployment, however, emerged during the Carter-Reagan presidencies.

The policy response of the CBC was to push job creation, not only economic stimulus bills. Thus, government jobs as the last-resort provision in the Humphrey-Hawkins bill were vital to Black lawmakers who believed that Black unemployment was caused by a complicated set of conditions that economic stimulus programs alone could not address. Wilson, in a later book, *When Work Disappears* (1996), advocated that Congress create jobs for those who need them along the lines of the Works Progress Administration (WPA) jobs program created by Roosevelt during the Great Depression. Eight million Americans were employed through this program (*CQ Almanac* 1982, 61). Because of the difficulty of winning government programs targeted to alleviate Black poverty, Wilson argues that such a program should be universal, eligible to anyone needing work, not only the poor, but the working and middle classes as well.

However, jobs creation programs are notoriously expensive, and the Comprehensive Employment and Training Act (CETA), a jobs creation program, was labeled by fiscal conservatives in Congress as a waste of taxpayer money. CETA provided as many as 750,000 jobs annually during the early years of the Carter Administration (*CQ Almanac* 1982, 61). CETA expired in 1982 under President Reagan.

A second element in the political agenda of the CBC was to address the problems of Black America by addressing conditions in urban America. Carter's only Black Cabinet-level official, Patricia Roberts Harris, served as secretary of Housing and Urban Development (HUD) between 1977 and 1979, and in 1979 she became secretary of the Department of Health, Education, and Welfare.

Thus, President Carter was subject to four years of strong criticism by Black lawmakers Some Black lawmakers even told reporters at the end of Carter's first term in office that they thought they'd be better served if some other Democrat held Carter's seat. The battles were over Carter's economic policies, but spilled over into defense spending, which the CBC believed was taking money away from badly needed domestic programs. The CBC continued this approach of public criticism through the Reagan-Bush years, but changed tactics once Bill Clinton was elected in 1992.

Some of the unruliness of the Caucus was the legacy of Watergate years when the Congress felt that presidents were usurping powers reserved to the people and the Congress in the way they sought to lead. But, as newcomers, Black lawmakers were outsiders in Washington, and they were forced to lean heavily on media coverage to get their agenda heard. The Democratic Party was still dominated by conservative southern interests. As the numbers of Black lawmakers increased, and as the party integrated Blacks better into leadership posts, things changed. The Carter, Reagan, and Bush years represented the CBC's best efforts to promote Black interests, albeit in a combative fashion.

Black Radical Interests in Washington

Black radical interests are defined as both racially oriented and extremely liberal (or progressive) but also defying the conventional liberal-conservative spectrum that covers mainstream politics promulgated by the Republican and Democratic parties. This radicalism is reflected in the CBC's political style. During the Carter presidency, not only was the opposition among Black lawmakers to Carter's reelection radical but there were many other issues as well where Black lawmakers openly defied their president or party.

The first area of contestation was over the federal budget. President Carter had defined himself as a fiscal moderate. Yet Black unemployment had skyrocketed under his administration, and Black Democrats wanted Carter to spend more money to reduce the Black employment rate. In addition to the budget battle was the Humphreys-Hawkins bill. Spearheaded by a Black House lawmaker from California, Augustus Hawkins, as well as a White senator from Minnesota, Hubert Humphrey, who had also been the Democratic Party presidential nominee in 1968, this bill represented the radical vision of Black lawmakers of that era. They wanted the government to create jobs for the unemployed as it had during the Great Depression under President Roosevelt. They wanted a Marshall Plan, the program of U.S. foreign aid to rebuild Europe after World War II, for Black America. This was a radical vision. It remains a radical vision but one that no longer commands the unified support of Black lawmakers today because it looks out of reach. The Marshall Plan approach had greater possibilities in the aftermath of the Black political and social unrest of the 1960s.

Finally, the CBC led the fight against the racial policies of White rule in Rhodesia and South Africa. The notion that the United States ought to make the African continent a priority regardless is also radical, since American national interests were not necessarily at stake. It reflected a Pan-African vision, where Blacks in the Diaspora work together to overcome horrible economic conditions and racism. Today, a pro-Africa policy fits more with a humanitarian vision. Then it did not. Thus, the promotion of a clear pro-Africa foreign policy in the United States rests midway between radical and liberal philosophies. In this section, I provide descriptions of these three areas of contention to show how they reflected the radical visions and radical strategies of the CBC.

CBC Opposition to Carter's Budgets

Carter, plainly, was a fiscal moderate. In this respect, he was compared unfavorably by House liberals to President Gerald Ford. Liberal Democrats in Congress had enacted big public works programs over the vetoes of Presidents Nixon and Ford (*CQ Almanac* 1982, 61). Some even compared his economic policies as being slightly to the political right of President Nixon. Carter's fiscal conservatism irked the CBC mightily. They claimed that Carter was fighting inflation and rising deficits at Blacks' expense. President Carter found some resistance by Black lawmakers to all four of his budget proposals.

The Democratic-controlled Congress began with their first Carter budget by requesting more spending and a larger deficit than requested by Carter. Some of the difference between the House proposal and President Carter's was the House's gloomier assessments of the upcoming fiscal year. The House also proposed less for defense spending than requested by Carter. There were increases in spending on programs in health, education, transportation, community development, and veterans, but reductions in international assistance. Then Carter withdrew his support for $50 rebates to stimulate the economy in order to make the budget resolution passable. Now liberals were really upset since they had agreed to accept fiscal restraint in the overall budget because of the $50 rebate deal. The House passed, however, its compromise budget resolution May 5 by a vote of 213–179. Only Dellums and Conyers voted against the compromise budget, while the rest of the Black House members went along. A few, however, did not participate in the vote.

Republicans had not supported the Carter budget resolutions because of their concern about the level of deficits, and so Democratic support was crucial. The Senate then put in more money for defense. Although most Black legislators still supported the final budget resolution, Mitchell of Maryland, head of the CBC, and Stokes of Ohio, joined with Dellums and Conyers and voted "no."

High unemployment dogged the nation in 1978, and Carter proposed a $24.5 billion tax cut to stimulate the economy that year. Furthermore, California voters in June 1978 approved a state constitutional amendment drastically cutting property taxes, and thus Carter's proposal represented a response to growing voter anger over taxes. Still, Black members of Congress were upset by calls for a tax cut. While Carter won plaudits from Republican senators for his tax cut proposal, there was still significant opposition to his budget request in the House. Complicating this was that the Senate also sought to eliminate a $2 billion federal jobs program. The House, however, maintained the public works program in its budget resolution, backing tax cuts as well, albeit smaller than those proposed by the president. The House budget resolution that contained the $2 billion public works program won the unanimous backing of all the Black legislators who voted. And it turned out that the 11 votes the Caucus provided were necessary as it won by a margin of only four votes. The compromise legislation that finally emerged now only included $700 million for the public works program. Although the Caucus opposed the big cut in the jobs program, only Conyers voted against the compromise bill.

In 1979, the nation had entered into a recession. Carter announced that he had set a goal of reducing the federal deficit to below $30 billion as part of his anti-inflation program. In 1979, Carter proposed a 5 percent cut in domestic programs. The newspapers reported that Democrats were alarmed, including Tip O'Neill, Speaker of the House. The CBC pledged to fight Carter on his budget. They were especially outraged over the defense budget request in light of cuts to social spending programs. As the *Washington Post* reported, "Caucus members made it clear that they are most angered by the proposed increase in defense spending, which Rep. Ronald V. Dellums (D-Calif.) called 'potentially dangerous and intolerable'" (Walsh 1979). With Black unemployment rates twice that of national rates, the mood among CBC members was especially combative. The Congressional Black Caucus voted unanimously to oppose the budget resolution, "reasoning that no matter what happens things can't get much worse for blacks and believing there's nothing to gain mediating a fight among middle-class whites" (Russell 1979).

The national mood seemed to favor budget cutting, however. In fact, the Democratic House leadership reportedly went out of its way to court conservative Democrats to vote for its budget resolution, ignoring the CBC. Picking up southern Democrats who tended to be the least supportive of President Carter, the vote was substantially in favor of the House budget resolution—220–184. Black Democrats, however, stuck to their guns and 13 voted against its adoption.

The House was unable to sustain support for the 1979 budget plan after the Senate cut $2 billion from social programs. Losing the second vote on this resolution, a new one passed by a slim 212–206 vote. The House had increased defense spending by $1.9 billion, but critically increased federal assistance to local governments by $400 to $550 million. No Republican voted for it as it failed to reduce the deficit significantly. This resolution, however, passed with early agreement from Black liberals who claimed that they were responding to "political realities" (*Congressional Quarterly Almanac* 1979, 18). Still, Dellums and Conyers voted against it.

Inflation continued to soar out of control in 1980, adding to the cost of federal programs. Carter called for a small increase in spending over his 1980 budget, as there was a projected small surplus in fiscal 1981. Both parties, nonetheless, sought to appeal to fiscal conservatives who appeared to be major voices in 1980 congressional races. *Congressional Quarterly Almanac 1980* reports that the House budget resolution represented "the largest annual increase in military spending during peacetime" (1980, 108). Thus, in 1980, the CBC, once again, called a news conference to protest Carter's budget plan. Dellums and Conyers were expected to vote "no" on this House budget resolution, but the entire CBC delegation voted "no." Incidentally, Wyche Fowler, a White representative who had inherited Andrew Young's old seat in Georgia, voted "yes." A "yes" vote supported the president's position. The House approved House Congressional Resolution 307 by a 225–193 vote. Amendments rejected included ones for a defense increase and a domestic spending increase. A CBC substitute proposed by Parren Mitchell to increase domestic spending by $5.4 billion failed by a large margin, 74–313 (1980, 115).

President Carter and Speaker O'Neill in the House rejected the Senate-led compromise budget plan for 1981 as too lopsided in favor of guns over butter. The second resolution, which had a deficit, was crafted as Carter lost his bid for reelection and as Republicans won majority control of the Senate. One-third of the CBC voted for the conference report on December 3, notably Bennett Stewart, Conyers (surprisingly), Chisholm, Rangel, and Ford. The rest did not. It still passed by a huge margin of 334–45. The mood was somber as liberals fretted over president-elect Ronald Reagan's campaign pledge to significantly pare down government once he took office.

The Fight for the Humphrey-Hawkins Bill

The ideological battles involving the CBC in the Carter administration were fundamentally over jobs. As figure 5 establishes, Black unemployment was rising, and the CBC wanted to make full employment a policy priority in this Democratic administration. President Carter was resistant, as his policy experts warned him that full employment policies were inflationary (Weir 1992). And inflation was out of control during the Carter administration. The CBC, however, was adamant, and requested a number of times to meet with President Carter about the matter. Carter put the organization off in a manner reminiscent of Nixon, which had led to the CBC's boycott of Nixon's State of the Union address. Eventually, Carter granted the meeting in September 1978. However, matters were so tense that Conyers walked out during the meeting when the president rejected his proposal for a Camp David conference on unemployment (Walsh and Russell 1978). Carter held a second meeting four days later with the organization to smooth things over. The White House then issued a press statement calling for quick action on the Humphrey-Hawkins bill.

The full employment bill is named for Senator Hubert H. Humphrey (D-MN) and Rep. Augustus F. Hawkins (D-CA), a member of the CBC. The CBC wanted the legislation enacted in 1978, although Humphrey had recently passed away from cancer. The bill was signed into law by President Carter on October 27, 1978. The bill had been watered down, however, since it was originally proposed (Weir 1992). The most important of its original provisions had been the provision that created government jobs as the "last resort" for the unemployed. This was eliminated. Instead, the bill listed two national goals of reducing the unemployment rate to 4 percent by 1983 and reducing the inflation rate to 3 percent by 1983 and o percent by 1988. It required the Federal Reserve Board to report twice annually on its monetary policies and their relationship to the stated goals of the act. Opposition to even the watered-down version of the Humphrey-Hawkins Act was based on arguments that full employment would bring high inflation. Republicans, especially, made the inflationary impact of the Act their main criticism. With inflation goals alongside unemployment ones, the House vote was strong in spite of the long delay to its passage and the intensive lobbying against it. The vote was 257–152. The Senate also approved its version of the bill by a 70-19 vote (*CQ Almanac* 1978). Black efforts to win a full employment program crested in 1978. It was a radical agenda item that did not return over the next decades. The most liberal agenda item that occupied Congress after job programs ended were stimulus spending programs.

Meanwhile, existing jobs programs were under attack starting in the Carter years. The Kennedy administration had first created a jobs program reminiscent of those established during the Great Depression. In the 1970s, these billion-dollar public service and works programs became controversial. They were passed over the vetoes of Republican presidents Nixon and Ford. The Comprehensive Employment and Training Act (CETA) was originally enacted in 1973. Carter extended CETA for only one year in 1977, pledging to study the program and make recommendations as necessary during this time. In 1978, CETA was extended again, but this time for four years—through 1982. Its public service jobs were reduced from 725,000 to 660,000 positions. There was a fierce argument about the program as reports alleged widespread corruption and waste as run by local governments. One problem was that CETA didn't create new jobs, but governments transferred existing jobs to the CETA funds (*CQ Almanac* 1978).

President Nixon had wanted local governments to run CETA directly as part of his New Federalism initiative aimed at decentralizing the federal system. Funds, therefore, were given to localities directly based on a formula. Tension existed as members of Congress worked out the details of the formula; urban representatives wanted the money to go to the hardest-hit areas—the central cities. To keep governments from transferring their jobs to CETA jobs, the law mandated that workers could stay in the public service jobs for 18 months only and that salaries were to be held below $10,000 a year.

Senators across both aisles criticized CETA. Republican Jesse Helms of North Carolina called CETA "just another typical example of the futility of throwing tax dollar after tax dollar at a problem." Senator Adlai Stevenson III of Illinois, a Democrat, called CETA "grossly inefficient," and said the CETA funds should be used to reform welfare and reduce the federal deficit (*CQ Almanac* 1978, 295). The Senate passed the bill continuing CETA, however, by 66–10. There had been more criticism and debate in the House, but it too passed by a significant margin. President Reagan eliminated CETA during his presidency.

Did Black lawmakers back away from jobs programs because the policy environment became too conservative and too hostile? Or did they lose their ideological appetite for it as the Democratic presidents and the party pitched instead a vision of job creation through stimulus spending? Both forces were at play. The battle over the Humphrey-Hawkins bill, again, represented a radical agenda that all members of the CBC could agree upon. Today, that is no longer the case.

Rhodesia, South Africa, and Haitian Refugees

The CBC wanted President Carter to condemn the White Rhodesian government, which reserved political rights to White settlers only. The CBC pushed for President Carter's enforcement of United Nations sanctions against Rhodesia even after elections there had elected a biracial government (*Washington Post* 1979). These elections still reserved over one-quarter of the seats for Whites and banned Blacks imprisoned for their political views from voting. Carter announced that he was keeping the boycott in place as "in the national interest." Rhodesia formally changed its name to Zimbabwe and ended White rule in 1980.

South Africa required a larger campaign from Blacks. It did not become a racially integrated democracy until the 1990s. The CBC issued statements urging a different U.S. policy on South Africa. The CBC urged the president to recall its ambassador in disapproval of the South African crackdown on Black organizations and newspapers. The CBC sponsored a resolution that denounced the government of South Africa for its "'repressive measures against black and white opponents of its apartheid policy'" (McBee 1977).

On Haiti, the CBC charged the administration with racism (Hornblower 1980). Carter's refugee policy left Haitians eligible for food stamps and temporary work permits, but they did not qualify for political asylum as those fleeing communist countries had. In fact, a full refugee policy for Haiti never materialized.

Crafting better and fair U.S. policies for Black Africa and the Black Caribbean remained a lasting political achievement of the CBC. While a radical economic agenda favoring Blacks was lost after the Carter-Reagan presidencies, the group's efforts to improve U.S.-Black Africa/Caribbean relations proved more productive. In the end, a radical-liberal vision there survived perhaps because it suited the humanitarian spirit that was emerging in Western Europe as well.

Measures of CBC Presidential Support, Party Unity, and the House Majority under Carter

During his four years in office, Carter was unable to win the CBC over. In 1980, the CBC gave the president their lowest level of support of 63 after peaking in 1979 at 70. Blacks were less oppositional than Democrats as a whole, even as their support was as low. Democratic opposition to Carter was thought to be both a reflection of his leadership skills and the post-Vietnam, post-Watergate era. House Democrats as well as Black Democrats were unruly during this period. In 1979, however, Black Democrats' support of Carter's legislative agenda was noticeably higher, with a score of 70 in contrast to a score of 64 for all Democratic members of the U.S. House of Representatives.

Opposition to the president's policy agenda drove down his presidential success measures. *Congressional Quarterly Almanac* reports for 1977 that Carter's support scores from congressional Democrats were low for the first year of a president: "Since 1953, the highest presidential support score was 93.0 percent achieved by Johnson in 1965; the lowest, 50.6 in 1973 by Nixon" (*CQ Almanac* 1977).

Black House Democrats voted with the majority 45 to 61 percent of the time from 1977 to 1980. House Democrats voted with the majority slightly more of the time than Black Democrats, having House majority support scores ranging from 51 to 64 percent. The key votes, representing about a dozen bills each year identified by *CQ Almanac* as major, include a mix of economic, social welfare, defense and foreign policy, environmental and energy, and house ethics/election reform bills. During the Carter presidency, there was only one year that House votes on social policy legislation were included as major votes by *CQ Almanac*. In 1979, the House voted on a constitutional amendment to ban busing to achieve school integration. It required a two-thirds majority vote, but won 209 votes, almost a majority but nowhere near the 284 needed. It won 74 percent of the House Republican vote, and 35 percent of the House Democratic vote. One can see how this vote inflamed Black Democratic lawmakers.

Black Democrats divided some, but not on the one social or the economic issues identified as major during this time. On every other major bill, the CBC generally voted with less than one-third in disagreement. Because *CQ Almanac* designates bills as significant that reflect presidential politics, energy policy questions were included for most of the Carter presidency. Carter had created the Department of Energy during his presidency, making it a cabinet-level agency. In these energy bill votes, some Black House members refused to back Carter. Their votes on energy bills reveal that the CBC was working independent of presidential and party controls. Their disagreements on some energy bills also reflected regional and political differences, not ideological ones.

President Carter opposed some water projects as wasteful both in 1977 and 1978. In 1977, the water project won funding through a House majority vote, but the House was unable to override a presidential veto for water projects funding in 1978. The CBC division on the water works projects in 1977 and 1978 reveal an odd discovery. Dellums and Conyers, who represented strong ideologues, were opposed to them, and therefore, backed President Carter on this issue both times. Harold Ford Sr., a fellow southerner, generally supported and backed President Carter. The ardent liberals favoring the public spending projects both times were Hawkins, Mitchell, Clay, Chisholm, and Barbara Jordan, as they should, in light of how liberals generally see federal spending on public projects as helpful in combating unemployment.

However, because the spending was not targeted to urban areas, there may have a split based on region on this issue. Members from the Southwest, Southeast, and West wanted additional funding for water projects in 1977. In 1978, it was also cast as a pork matter, not an economic one.

Congress passed legislation creating the Department of Education in 1979 by a thin margin of 210–206. Many more Republicans were opposed to the creation of a new federal bureaucracy than Democrats; the new department had been strongly supported by the National Education Association, the interest group for educators. The NEA had spent $3 million backing Carter in 1976 (Stephens 1983–84).

Yet Blacks seriously divided over the matter. Blacks opposed to the Department of Education were in a CBC plurality of 43 percent. Black opponents backed the contention of Joseph A. Califano Jr., the secretary of Department of Health, Education, and Welfare (HEW), that having education policy alongside health and welfare made better sense for children, especially for the education of poor children. Later, HEW secretary Califano reluctantly asked Congress to pass the bill (Stephens 1983–84).

David Stephens (1983–84) contends that Democratic Party leaders urged support to increase President Carter's chances for reelection. This, however, did not matter as much to Black Democrats in 1979; it later became more appealing as their stakes in party control grew. Black opposition to the Department of Education, and later to bipartisan immigration reform in 1986 and to the No Child Left Behind legislation in 2001, reflected uncertainty about how these policies would affect the Black community, and thus reflect genuine divisions over the direction of radicals and liberals among Black House legislators. Black radical lawmakers will not support liberal policies that on their face appear to not be responsive to the policy concerns of Blacks and minority groups.

Members of the CBC also divided over whether to expel one of their members for corruption. The House voted to expel Diggs in a vote requiring a two-thirds majority, and the vote won only 45 percent of the House majority. There was also the personal involved in these votes. Adam Clayton Powell had been denied his seat in 1967 by a House vote; later the Supreme Court ruled that Congress had acted unconstitutionally in denying Powell his seat as an elected official. In 1978, Diggs was indicted on charges of cheating the U.S. government of more than $100,000 by falsifying office payrolls. Fifty-five years of age at that time, at first he claimed innocence, but he was convicted of mail fraud. He still won reelection in 1978, and appealed his conviction. Diggs was chairman of the House International Relations Subcommittee on Africa. Then he admitted his guilt and promised to repay the U.S. Treasury the roughly $40,000 he had taken plus interest (*CQ Almanac* 1979). In 1979, a unanimous House voted 410–0 to censure Diggs. Four House members voted present, including Diggs, Hawkins, and Mitchell. Republicans had been unable to get the House to vote on expelling Diggs. Diggs resigned in 1980 to serve a three-year prison sentence.

In 1980, the House voted to expel a White member, Michael Myers (D-PA), who had been implicated in accepting bribes from FBI agents masquerading as Arab businessmen and sheiks as part of the Abscam scandal. Seven members of Congress had been implicated, including some committee chairmen. The vote to expel Myers was overwhelming. Only 30 House members voted not to expel Myers, and nearly half of the CBC, or 47 percent, voted with that group. Those voting not to expel Myers argued that such a decision should be delayed until after he was convicted.

Black lawmakers divided over other House ethic issues. In 1977, the Democrats attempted to adopt new ethics standards that included a grievance panel to hear discrimination complaints from House employees and an auditor to review the accounts of members. The reform measure lost by a vote of 160–252; every House Republican opposed it. Democrats divided 160–113. Sixty-two percent of the CBC voted for it; opposed were Hawkins, Metcalfe, Clay, Stokes, and Jordan. In 1978, the House voted on a measure to toughen disclosure laws governing lobbying. Interest groups donating more than $3,000 to a lobbying firm must be listed and the bill required disclosure of grassroots lobbying activities. The measure passed the House by 259–140, but it was killed in the Senate. About 58 percent of the CBC voted for it. Jordan was against both reforms, but members of the CBC generally split their votes on this issue. Thus, there were divisions within the CBC, but these divisions were nonideological and reflected also the tenor of the times.

UN Ambassador Andrew Young's Resignation

An important matter during the Carter presidency was Andrew Young's appointment and subsequent resignation as the nation's first Black United Nations ambassador. Young's leadership reflected the sensibilities of many in his generation, new to the Democratic Party, but who later were purged as the Democratic Party sought to appoint less aggressive racially oriented Black leaders. Clinton and later Obama kept out of their presidential administrations Blacks who had radical racialized views.

President Carter picked Andrew Young for UN ambassador in 1977. Young then was a House representative in Congress, having won office originally in 1972. When Young resigned to work in the Carter administration, a popular White Democrat won his seat. Young's resignation from this post was a significant event in the Carter presidency for African Americans. Days before his resignation was announced in August 1979, the *Washington Post* reported:

> For a while it seemed Young was always in hot water. The reporting on his quotes outpaced the reporting on the effectiveness of his diplomacy.

To the dismay of his fellow diplomats, conservative politicians and, at times, the White House, Young was reported as saying:
The British were "a little chicken" on race issues.
That former presidents Richard Nixon and Gerald Ford had racist attitudes.
That the Cubans were a "stabilizing influence" in Africa.
That U.S. jails had "hundreds, maybe even thousands of political prisoners."
That the Ayatollah Khomeini was "a saint." (Trescott 1979)

Young's 1978 assertion to a French interviewer that there were "political prisoners" in U.S. jails also inflamed Washington. The remark prompted a telephone call from President Carter and Secretary of State Cyrus R. Vance. Young clarified his statement by saying that he never meant to equate U.S political freedoms with those in the Soviet Union and that he condemned the persecution of Soviet dissidents. In response to this statement, however, one southern Democratic member of the House moved to propose that Young be impeached, but that proposal was shut down by Majority Leader Jim Wright (Russell and Kaiser 1978). Minority Whip Robert Michel of Illinois called for the president to fire Young. There had been criticism of Young in the State Department concerning his meeting with a Palestine Liberation Organization (PLO) aide. The PLO had refused to recognize the right of Israel to exist and was considered a terrorist organization. There was also some praise for his improving America's image among developing nations in the Third World. President Carter backed Young solidly during his tenure as UN ambassador. Young also reciprocated and backed Carter for reelection and asked his former Black colleagues in the House to stick by the president.

Because Andrew Young was a member of the civil rights movement's elite, as a former aide to Martin Luther King, he had legitimacy as a Black radical. The Carter years were the last years Black national leaders might speak their mind freely about what they thought about race relations. Parren Mitchell, who headed the CBC during the Carter years, told a reporter that watching *Roots*, a television series based on Alex Haley's gripping novel about the unmerciful hardships of an African slave in America and of his descendants, made him angry. He turned the program off after two days of watching it, adding that "If I had met any of my white friends I would have lashed out at them from a vortex of primeval anger" (Trescott 1977b). There was less tempering of style and tone for Black leaders in Washington in the 1970s.

African Americans and President Carter: A Retrospective

As the governor of Georgia, Carter did not support a holiday for Martin Luther King's birthday, but in 1979, as president, he supported the proposal. Blacks, nevertheless, felt that their votes had been taken for granted—a sentiment that only deepened as the decade progressed. Cardiss Collins, as the new head of the CBC, enthusiastically explained to a *Washington Post* reporter in September 1979, before the start of the 1980 campaign season, why she felt that Carter should resign before seeking reelection. She wanted vice president Walter Mondale to run for his office. "Actually I have never been gung-ho Carter . . ." she said. "Carter should become a statesman and resign. And you would be surprised the number of people privately who are with me on this" (Trescott 1979).

Senator Edward Kennedy challenged President Carter in the 1980 presidential primaries and aggressively campaigned for Black votes. Although Carter had secured enough votes for victory, Kennedy kept his campaign alive through the August Democratic convention (Abramson, Aldrich, and Rohde 1982). To thunderous applause at a CBC event, civil rights leader Jesse Jackson warned Black voters to keep both Kennedy and Carter at a "safe political distance" (Brown 1979). Decades later Jackson urged Blacks at the party's national convention to support the reelection of President Clinton, a moderate Democrat. Pointing out that the "stakes are high," because Republicans now controlled Congress, Jackson praised President Clinton, despite his conservative policy record (Barker, Jones, and Tate 1999, 229). However, 1979 represented a period when Blacks were aggressively pursuing new avenues of power with the Democratic Party.

The newspapers reported that Blacks booed and hurled bottles at President Carter's motorcade in an inner-city section of Miami during the 1980 presidential campaign (Walsh 1980). However, Blacks lined up to vote massively for Jimmy Carter in his campaign against conservative Ronald Reagan. Although many analysts did not consider Carter's domestic presidency to be especially successful, he later won the Nobel Peace Prize in 2002 for his peace-building efforts in the Middle East.

CHAPTER 3

Black House Democrats
in the Reagan-Bush Years

*The combination of the new [Reagan] executive administration and
[Republican-controlled] Senate can have a totally devastating effect unless
blacks are ever vigilant.*

　　—Rep. Cardiss Collins, chair of the CBC

*It seems that a conservative element in this country is looking at the
election as a mandate for retrenchment . . . and that there is a coalescing of
ultraconservatives to turn back the clock.*

　　—Rep. William H. Gray III, member of the CBC

*Rep. Parren Mitchell of Maryland believes that there will be no "meat-ax
approach" to social programs.*

　　—"Worry Time for Blacks," *Newsweek*, December 1, 1980

The CBC won its most important victories during the Reagan-Bush
years. There was the 1982 extension of the Voting Rights Act, which was
strengthened by lawmakers in spite of President Reagan's initial opposition. President Reagan also signed into law the Martin Luther King holiday bill in 1983, making King's birthday a federal holiday. Furthermore,
the CBC remained radical over South Africa, and in part through the
group's efforts over the decade Black political activist Nelson Mandela was
released from prison in 1990 (Tillery 2011). President Bush supported the
1991 Civil Rights Act, which strengthened the legal claims made by those
discriminated against in the workplace but also imposed ceilings on awards
through discrimination lawsuits. The caps were imposed to help small
business and win bipartisan support. The victories were achieved with

better, more united Democratic Party support. But they also reflect a period in which Blacks had won decisively the battle over their civil rights in America. The segregationists were no longer in power, and those who had backed segregation in the South and remained racial conservatives, such as Senator Strom Thurmond (R-SC), had switched to the Republican Party.

The Republican Party no longer debated whether Black demands for civil rights were constitutional. Support for symbolic legislation for Blacks grew, too. In 1989, John Conyers introduced his reparations for U.S. slavery legislation in the House, and that was radical. Later, some southern states, including Alabama, Maryland, North Carolina, and Virginia, passed symbolic legislation apologizing for Black slavery. Thus, some watchful critics of this era might claim that the CBC won at best symbolic victories, including even the 1965 Voting Right Act's extension. Symbolic victories for minorities, however, still improve race relations and increase minority group power.

While Blacks won their public battle over civil rights, they lost in their efforts to redress disadvantages that faced Blacks because of racial discrimination, segregation, and poverty. This second agenda on social policy justice was also aggressively countered through racial politics practiced by the Republican Party. The GOP solidified over the party's opposition to affirmative action. Presidents Reagan and Bush also benefited from a conservative tide against a generous welfare state and favoring an expansion of tough sentencing laws. Democrats divided over such policies, and President Clinton successfully embraced some of the conservative elements of the debate to win election in 1992.

The period reflected remarkable, continued solidarity among the CBC. There was no signs yet of the divisions among the CBC between "moderates" or "liberals" that emerged over time. Some members of the CBC still opposed Democratic House budgets. During the twelve-year period, members of the CBC divided significantly only once, over the Democratic House budget resolution in 1989. In 1981, the CBC began presenting its alternative budget requests, which won unanimous support over the decades, except in a few instances when only three CBC members who voted "present." Dellums won impressive CBC solidarity for his campaign against a defense buildup under President Reagan.

CBC members showed ever increasing party loyalty as the Democratic Party began promoting them into more leadership positions. On tax policies, Black Democrats began to support party leadership to cut American taxes. While all Democratic Black House members united in opposition to the 1991 Gulf War, they later divided over a second resolution extending support to the war.

But a different and more diverse CBC emerged post Reagan-Bush. These differences, I contend, emerged in the CBC as more supported Democratic presidential and House leadership, backing, also, more conservative bills under divided government. Radical policy objectives, radical strategies, and radical leaders, I contend, are sacrificed once minority groups achieve incorporation. Thus, the main thesis of this chapter is that Black Democrats sought during this time more influence over the legislative process and retained a radical posture during the Reagan-Bush years, but quietly began backing the legislative process.

Rising Racial Divisions and Party Politics

In 1980 Republican Ronald Reagan was elected with a powerful antigovernment agenda. He intended to shrink the size of the federal government, not merely tamp down spending. Whereas the CBC had a clear political agenda during the Carter administration—reduce double-digit Black unemployment and fix the cities—its members appeared uncertain in their response to the Reagan Revolution as their friends, the Democrats, appeared ready to play ball with Team Reagan. Charles Rangel in his memoirs explains that things got so cozy between House Democrats and the Republican presidents, that Dan Rostenkowski (D-IL, and also the chairman of the House's powerful Ways and Means Committee during this time) was even advising Bush how to get reelected (Rangel and Wynter 2007, 231).

Writ large, however, the 1980s represented an internal battle within the Democratic Party as Black Democrats had to reckon no longer with the old segregationist fixtures who once dominated their political party but young fair-weather friends calling themselves the "New Democrats." The New Democrats were moderates disenchanted with President Johnson-era social welfare policies.

Furthermore, racial divisions expanded, and did not contract, during the 1980s. The Reagan-Bush years represented a period of a widening gulf between Blacks and Whites, as Black voters rallied behind Democrats and White voters pulled away. Reagan was enormously popular in 1980 and 1984 among White voters, but immensely unpopular among African Americans. A number of books focused on the racial polarization that emerged in the electorate during the 1980s (e.g., Huckfeldt and Kohfeldt

1989). Democrats accused Republicans of exploiting White resentment of Blacks through the use of code words in the 1980s (Mendelberg 2001). Reagan campaigned on fraud and waste in government services used "immoderately" by African Americans. He began his campaign in 1980 in a county in Mississippi where three civil rights workers had been murdered. He also stated his preference for "states' rights," a symbol of White southern resistance to ending Jim Crow laws.

George H. W. Bush also alienated Blacks through his exploitation of racial politics in his 1988 campaign. The campaign used Black convict Willie Horton as a symbol of his opposition to liberal criminal justice policies. In 1988, Bush ran a television ad showing a Black criminal being released. Bush also vetoed civil rights legislation just before the 1990 midterm elections, denouncing it as a "quota bill"; the bill was also used in an anti-affirmative-action ad by Republican senator Jesse Helms in 1990 indicating that the law would put Blacks in jobs that Whites desperately needed. President Bush later signed the measure into law in 1991.

Adding to the racial tensions roiling the electorate were the presidential bids of Black civil rights activist Jesse Jackson Sr. in 1984 and 1988. Jackson's campaigns followed a strategy later outlined by political scientist Ronald Walters in his book, *Black Presidential Politics in America* (1988). Walters, who had served as a deputy campaign manager for Jackson in 1984, argued that Black presidential bids benefit Black Americans, assisting in the institutionalization of Black politics. Not only will campaigns by Black leaders help organize the Black vote every four years, but a Black presidential contender can issue policy statements that could become part of the party's policy platform at its national conventions. Jesse Jackson's 1984 presidential bid, however, was met by a lack of a support among Black members of Congress. Black lawmakers favored Vice President Walter Mondale. Jackson did very well among Black Democratic voters, nonetheless. Many Black lawmakers consequently endorsed Jackson's second bid in 1988 based on his popularity in the Black community (Barker, Jones, and Tate 1999; Tate 1994).

Black leaders in Washington during the 1980s also emphasized the problem of racism there. Harold Ford Sr. was quoted as stating, "We're very disappointed with the leadership. . . . The leadership did not see fit to address the unemployment among blacks or youths or in urban central areas." Parren Mitchell was quoted in the same article as stating that Congress would not move on the problem of Black unemployment until it became a White problem too. Charles Rangel, touching on the invisibility of Black members of Congress within the House, stated that one White colleague expressed his surprise to learn that Rangel was chair of a committee (see Tolchin 1983). These critiques ended by the 1990s. The problem of racial discrimination became less profound. Even among Blacks generally, discrimination as a problem fell to third place behind crime and unemployment in a 1996 national telephone survey of Blacks. In 1984, however, unemployment and discrimination ranked first and second, while crime placed third. Racial issues, therefore, were still very prominent during the 1980s.

In addition to race-card politics by the GOP, Jackson's rebellious presidential bids, and racism (Marable 1991), another important development during the 1980s was the emergence of Black conservatives. Although their actual numbers were small, they obtained a special prominence as Republicans sought them out. The media also gave them special attention. Reagan fired White moderate Republican Arthur Fleming as chair of the Civil Rights Commission in 1982 and appointed Clarence Pendleton, a Black conservative who was a friend of Reagan's attorney general, Edwin Meese. Pendleton argued against government action to address critical problems in the Black community such as unemployment; he was also an opponent of affirmative action, and used his platform as chair of the Commission to promote these views (Walters 2003). Reagan met with the CBC early in 1981, but then never met with the group again. Reagan's snub of the CBC was based on the hope to cultivate new Black political leadership through his attention to Black Republicans and Black political conservatives.

Although Bush pledged to meet with the CBC regularly (Devroy 1989), the entrance of Black conservatives into Black politics was facilitated greatly by his appointment of Black conservative Clarence Thomas to the Supreme Court in 1991. Thomas was picked to fill the vacancy created by the retirement of Thurgood Marshall, the Black liberal Supreme Court justice. During this time, Gary Franks won his election in a majority-White district in Connecticut in 1990 as a Black Republican. With their second entry onto the national scene in the 1980s, the growth in the number of Black Republicans has been slow, but it is picking up. The country's first Black secretary of state, retired general Colin Powell, is a member of the Republican Party, as is the second Black secretary of state, Condoleezza Rice. In 2009, the Republican National Committee picked a Black, Michael Steele, a former lieutenant governor from Maryland, to head its organization. A record number of Blacks ran for House seats as Republicans in 2010, and two were elected in majority-White southern districts.

The pressure from Blacks to bring them into the upper-echelon of leadership got a positive response from the Democratic Party. During the 1980s and early 1990s the party elevated more Blacks into committee chairmanships and party leadership positions. In 1985, CBC member William H. Gray III won Democratic Party support in the House to become the chairman of the powerful Budget Committee, replacing a White chair who had served six years. He had been termed out under a rule that Democrats sought to enforce. In 1985, CBC members chaired a total of five of the 22 standing committees in the House. Under Gray's leadership, the CBC supported the Democratic House budget resolutions, even as Gray voted "present" for the CBC's budget alternatives. The party was able to demonstrate tighter discipline over CBC members during the Reagan-Bush years than under it had under Carter.

Except for 1989, throughout this period only a few Black House members, notably Black radicals such as Conyers and Dellums, voted against the Democratic Party's budget resolutions. And Black support for Democratic Party budget resolutions under Republican presidents undercut the dream (for now it looked farfetched) of a government-backed jobs program. Black public support for a government jobs program as measured in public opinion polls fell during the 1980s as well, a trend Tate (2010) argues is rooted in the political moderation of the CBC.

Budgetary Politics under Presidents Reagan and Bush

President Reagan won an impressive victory with his budget request to Congress 1981, but his later budget proposals were not supported. The 1981 victory, however, was important, for Reagan obtained tax cuts that critics blamed for the record-high federal deficits that plagued his administration. In 1981, the president pledged that he would provide the public and businesses with tax relief, and take them out of an "economic swamp" by stimulating the economy and thereby achieve a balanced budget by 1984. Shortly after winning his budget/tax victory in 1981, President Reagan admitted that a balanced budget was unachievable by 1984. He blamed the recession, which persisted until 1985, as well as rising interest rates, for the ballooning federal deficits, rather the tax cuts, which he maintained were necessary for economic recovery.

Another important discovery in this chapter is that Black members of Congress backed nearly every Democratic-controlled House budget resolution during this period, with regular challenges by a few old guard Black legislators. An exception occurred in 1989, under President Bush, when 60 percent of Black House members opposed the budget resolution put forward by Leon Panetta, Democratic chair of the Budget Committee, which I will discuss further. Mostly, however, Black lawmakers supported these budget agreements even after these House budget resolutions were modified by the more conservative Senate. They proffered their alternative budgets, which they claimed would close the deficit through rescinding the 1981 tax cuts, raising taxes, and cutting defense spending. The Democratic-led Houses refused to rescind Reagan's popular 1981 tax cuts, except for a few business taxes in 1982. But revenues were raised by imposing new taxes during this time.

Why did Black legislators back House budget resolutions, and not fight as a group, as they did under President Carter? One reason was Black legislators showed increasing loyalty to the party, as they rose in the ranks and had better ties to the party. An important reason was the party's decision to elevate a CBC member, William Gray (D-PA), to chair the House Budget Committee in 1985. Gray served as a pragmatic, self-declared bipartisan-oriented chair for four years. Another reason was conservative Republican rule, which makes it difficult for Black Democrats to maintain a united radical stand in budgetary politics.

Reagan used the reconciliation process to get Congress to accept his economic recovery plan. Phil Gramm (D-TX) and Delbert Latta (R-OH) formulated a plan that was consistent with the president's budget request. Boll Weevils, or conservative Democrats, backed it and it won over the House Budget Committee's resolution with a vote of 253–176. All the Black members of the House voted against the Gramm-Latta plan.

In spite of the ideological talk, moderate Republicans in the Senate refused to back Reagan's spending requests. In addition, twice the Congress also passed emergency spending measures that included additional funds for domestic programs such as food stamps and guaranteed student loans in 1982 and 1983, which Black members favored. Thus, while the economic talk in Washington was uncomfortably polarized under Reagan, Democrats manfully stayed in control of the purse with support from moderate Republicans in the Senate as much as possible from 1982 on. Democrats also regained control of the Senate under Bush.

President Reagan's budget requests remained ideologically consistent through his two terms in office. Reagan was never pretending to be a pragmatist. Reagan favored a strong national defense for the nation. Thus, he continually asked for large increases in the defense budget in spite of rising deficits. Only for his last budget request in 1988 did he reduce the amount of funding he wanted for defense. Claiming the requests were impractical, Congress largely ignored these large requests. Still, defense spending expanded over the eight years while discretionary social spending shrank as a portion of the federal budget. Critically, overall government spending was not contained even though Reagan had sought to fight "big government." The Democrats demanded that taxes be raised to fight the deficit. Staunchly opposed to rescinding his 1981 tax cuts, Reagan supported efforts to generate more revenue through new taxes in 1982, 1985, and 1987. However, the federal deficit was not tamed with the addition of these new revenues.

Afterward, Congress took back the budget process from Reagan. Thus, in 1982 the budget resolution contained new taxes, rescinding only a few business tax breaks that had passed in 1981. For many compelling political reasons, the House agreed to back the Ways and Means Committee plan by a vote of 208–197. Passage meant that the House agreed to a lesser role in shaping the final legislation. Only Harold Washington voted against it. Washington later ran for mayor of Chicago in 1983, and may have intended to fight congressional budgets that hurt American cities and urban voters.

In 1983, *CQ Almanac* calls the Budget Committee's resolution a "Democratic Manifesto" (*CQ Almanac* 1983, 435). It won support from moderate Republicans in the Senate, and from all Black members except for Dellums. The rising deficit problem challenged Democratic leadership, nevertheless. In 1984, the Republicans in the Senate insisted that Congress pass a resolution that included deficit reduction. There was anger still among Blacks that the defense budget was spared, while the budget resolution imposed Cost of Living Adjustment (COLA) delays for federal retirees. Four Black urban, northern members voted against the final conference report: Gus Savage, Charles Hayes, Conyers, and George Crockett. Dellums failed to cast a vote.

The deficit control group won an important victory in 1985, getting the Gramm-Rudman-Hollings bill passed. This antideficit measure imposed automatic cuts across the board to reduce the deficit unless Congress acted otherwise. Later, the Supreme Court upheld a lower court ruling declaring it unconstitutional. President Reagan had also sought a line-item veto from Congress, but failed to get it. Overall, the deficit control faction in Washington was a powerful check on Black radicalism.

In 1985, with all the knives out, Congressman Gray was now chair of the House Budget Committee. Gray sought but was unable to deliver a bipartisan agreement from his committee. Only one Republican on his committee supported it. While Gray supported deficit reduction efforts, conservative Democrats on the committee voted for his budget plan only after getting agreement that their tougher alternative would be presented on the floor. This tougher alternative included eliminating Social Security COLAs. In the end, Democrats, however, lacked the will to impose the cuts on Social Security recipients, and backed Gray's budget plan by 258–170. Conyers was the only CBC member to vote against it.

From 1986 through 1989, Black lawmakers supported the committee's budget resolutions even though Gray publicly stated that he sought to work with everyone, including House Republicans. But his appointment obviously played a role in keeping the peace between Black House Democrats and the party. Gray continued his moderate approach to the federal budget the following year, in 1986.

Reagan's budget proposal still permitted the defense budget to grow. Congress pledged instead to respect the deficit targets under the Gramm-Rudman law. Under the Democratic Party's, including Gray's, leadership, the House adopted the final conference report by 333–43 in 1986. Conyers backed this budget, but Dellums and Mitchell voted against it. Dellums was a noted critic of the big defense budgets. Gray continued to pledge support to the Gramm-Rudman's automatic reductions language, reasoning that this forced President Reagan into more serious budget negotiations. However, it forced Democrats to agree to further budget cuts in domestic programs as well. While Republicans sought a freeze in government spending, Gray rejected it. In 1987, he was only able to get his budget resolution passed by a party-line vote of 230–192. All the Black members in 1987 backed the House plan. In 1988, Reagan tempered his hard-line budget requests, scaling back his demand for defense budget increases. The parties cooperated in the budget process in 1988, and the House budget resolution put together by Gray won by a large margin of 319–102. Only 24 Democrats opposed it. Again, not a single Black member objected to Gray's budget.

President Bush entered into the fray over budgetary politics severely handicapped as a nonideologue. In his initial budget, Bush proposed defense cuts, something Reagan did not do, and also cuts in Medicare and agriculture. Leon Panetta (D-CA) now chaired the House Budget Committee, and although his budget plan included an increase in domestic spending, it still protected defense spending. The looser, nonideological justification for the budget plan upset liberal Blacks. In the final conference report, 14 out of 23 Black House members rejected it. Those backing Panetta, for example, included Bill Gray, Hawkins, and CBC members from the South, John Lewis, Mike Espy, Ford, and Leland. Charles Rangel generally supported the party, but voted against the final budget measure, as did Collins, Savage, Hayes, Kweisi Mfume, Conyers, Crockett, and Stokes, members from the urban North.

Panetta, however, won better support from the CBC for the remaining three years of his budget leadership under Bush. Just as Reagan accepted some new taxes in 1982, Bush accepted a tax hike in 1990. However, these new taxes broke Bush's 1988 campaign pledge, and were considered to have cost him reelection in 1992. The budget agreement included raising the tax rate for the wealthiest from 28 percent to 31 percent. To make this a bipartisan agreement, real cuts were made to Medicare, as increases in deductibles and copayments were imposed. It passed 227–203, with only Savage and Hawkins, presumably upset over Medicare, voting against it.

President Bush's budget proposals still took a nonideological tone as he sought a mix of cuts and increases in his effort to reprioritize government spending programs. Republicans plainly rejected Bush's budget plans on the floor, with his budget being rejected by a vote of 89–335. In 1992, a Bush budget plan got even fewer votes still, even though he sought a capital gains tax reduction, a spending freeze, and the elimination of unnecessary programs for the poor. In 1991, Democrats added an additional $200 million for education to the budget in an amendment. The CBC backed the budget plan unanimously. The politics in 1992 were a bit more difficult, as liberals wanted a "peace dividend," or the transfer of these cuts on defense spending to domestic programs. The Democratic-controlled Congress in the end instead chose to put the defense cuts into deficit reduction. Republicans rallied in this election year against the Democratic-dominated plan, and the final measure barely survived in the House by a vote of 209–207. Still, three CBC members (Dellums, Savage, and Conyers) voted against their party on this final bill.

Although the CBC remained a key liberal group in Congress, it was no longer protesting against the way the two parties worked together to pass budgets. In budget politics, I contend that the ardent ideology of liberal Black members was cooled by the pressure for strong party discipline against an ideological president, their inclusion and growth, and the presence of a Black chair on the Budget Committee.

The CBC's Alternative Budgets

The mystique of a rebellious CBC is maintained through the ritual of its annual alternative budget request. Permitted a floor vote on its alternative budget, this also helps the CBC keep its organizational cool. The Democratic Party gave Black members greater deference in agreeing to accept the CBC amendment challenge to the committee-backed budget resolutions year after year. Since it did not keep Black lawmakers positioned to seriously challenge the party over the defeat of their alternative budgets, the alternative budget has lost a lot of its bite over time. It currently helps only the organization, and no longer those in the electorate wanting a budget statement that reflects a belief in a progressive taxation system and a commitment to the nation's social welfare programs over defense.

The alternative budget initiative still keeps the CBC in the political spotlight, bringing recognition to its members. The press probably accords less attention over time to the budget as it appears to serve purely as a symbol of Black unity, and less the ideological fervor of Black members. Importantly, the Democratic Party is likely rewarded with greater support from Black legislators for its deference to the CBC on this matter. The Democratic Party agreed to accept the alternative budget requests as its own pledge to recognize and incorporate Black lawmakers. Thus, the alternative budget may be a bigger win for the party than for the CBC today.

In 1981, the CBC proposed its first alternative budget. It won 69 votes. Table 1 shows the votes for the alternative budgets from 1981 to 1988. In 1982, it obtained 86 votes. In 1983, the CBC formulated its own budget resolution, but decided not to have it voted on by the full House. In 1984, however, it did present its budget plan for a vote, winning 76 votes, impressive for a group of about 20 members. Their large budget request dared to do the opposite of Reagan's equally immodest economic agenda. It raised taxes, increased domestic spending significantly, and pared down defense spending. It was rejected along with several modest alternatives that aimed to reduce the federal deficit by cutting discretionary spending programs or raising taxes. Conservative Democrats, along with Republicans, liked the defense spending, and raising taxes was unpopular.

The CBC's budgets in the late 1980s were strongly liberal. They raised taxes and sought to restore spending to domestic programs while cutting back on defense. The CBC alternative budgets won fewer votes in 1986 and 1987 than it had won in 1984 (see table 1). He felt that voting for the measure limited his ability to chair a bipartisan committee and reach agreement on the budget. House Democrats worked openly for a bipartisan agreement that cut spending equally across domestic and defense programs. House Democrats were on the defensive, favoring tax increases only if the popular Republican president backed tax increases as well. There seemed to be an implicit antigovernment strategy in the budgetary politics—that by being the fiscally irresponsible party, Republicans removed all hope that domestic spending levels could be restored in light of the growing deficit.

In 1989, the CBC alternative budget boldly raised taxes by $25.3 billion and cut defense to gain funds for increasing domestic spending. Support picked up slightly for the Black alternative budget, probably because Congress felt then that defense should be cut. The vote was 81–343. The liberal and conservative alternatives were far apart, as liberals sought to raise revenues, while conservatives still championed spending freezes. There was a consensus only on reducing government spending on defense.

Key Issues for Blacks in the Reagan-Bush Administrations

Black lawmakers were united against Reagan's defense budgets and the Gulf War in 1991 under Bush. The other issues where Black lawmakers pressured both administrations were over the 1982 Voting Rights Act and U.S. policy on South Africa.

TABLE 1. Total Floor Votes for the CBC Alternative Budget

	Floor Vote	Black Division
1981	69–356	
1982	86–322	
1983	*None submitted*	
1984	76–333	
1985	54–361	Gray voted "present"
1986	61–359	Gray voted "present"
1987	56–362	Gray voted "present"
1988		
1989	81–343	
1990	90–334	
1991		
1992	77–342	
1993	87–335	
1994	81–326	
1995	56–367	Bishop voted "present"
1996		
1997	72–358	Bishop voted "present"
1998		
1999		
2000	70–348	
2001		
2002		
2003	85–340	
2004	119–302	
2005		
2006	131–294	
2007	115–312	
2008	126–292	
2009	113–318	Davis voted "present"

Source: Based on *CQ Almanac*, various years. Data are shown for years when there was coverage of this issue.

Defense Spending and the Nuclear Arms Race

A radical objective of Black lawmakers was consistent with a vision that the U.S. government should stop building weapons of mass destruction. Black Democrats were united around this objective at the beginning, and backed notably Ron Dellums's efforts against the arms race. Dellums influenced as well his White Democratic colleagues.

A clear victory for President Reagan's agenda was increasing federal spending on defense. The Democratic-controlled Congress gave Reagan most of what he wanted during his eight years in office for defense. Reagan sought to build up American weapons, as part of what analysts saw was an arms race between the United States and the Soviet Union. The MX missile was a controversial element of Reagan's defense plan, the deadliest and costliest nuclear weapon in the U.S. arsenal. One hundred of these missiles could wipe out 30 percent of the Soviet population, or 75 million people (CQ Researcher, June 5, 1981). Although the missiles were part of a mobile system, some Western states objected to having them placed in their states for environmental and economic-cultural reasons. The Carter administration, however, was the first to favor the stockpiling of MX missiles. He apparently favored the MX missile plan as efforts to achieve an arms control agreement under the SALT II talks stalled and as the Soviets invaded Afghanistan in 1979.

In light of the controversy, in 1981 President Reagan decided not to include additional funds for the MX missile because a decision on deployment was still pending. However, CBC member Ron Dellums (D-CA) introduced a floor amendment to kill the MX project altogether. It was firmly rejected in a 96–316 vote. Dellums secured the support of all the CBC members for his amendment, however. The House rejected an amendment by Paul Simon (D-IL) requiring that Congress vote in concurrence with the president's decision on the MX missile. It failed by 201–207. Again, as a bloc, the CBC voted for this amendment. Black legislators voted unanimously with other efforts by their Democratic colleagues to delete MX money from the budget in 1981. There were also some efforts in the House to eliminate $1.8 billion for the B-1 bomber through an amendment sponsored by Joseph Addabbo (D-NY). The B-1 bomber had its share of critics because of its expense, and there were reports it was quickly going to be replaced by another stealth system. In this instance, two CBC members, Hawkins of California and Crockett of Michigan, opposed this amendment, while every other CBC member favored deleting the B-1 bomber from the budget.

Congress in 1982 generally accepted Reagan's large increase in the defense budget, imposing only a small 7 percent cut (*CQ Almanac* 1982, 277). Congress scrapped, however, Reagan's request for more money for the MX missile. Now called the "Peacekeeper" by President Reagan, efforts to kill the MX missile outright in Congress were defeated. In 1982 Dellums sponsored an amendment to delete funds for the Pershing II ballistic missiles—nuclear-tipped missiles used in Europe. Dellums received 100 percent of the CBC's votes for this amendment. Nevertheless, it was rejected by the House by a vote of 74–311.

In 1983, Reagan made the MX missile an important part of his defense plan. Al Gore Jr. (D-TN) in the House was among those fighting to reduce the number of proposed MX missiles, but opposition had weakened in Congress. Reagan's tough stance toward the Soviet Union was more popular, even though House Democrats had gained more seats in the 1982 elections. The House, however, in 1983 approved a nuclear freeze statement that the Senate rejected. The majority favored the lengthy resolution proposing that the United States and the Soviet Union enter into talks with the objective of negotiating an immediate and verifiable freeze on the testing, construction, and deployment of nuclear weapons. It passed by a 278–149 vote. Among those voting for the nuclear freeze were all of the CBC members. Reagan responded to the nuclear freeze resolution by calling it "'a very dangerous fraud . . . merely the illusion of peace'" (*CQ Almanac* 1983, 207). Although it was not endorsed by the Reagan administration, one southern House Democrat proposed a "build down" plan that retired two warheads for every new one built, including Pershing II and MX missiles. All the Black House Democrats rejected the build-down proposal along with the House by a vote of 190–229. By a razor-thin margin, centrist Democrats helped keep the MX missile in production in 1985. Democrats, however, barred further tests of Reagan's antisatellite (ASAT) missiles in 1985 (missiles shot from a fighter plane that were designed to destroy Soviet space satellites), citing the Soviet's moratorium on the testing of nuclear weapons.

In 1985, Reagan was successful again in winning support for the MX missile. He lost the next year as opposition in Congress to Reagan's large defense budget requests grew in response to the rising deficit. The nuclear freeze camp in the House also won several key victories. In 1987, Reagan won an agreement with the Soviet Union banning intermediate-range nuclear force (INF) weapons. And in 1988, liberals in Congress supported the INF ban. Dellums was still part of the progressive contingent aiming to reduce funding for the MX and Midgetman nuclear missiles in 1988, but the amendment was soundly defeated, as centrists sustained the programs over the objections of liberals.

Confronted with a large federal deficit now, President Bush's relationship with Congress on defense began to encounter difficulties. Opposition to big defense programs such as the Strategic Defense Initiative (SDI), a space-based antimissile system, grew in Congress. Furthermore, the Senate rejected John Tower's nomination to be secretary of defense by a 47–53 vote. Dick Cheney, a House Republican from Wyoming, was later confirmed to that post. In April 1989, House members from states scheduled for military base closures sought passage of a resolution disapproving a House committee's recommendation for 91 base closures. It failed by a 43–381 vote, and only Gus Savage of Chicago, among CBC members, voted for it.

President Bush requested a zero-growth budget for defense in 1990, but he also sent U.S. troops to Kuwait and Saudi Arabia to defend it from Iraq in January 1991. The end of the Cold War came that year as well, with Mikhail Gorbachev's resignation as the last leader of the Soviet Union, putting the United States in what Bush called a "New World Order." As a member of the Armed Services Committee, Dellums still led the charge to reduce funding for the Strategic Defense Initiative (SDI) and eliminate the SDI program office. Even though Dellums's May 1991 amendment was rejected 118–266, he got all of the Democratic CBC members to support it. The CBC now had 25 members (including the Washington, DC, delegate, Eleanor Holmes Norton, and Black Republican Gary Franks).

In 1992, Congress cut the SDI program significantly. Congress also passed a nuclear test ban in response to all former Soviet states except Russia renouncing nuclear weapons, and Russia having announced its own test ban in 1991. Maxine Waters (D-CA) along with Dellums (D-CA) sponsored an amendment to reduce the defense authorization bill by 10 percent. It was rejected by 90–283.

Overall, the CBC was defeated in its effort to block the massive expansion of the federal government's defense budget and its production of nuclear weapons. Reagan's persuasiveness and events shaped congressional behavior. But the Democratic Party liberalized in time over this issue. With Dellums leading the fight against the production of the nuclear missile, the MX, other liberals, such as Al Gore, joined in. In the post-Soviet empire world, the defense budget stopped growing and expensive defense programs, like SDI, were cut under President Bush. Remarkably, the CBC stayed united under Dellums against the nuclear weapons build up and defense spending during the Reagan-Bush years. Only one southern Black Democrat seemed likely to defect to the Democratic centrist cause, Mike Espy (D-MS). The other new members of the southern Black delegation elected in 1992 remarkably stood with Dellums to oppose big defense programs. Espy later was appointed to Bill Clinton's administration in 1993. And later, some southern Black members of the House supported Clinton's big defense budget requests.

The 1991 Gulf War

President Bush sent American troops January 1, 1991 to Saudi Arabia and Kuwait to defend Kuwait against Iraq's invasion, which had began in August 1990. While some debated whether it was constitutionally necessary or not, Congress was asked to authorize the president's declaration of war against Iraq. The Congress initially sharply divided. The Senate authorized the use of military force against Iraq on January 15 by a narrow 52–47 vote. The House also backed the president by a vote of 250–183. Not one Black House Democrat supported the resolution. In the newspapers, John Lewis (D-GA) said "war is obsolete as a tool of American foreign policy" (Garrett 1991).

After the Gulf War began, Congress, however, passed a second resolution warmly backing the president and supporting his leadership as commander in chief in the Gulf War. Unlike the first, there was unanimous support for it in the Senate, and overwhelming support in the House. Ten of the 12 members of the House who voted "no" or "present" Were Black lawmakers. "I do not support the president's action and never will," Charles Hayes (D-IL) told reporters. "The resolution, he said, amounted to saying 'Amen, you're right, Mr. President'" (Garrett 1991). Five Blacks voted present, five voted against the resolution, while ten supported it. The ten supporting it included John Conyers and Barbara-Rose Collins of Michigan, John Lewis of Georgia, and Alan Wheat of Missouri. Rangel, who opposed it, was quoted in *Congressional Quarterly Almanac* as having said on the floor during debate, "We can support the men and women in the military and still disagree vigorously with the president of the United States. Nobody in this country is going to browbeat me into agreeing with the president on the Persian Gulf" (*CQ Almanac* 1991, 444). The war ended with President Bush's announcement of a cease-fire after six weeks of war.

The CBC and U.S. Africa Policy

Alvin Tillery's (2011) book on Black leadership and U.S. foreign policy establishes that the CBC played a crucial role in the formulation of U.S. foreign policy toward Africa. White minority rule ended in Rhodesia, now Zimbabwe, in 1980. However, it was not until the 1990s that South Africa held discussions to formally end White minority rule and abolish its system of state-sanctioned discrimination against its majority-Black citizens. Antiapartheid activist Nelson Mandela was released from prison by the White-led regime in 1990. This was an important victory for the CBC, and Mandela visited the United States to a tremendous showing of American fans. Frederik W. de Klerk, the White ruler of South Africa, also visited the country for talks with President Bush in 1990 to set a new U.S. foreign policy with South Africa, which was now intent on opening its regime to its Black citizens.

The CBC accelerated its program of changing U.S. policy on South Africa during the Reagan years. The organization's style, in fact, became radical, but won plenty of White support from left-leaning groups as well as student activists. The drumbeat over changing U.S. policy on South Africa was steady. First, in 1981, the CBC issued a statement that UN ambassador Jeanne Kirkpatrick should be fired for meeting with South African military officials (DeVries 1981). In a separate news conference, CBC member Julian C. Dixon said that he planned "to introduce a resolution asking President Reagan not to invite Prime Minister P. W. Botha of South Africa to visit the United States 'until that country renounces its policy of apartheid'" (*New York Times* 1981). Second, in 1981, the CBC denounced the U.S. veto of a United Nations Security Council resolution condemning South Africa. The CBC kept up its lobbying pressure on the Reagan administration.

TransAfrica was deeply involved in the campaign to isolate South Africa until it ended its system of racial apartheid. TransAfrica was started with the help of the CBC in 1977 (Remnick 1985). In 1982, the CBC wrote a letter to President Reagan protesting a planned International Monetary Fund loan to South Africa. Some CBC members participated in the picketing of the IMF in Washington. In 1984, some CBC members were among 25 members of Congress who were arrested for protesting at the South African Embassy. In 1984, South African bishop Desmond M. Tutu, a leading critic of apartheid, won the Nobel Peace Prize. President Reagan met with him, but his administration also issued a statement that the meeting would not alter U.S. policy toward South Africa. The Reagan administration continued to insist on "quiet diplomacy."

In 1985, the House voted for economic sanctions against South Africa. The margin in the House was large. This vote was a setback for the Reagan administration, which had opposed sanctions. Finally, in 1990, South Africa released Nelson Mandela. In 1991 President Bush announced that his administration was seeking the lifting of sanctions against South Af-

rica. The CBC had wanted the Bush administration to "go slow" on end-
ing sanctions, but feared that they didn't have the votes to continue them.
However, Bush's decision angered the CBC. Yet just like in the case of the
Voting Rights Act, the CBC won a major victory in getting the United
States to pressure South Africa to end apartheid.

The 1982 Extension of the Voting Rights Act

The 1965 Voting Rights Act was radical law, but it was sustained as constitutional by the Supreme Court. Its extension in 1982 constituted a major
victory for the CBC. The 1965 Voting Rights Act (VRA) had been extended
two times, in 1970 and 1975, but the law was set to expire in 1982. In every
instance, a Republican president (Nixon, Ford, and now Reagan) presided
over its reauthorization, offering objections, but each was forced to support
its extension nonetheless in light of weak Republican opposition.

By 1982, the traditional opponents of the VRA were no longer southern
Democrats, but southern Republicans. Strom Thurmond, who had led the
Dixiecrat revolt against the liberalizing Democratic Party on civil rights in
1948, had switched parties, and now chaired the Senate Judiciary Committee as a Republican. Jesse Helms (R-NC), who had once been for a Democrat, sought to filibuster the legislation. Only 17 House Republicans and
seven House Democrats voted against it. President Reagan had supported
only a ten-year extension, but signed a 25-year extension into law in 1982.
The U.S. Senate had voted for the measure by 85–8 (*CQ Quarterly Almanac*
1982). Not only was Section 5, which required federal preclearance of voting changes in the affected states, extended for an unprecedented amount
of time, but the language of Section 2 was strengthened to make it easier
for courts to find violations of minority voting rights. Opponents of the
new amended Section 2 complained that this change made it into a "results
test," where the absence of minority officeholders in a given jurisdiction
was considered a violation of the Act.

While Republican Senators Jesse Helms and Strom Thurmond objected to the Act's constitutionality in 1982, Republican opposition to the
Voting Rights Act was more symbolic. Its popularity in Washington, according to one scholar, reflects the growing importance of the Black vote
and the expansion of it beyond its original jurisdiction to include other
minority groups. Abigail Thernstrom (1987) contends that the 1982 extension revealed the core strength of liberal interests in Washington at that
time.

Moreover, the segregationists who had worked southern White voters into a fever pitch during the civil rights era were absent in 1982. They still managed to help Republicans win presidential elections through the political conversion of White voters to the Republican Party in the South by promulgating racial conservatism. Yet Republicans refused to mount a strong challenge to its extension. Some contend that the Republican Party backed the VRA's extension because it benefits from redistricting that favors minority groups. Increasing the size of the minority population to a majority in one district can increase political opportunities for Republican candidates in adjacent districts.

Divisions within the CBC

Divisions initially within the CBC were over water projects and environmental issues as they had been under Carter, but in 1986 the CBC divided over two major achievements of the Reagan presidency: the Tax Reform Act of 1986 and the 1986 Immigration Reform Act. The Tax Reform Act substantially reduced the tax rate from the top earners from 50 to 28 percent and taxed the rest of the population at 15 percent. It eliminated special tax breaks for the wealthy, but also slightly reduced the top corporate rate. Reagan celebrated the ending of "the steeply progressive income tax" (*CQ Almanac* 1986, 491).

Conservatives in the Senate nearly derailed the tax cuts because of the growing federal deficit problem, but in the House 116 Republicans for it, with 62 against. Democratic House members were overwhelmingly in favor of it, voting 176 to 74 for the new tax codes. Democrats wanted credit for the tax cuts as much as Republicans. To win liberal support, Democrats explained that the new reform took millions of poor workers off the tax rolls. Opposition still persisted among liberals who felt that the tax cuts for the wealthy were too extreme. Still, 63 percent of CBC members voted for it, and those opposed mainly consisted of old guard members such as Mitchell, Conyers, and Clay, as well as newcomers such as Dixon and Leland.

The 1986 immigration reform law passed by a smaller margin than the bipartisan tax reform act. This law was the first major reform of the nation's immigration laws since the 1965 Immigration Act. It passed with a vote of 230–166. Republicans, this time, were generally opposed to the new law, which granted amnesty to undocumented immigrants who could prove that they worked in agriculture and legalized three million undocumented immigrants who entered the United States before January 1, 1982, and had resided there continuously since then. They had to pay a fine and back taxes. The law was the first time the nation imposed penalties on employers for hiring undocumented workers. The House Republican vote was 62–105 opposed. The House Democratic vote was 168–61 in favor. Again, the CBC split on this reform legislation, as 65 percent voted in favor of it. Several old guard members (Mitchell, Conyers, Crockett) chose not to vote on this landmark legislation. Those opposed to the new law were mostly from states having large Latino populations (Hawkins, Mervyn Dymally of California, Leland of Texas, Edolphus (Ed) Towns of New York, and Savage and Hayes of Illinois). Their argument against it was similar to arguments by Latino lawmakers that the new employer sanctions might lead to discrimination against foreign-looking job applicants. Latino lawmakers in favor of it, such as Bill Richardson (D-NM), favored amnesty, stating, "It was the last gasp for legalization to take place in a humane way" (*CQ Almanac* 1986, 67). Still, only five of the 11-member Hispanic Caucus in the House voted for it.

In 1987, there were no significant divisions in the CBC. The "key votes" legislation consisted of five key social policy bills in 1987. Notably, Reagan signed into law reparations for the Japanese Americans who had been forced into internment camps during World War II. The Act came with a government apology and token repayments. Congress also overrode a presidential veto by Reagan to pass civil rights legislation in 1987. The House also passed a law approving the death penalty for drug traffickers. The CBC was solidly against it, with only Espy voting for it. The House also passed a bill that barred the District of Columbia from using its own funds to pay for abortions. The House voted to eliminate the seven-day waiting period for the purchase of handguns from an antidrug/crime bill. Only Espy voted for this amendment eliminating the waiting provision. Most of the Democratic Party now was hostile to the growing social conservatism of the Republican Party, which helped unite Black Democratic lawmakers with their party.

The CBC split three times in 1989 on legislation that the House wildly supported in two of the three instances. The first key vote was on Bush's bipartisan budget resolution. It passed by a vote of 263–157 with nearly half (45 percent) of the CBC voting for it. The old guard divided in this instance. For example, Conyers, Rangel, and Stokes voted for it, while Dellums, Collins, and Clay did not. There was liberal opposition to cuts in social programs, but Bush had agreed to cuts in defense spending. The second area of division on key votes for the CBC was on the repeal of a provision of the tax reform act. Small businesses had objected to the provision, called Section 89, which made it difficult for employers to discriminate against their workers in the provision of employee benefit plans. Most of the CBC voted against its repeal, but 33 percent favored it. Supporters included a mix of new CBC members, such as Lewis and Wheat, but also Gray.

The final division emerged over the repeal of the new catastrophic-illness insurance plan for Medicare. It had passed in 1988, but senior citizens revolted over having to pay for it. The CBC split evenly over the matter. It is difficult to see an old guard or ideological basis to the vote. Like the repeal of Section 89, the repeal of the catastrophic-illness insurance plan was wildly popular in the House. It won by a vote of 360–66. Four CBC members voted to oppose all three key bills: Savage and Hayes of Illinois, Donald Payne of New Jersey, and Towns of New York.

In 1990, the key votes included six social policy bills. While African American House legislators had divided some in 1986, only Savage voted against a 1990 bill that significantly increased immigration to this country and provided amnesty to the dependents of those granted amnesty through the 1986 Immigration and Control Act. Blacks were largely in agreement on the other social policy bills, including the defeat of a constitutional amendment to prohibit flag burning, support for the Family and Medical Leave Act for workers caring for sick relatives or children, opposition to a ban on abortions at overseas military facilities, support for a ban on federal funding for obscene or homoerotic art, and support for the successful House effort to override President Bush's veto of 1990 civil rights legislation. In 1990, all but Conyers voted for the key bill adopting a budget agreement that included new taxes, combined with cuts in social programs. This agreement reached with the White House meant that Bush had abandoned his 1988 campaign pledge of "no new taxes."

In 1992, Conyers introduced his "budget walls" bill, which was rejected in the House by a vote 187–238. The bill proposed to knock down the walls between defense and social programs, so that savings from cutting defense could be transferred to domestic spending programs. No Republican favored it, but he won most of his Democratic House colleagues for the measure. At this time, Conyers was chair of the Government Operations. Again, this is an example of the new concordance achieved during this time given the high level of House Democratic support for Conyers's "budget walls" measure.

Conclusion

President Reagan's popularity appeared so persistently strong that he was called the "Teflon president," because blame and criticism did not really stick to him. Studies of his popularity as president reveal that Reagan's was not that exceptional. It was battered by fallout over the Iran-Contra scandal, but lifted by support following the *Challenger* disaster and the invasion of Grenada (Lanoue 1989). He did not get all that he wanted from the Democratic-controlled Congress. However, the 1981 Reagan tax cuts were historic, and the Republican economic plan to restore economies through tax cuts now enjoys the support of many.

Tense racial politics remained in the air through the mid-1990s, also as Blacks continued to win elections in historic contests in the nation. The defeat of conservative Robert Bork in 1987 as a Supreme Court nominee by President Reagan, while it took place in the Senate, was an important development in political relations between the major parties. However, the Senate confirmed by a narrow margin a conservative Black, Clarence Thomas, to replace retiring liberal Black justice Thurgood Marshall in 1991. Belatedly, basically after 1994, the Democratic Party began to aggressively counter the ideological immoderation of the Republican Party in Washington. Yet Republican dominance ultimately took a toll on the unity of the CBC. Although it responded aggressively and singularly as a group to conservative policies promulgated by Presidents Reagan and Bush, the CBC channeled its later oppositional responses to Republican national leadership through the Democratic Party because the party continued to liberalize.

CHAPTER 4

President Clinton and the New CBC

We want a first-class partnership.

—CBC chairman Kweisi Mfume, referring to the CBC's
policymaking role with President Clinton

The 1992 elections brought a Democrat back to the White House after a long hiatus of twelve years. Arkansas governor Bill Clinton defeated President George H. W. Bush in his reelection bid. The 1992 elections also increased Black political power in the U.S. Congress significantly, as 13 new Black lawmakers were elected along with the first Black female U.S. Senator, Carol Moseley Braun. This new Democratic president, coupled with the enhanced political power of African Americans in the U.S. Congress, in theory could have been used to restore the nation's domestic policies that had been assaulted during the Reagan-Bush years. Clinton, however, was a "New Democrat," one who had a distinctive policy agenda that combined conservative objectives with liberal ones. He sought comprehensive health insurance coverage along with conservative welfare reform that ended the federal entitlement to welfare for families in need. He favored increased spending on crime prevention along with "three strikes" legislation that mandated life imprisonment for those convicted of a third felony.

As president, Bill Clinton was enormously popular among Black voters (Tate 1994). He criticized Black radicalism, which some attributed to Jesse Jackson's activism within the Democratic Party, by denouncing Sister Souljah. Sister Souljah had made a racially insensitive statement about Whites in an interview about the 1992 Los Angeles riot. However, during the campaign, he promised Blacks that he would work to heal racial divisions in the nation. He stated: "My whole career, my whole campaign, is about unity, not division" (Ayres 1992). Divisions on racial issues still were great in this country. Clinton delicately campaigned in soft support of affirmative action in 1992 by proclaiming "Mend it, don't end it." Ironically, as much as surveys show that the vast majority of Whites don't like affirmative action programs, one 1995 poll revealed only 17 percent of Whites, Latinos, Asians, and other minorities responded that "it is time to eliminate all affirmative action programs for minorities and women" (Tate 2010). Thus, this moderate president spoke to Black voters while attempting to maintain a broad base of support within the White community. In 1997, President Clinton established a panel for a "national conversation on race" that was chaired the Black historian John Hope Franklin (Barker, Jones, and Tate 1999).

Several changes worked especially in President Clinton's favor. Black public opinion had grown more moderate and economic conditions within the Black community had improved. A majority of Blacks favored Clinton's welfare reform initiative that ended the federal guarantee of a welfare check for families in poverty. Majorities of Blacks also liked "three strikes" legislation, which laid down mandatory sentences of life for a third felony conviction (Tate 2010). Black unemployment and poverty rates fell sharply during the 1990s. In 1970, one-third of all Black families were in poverty. By 2001, roughly 23 percent of Black families resided below the poverty line. Figure 6 shows the national poverty rate and the Black poverty rate over time. Beginning in 1994, when the Black family poverty rate fell below 30 percent, there are steady decreases. In 1997, the percentage drops to 25.5 percent and by 2000 fell to 21.2 percent. The percentage of Black families in poverty increased slightly in 2002 through 2006, but remains lower than the rate during the 1980s when one-third of all Black families were in poverty.

Moreover, the political style of the CBC was strikingly different than it was the last time a Democrat sat in the White House. The Caucus was less adversarial and more cooperative. Several reasons explain this change in style. First, with the addition of 13 Black lawmakers to the House, one could almost talk about a new CBC, one consisting of a new generation of Black legislators along with the old guard. David T. Canon (1999) documents the changes in the political style of Black lawmakers after the new post-1990s districts were constructed. The old guard did not back President Clinton as often as the new Black House members. But they were not as openly critical of Clinton as they had been of Carter. Conyers, for example, pledged support to Clinton especially in the aftermath of the Re-

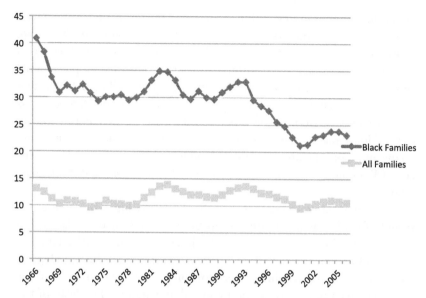

Fig. 6. Percentage of all families and of Black families in poverty. (Data from www.census.gov/hhes/www/poverty/histpov/histpov2.html.)

publican control of the U.S. Congress in 1994 and when the Republican-controlled House voted to impeach Clinton in 1998. Thus, even members of the old guard had changed their approach to working with Democratic presidents. They gave deference to electoral considerations as they strived to win policy concessions from the White House. Secondly, Clinton was persuasive, too, and courted the new CBC. In addition to meeting with the CBC frequently, Clinton also faithfully attended CBC fund-raising dinner events.

A third factor in Clinton's favor was an expansion of Black clout in the new Clinton administration through committee service. Ronald V. Dellums (D-CA) became chairman of the House Armed Services Committee in 1993. John Lewis (D-GA) became one of the Democrats' chief deputy whips, a position that could lead to Majority Leader. John Conyers Jr. (D-MI) chaired the Government Operations Committee. Rangel and Conyers were poised to head the House Ways and Means Committee and the Judiciary Committee, respectively. All this new and potential Black power on committees was taken away once the Republicans seized control of the House and Senate, having majorities in 1995. Thus, a fourth important change was Republican dominance in Congress. Newt Gingrich talked about the Republican Revolution in 1994, and the ten-point Contract with America. This was the first time that the GOP had control of the House of Representatives in forty years. Blacks' party unity scores had increased since the Carter years, and Clinton earned significantly higher presidential support scores from Black legislators than had Carter. The policymaking process in the House was no longer loosely bipartisan for Democrats, as Rangel had characterized the process under Reagan. Republican control of the House made support for President Clinton mandatory. Thus, new, young ambitious members, senior and influential Black ones, and the menace of Republican dominance helped favor the president and the Democratic Party.

It is not accurate to say that the CBC's relationship with Clinton was trouble free, but it was more successful than the Caucus's relationship with Carter. Clinton had abandoned his liberal appointee, African American Lani Guinier, to head the civil rights division of the Justice Department. Her academic writings on proportional representation in elections were perceived to be too radical by his administration. The head of the CBC, Kweisi Mfume, said that this retreat on her nomination would have "dramatic fallout in the Black Caucus, among progressive groups, among women's groups and among individuals in the nation who believe everybody ought to have a day in court" (Lewis 1993). A day later, Mfume called the president's decision to withdraw the nomination "reprehensible," adding, "The president has succumbed to fear, innuendo and a whispering campaign by a few nameless and faceless senators and members of the far right. . . . The Congressional Black Caucus must now reassess and re-evaluate its relationship and future role with this administration" (Seper 1993).

However, a review of the legislative record and newspaper accounts of the CBC and Clinton reveals that Clinton kept the CBC close to his administration and consulted with the organization more frequently than the CBC admitted. All accounts described the president as persuasive. The voting behavior of the CBC revealed internal divisions within the CBC, and, notably, even the most radical members of the CBC showed greater deference to the policy agenda of this president.

Some of this might be due to senior members holding chairmanships, or being in line for important chairmanships, and holding party positions or seeking party positions. Yet the later analysis reveals that senior members and legislative leaders were among the most liberal members of the CBC. It was due to both stronger presidential leadership and the nature of the times. Republican presidents could refuse to meet with the CBC without any significant fallout from constituents. New CBC members wanted this new audience with the president. All wanted a new partnership in national policymaking that a Democratic president offered.

Clinton, certainly, appointed more Blacks to his administration than Carter, who had been criticized for having only one Black cabinet member. Five Blacks held cabinet-level posts in the first Clinton administration. These Black cabinet members were Mike Espy of Agriculture, Ron Brown of Commerce, Energy Secretary Hazel O'Leary, Veterans Affairs Secretary Jesse Brown, and Lee P. Brown, director of the Office of National Drug Control Policy.

Agricultural Department head Mike Espy was a former CBC member and also the first Black congressman from Mississippi since Reconstruction. His politics as a Black lawmaker was more conservative than his CBC colleagues since he opposed gun control laws and favored the death penalty. Clinton also appointed an African American, Deval Patrick, to head the Civil Rights Division of the Justice Department after withdrawing Guinier's name for that post. Clinton sought to lead, however, by engaging both the Left and the Right and proposing centrist solutions to policy debates. His political adviser Dick Morris coined the term "triangulation" to describe the president's policies that were a blended form of liberal-conservative policies that included welfare reform, crime control, and balanced budgets.

In the end, Clinton was most successful in his policies that won Republican backing. Most Black legislators voted against welfare reform, but saved votes for Clinton's budgets. They also didn't denounce President Clinton as too conservative, but rallied to see him reelected in 1996. Policy divisions between the CBC and Clinton were handled out of the public's eye. Thus, while Black radicalism fell as the policy rhetoric was relocated to a Left-Right dimension, it also fell as Black lawmakers abandoned Black radical strategies. These Black radical strategies include the protest Black lawmakers showed on the issue of South Africa and the unified bloc voting they had once used for leverage over budgetary matters. The one major exception was Black lawmakers' failed attempt to reshape Clinton's omnibus crime bill in 1995.

The CBC and Clinton's Fiscal Policies

President Clinton was only able to propose two budgets before the House was taken over by a Republican majority who dictated their own budget plans in 1995 and thereafter. Clinton proposed spending cuts but boldly raised taxes as his effort as a moderate Democrat to reduce the federal deficit. African American House legislators backed his 1993 and 1994 fiscal policies strongly, with mild threats that they would break party ranks if necessary to protect vital programs for the poor. Clinton consulted the CBC aggressively as well, and party unity for this Democratic president was significantly higher than under Carter.

As the nation's first Democratic president in 12 years, the Democratic House mostly followed Clinton's budget plan that raised taxes, cut spending, but also increased spending in key areas such as children's health programs. Although it contained spending cuts, Republicans, nonetheless, did not go along with Clinton's proposal. On the first budget for fiscal year 1994, Clinton met with members of the CBC to ensure their cooperation. Later, the CBC refused to meet with the president any further over the first budget, which they pledged to block, if his administration compromised with the Senate to include cuts to Medicare, the earned income-tax credit, child hunger programs, and summer jobs for youths (Clymer 1993).

All 37 Black Democrats nevertheless voted for Clinton's first budget. Clinton's budget plan was aggressively opposed by Republicans. The House voted largely along party lines, adopting the budget on a 243–183 vote. In the end, the Clinton stimulus bill was killed in the Senate. Clinton also met with the CBC just prior to the budget vote. The CBC still proposed its alternative budget, cosponsored with the Progressive Caucus, which was defeated 87–335. The compromise legislation reduced some of the spending cuts. Black legislators, thus, backed the conference bill unanimously, showing strong party unity as it obtained no Republican support.

One reason Clinton obtained unanimous CBC support for his first budget plan was because of his aggressive 1993 stimulus bill, which was approved by the House. This plan included public works projects to stimulate the economy and produce jobs as well as summer jobs for the young and job training programs. The Congressional Black Caucus fought to resurrect Clinton's stimulus bill after it died in the Senate. What they got was only a fraction of the original stimulus measure—a package of emergency appropriations for extended unemployment benefits. Republicans still opposed the bill, arguing that it wasted taxpayers' money or should be offset by cuts in existing programs. However, the scaled-down measure was signed into law by President Clinton in April 1993.

Democrats had pledged their support to reduce the federal deficit during the Reagan years. Democrats under Clinton's leadership, therefore, sponsored a reconciliation bill that was aimed at deficit reduction. The

1993 Omnibus Budget-Reconciliation Act (HR 2264) still raised taxes to drive down the deficit. The new taxes came from the wealthiest tax payers, but there were increases in the Social Security benefits subject to taxation as well as an energy tax. But it also added spending on new and expanded social programs to win votes from liberal Democrats. The CBC warned Democratic lawmakers that they wanted programs for poor Americans protected from cuts or they would unite with Republicans to sink the bill (*CQ Almanac* 1993, 118). Republicans opposed the plan unanimously. In the end, Clinton needed every single Black legislators' vote as on August 5, 1993, the reconciliation bill passed by 218–216. Forty-one Democrats defected to vote against the new tax increases, but not one Black Democratic legislator.

The budget resolution for the fiscal year 1994–95 budget, voted on in 1994, was again based on President Clinton's proposal. Even though the Senate added additional spending cuts to the budget approved by the House, the CBC unanimously voted for the conference report. Democratic CBC members also voted unanimously for their own alternative budget in 1994. It was defeated 81–326. Clearly, while there were mild threats from the CBC, the CBC chose to work in a united fashion with President Clinton. And in budget matters, their votes were critical to winning passage of Clinton's moderate budget plans.

Things changed dramatically as the House prepared its budget plan for fiscal year 1996. The House was now under Republican control. Thus, congressional Republicans proposed a "bold seven-year plan" that promised the largest tax cuts since the Reagan era. Writers for *CQ Almanac* stated that "the plan was a manifesto of the Republican vision of the federal government that was far smaller, much cheaper and far less intrusive than the one that existed in 1995" (*CQ Almanac* 1995, 2–20). The federal budget had not been balanced since 1969 (*CQ Almanac* 1995, 2–3). In order to finance its tax cuts, Republicans proposed to cut both Medicare and Medicaid. The President campaigned against the plan, offering his own, which had a timetable of ten years instead of seven and also contained deep cuts in spending programs as a means to erase the deficit by 2005.

Congress passed the Republican budget resolution. Democrats got to vote on a conservative Democratic plan and the CBC's alternative budget proposal. While voting for their own plan unanimously, 29 percent of CBC members also voted for the conservative Democrats' plan. Surprisingly, Conyers favored the plan, along with Dixon, William Jefferson, Carrie Meek, Albert Wynn, Eva Clayton, Melvin (Mel) Watt, Robert Scott, and Sheila Jackson Lee. Then Republicans fell behind schedule on other appropriations and fiscal matters. With Clinton refusing to budge, most of government was shut down from November 14 to 19 and from December 16, 1995, to January 6, 1996. The nation blamed Republicans in Congress for the shutdown, and they had to give up their effort to completely remake the federal budget.

In 1996, Clinton's budget plan proposed to balance the budget in 2002. With the Republicans in control of the House, Clinton's plan failed to pass. In contrast to last year, some liberal and moderate Democrats—78 in all—lined up to vote with Republicans and reject it (*CQ Almanac* 1996, 2–23). The vote was 117–304. About two-thirds of the CBC members voted for the president's budget, while one-third, predominately of the old guard, voted against it as contained too many spending cuts. The minority old guard list included Dellums, Conyers, Clay, Rangel, and Stokes, as well Black "newcomers" such as Waters, Wynn, Elijah Cummings, and Towns. Sanford Bishop voted against the Clinton alternative budget as well, but as a new Black moderate. Clinton's plan had billions of cuts proposed for Medicare and Medicaid, even as it spared education programs such as Head Start. The Republicans claimed the Clinton plan was based on gimmicks, and proposed their own that also balanced the budget in six years. However, in the end the Republicans passed a budget resolution that writers for *CQ Almanac* claimed was similar in discretionary spending to what Clinton had originally proposed (1996, 2–3).

In 1996, Democrats also voted for the Blue Dogs' budget. More than one-half of the Democrats favored it, and 72 percent of the Democratic Black legislators voted for it as well. Most of the CBC members voting for the 1996 Blue Dog budget were from southern districts, while Rangel, Conyers, and Dellums were among those who rejected it.

President Clinton sought a bipartisan budget plan for fiscal year 1998 in 1997. The budget resolution was a deficit reduction one that included spending cuts but also added money to Clinton's new social policy initiatives such as children's health care. The deal between the GOP House and Clinton won more than half of Democratic legislators' support. Many Republicans backed it as well because of the tax cuts. This time, in contrast to the previous year when two-thirds of Black Democrats voted for Clinton's budget, nearly two-thirds of them voted against his bipartisan conference report that was supported by the president in the House. Focusing on those Blacks who supported the bipartisan budget resolution, the list includes many from the South such as Meek, Bishop, Cynthia McKinney, Clayton, Jim Clyburn, Harold Ford Jr., Jackson Lee, and Eddie Bernice

Johnson. Northern Blacks who supported the bipartisan agreement as well include Julia Carson, Cummings, Wynn, Floyd Flake, and Chaka Fattah. Lewis, notably serving as a whip, voted against it as a member of the old guard along with mostly northerner newcomers.

In 1998, Congress failed to enact a budget resolution, and adjourned without one. In 1999, with a new House Speaker, J. Dennis Hastert of Illinois, the Republicans crafted legislation included tax and spending cuts as well as some of President Clinton's spending priorities that ultimately added to the federal deficit. It did not win the president's endorsement because of the tax cuts, and all members of the CBC voted against it. The moderate Blue Dogs were permitted to submit an alternative budget for a floor vote. It transferred a Social Security surplus toward reducing the national debt, and was defeated by 134–295. Nearly one-third of Black Democratic legislators voted for the Blue Dog plan. Most of these legislators were from southern districts. The House Democrats also submitted a plan that had higher spending but also significant tax cuts. It also addressed the solvency of the Social Security and Medicare trust funds. It was rejected by a vote of 173–250. Approximately 92 percent of the Democratic Black House members voted for the House Democratic plan.

In 2000, Republicans dominated the budgetary process and won passage of a bill with a straight party-line vote. Black Democrats voted in 2000 as the vast majority of House Democrats had—against the House resolution and its conference report. The House Democrats submitted an alternative that was defeated by 184–233. It had slightly higher levels of discretionary spending than Clinton's original plan, and more than the Republicans' budget as well. All the Black House Democrats voted for it. The Blue Dogs also submitted a plan that focused on debt reduction; it was defeated 171–243. Thirty-nine percent of Black House Democrats voted for it. Finally, the Progressive Caucus also submitted a plan that garnered 61 votes while the CBC's alternative budget netted 70 votes. The Progressive Caucus plan got 88 percent of the Black Democratic vote, while the CBC alternative budget received 100 percent.

The 2000 budget votes illustrated how Black House legislators became divided in the aftermath of the rising federal deficit. The easy unanimity of the CBC over budget issues in opposition to Carter's budgets and in solidarity with the House Democrats in the Reagan era had ended. Only through powerful presidential persuasion and a lack of credible alternatives can they be counted on to vote as a bloc now. Thus, senior Black leaders, such as Lewis and Rangel, sometimes opposed President Clinton's tricky efforts of mixing cuts with spending priorities for health care and education. But hardened liberals such as Conyers and Waters sometimes favored the president's budgetary leadership.

Blacks from the South were more likely to support moderate Democratic efforts to address the federal debt. Black Democratic support for the Blue Dog plans ranged from 72 percent in 1996, to 33 percent in 1999, to 39 percent in 2000. This moderate Democratic caucus won surprisingly high levels of Black support during the George W. Bush administration as well. The Progressive Caucus still won high levels of support in 2000 from Black legislators at 88 percent. Only four Black legislators failed to vote for the group's liberal plan—Bishop (D-GA), Clay (D-MO), Johnson (D-TX), and Scott (D-VA).

The CBC's Alternative Budget

In 1993, the CBC changed its proposals. Now it sought tax relief for the middle class while imposing higher taxes on the wealthy and corporations. The formula for spending on defense and domestic programs remained the same as savings through reductions in military expenses would go to domestic programs. In 1994, the CBC proposal was identical to Clinton's budget proposal in this way, while imposing steeper taxes. Thus, this mix of new taxes with tax cuts was more dramatic under the CBC than under Clinton. In 1995, the CBC dropped its tax cut proposal, seeking to balance the budget through raising corporate taxes and cutting defense spending by a significant amount. Bishop (D-GA) voted "present" in 1995 and 1997 on CBC budget substitutes presumably in solidarity with the antitax pledge Republicans had begun to formulate.

Changing Legislative Behavior and Divisions within the CBC

While Clinton enjoyed higher presidential support from Black members than Carter, the individual scores of a few members don't dramatically improve for presidential support until the 106th Congress in 1999. Scores for Clay, Collins, Conyers, Ford, and Stokes fell to the 60s for President Clinton in some years. There was a noticeable increase in this group's presidential scores in 1995, following Republican control of the House. In 1995 all of the old guard CBC members have scores of 85 or above.

The scores are affected by vote participation rates, which have improved since the Carter years for members of Congress generally. Lack of vote participation depresses scores, and thus Harold Ford's scores are generally lower than the others in 1993, a year he was on trial for bank fraud and conspiracy. Ford was charged originally in 1987 for accepting over one million dollars in phony bank loans. In the first trial in 1990, the jury deadlocked, but Ford was acquitted of the charges in 1993. The Black members with lower presidential scores for President Clinton retired during his presidency. Like Cardiss Collins, Ford retired after the 104th Congress. He was succeeded by his son, Harold Ford Jr. Ron Dellums and Louis Stokes also retired during Clinton's second term in office. These members were replaced by new Blacks having much higher presidential support and party unity scores. Clinton appeared to have gained his greatest loyalty and party unity support from Black newcomers. There was not, therefore, a dramatic conversion of these Black congressional seniors. They remained among the least persuaded by Clinton's efforts to compromise with Republicans to pass legislation, and most retired during Clinton's second term.

Black voting with the House majority rises considerably from levels under Carter to .71 in 1993 and .68 in 1994. When the Republicans commanded a majority in the House in 1995 to the end of Clinton's term in 2000, the CBC effectiveness scores plummet to an average of about .52. Thus, CBC members voted with the House majority under Republican rule a little more than half of the time on average.

The Clinton presidency was a moderate one, not unlike Carter. The House was poised to enact moderate legislation under his presidency, therefore. This time, unlike the last time a Democrat sat in the White House, a number within the CBC responded positively to pressure to support moderate legislation. It caused new divisions within the CBC.

Clinton refused to lower his request for defense spending, even though some Democrats demanded that it be reduced. The CBC had been a fierce critic of the Reagan budget requests and had remained unanimous over their opposition to them for the most part. While still constituting the minority, 41 percent of the Black Democratic House legislators nevertheless opposed Barney Frank's (D-MA) amendment to cut defense in 1994. These CBC members were generally from the South, and included Bennie Thompson (D-MS), Clay (D-MO), Wheat (D-MO), Clyburn (D-SC), Johnson (D-TX), and Scott (D-VA). Lewis and McKinney of Georgia voted to cut defense spending, but Bishop, their colleague, voted to block that amendment.

The crime bill of 1995 had involved a major showdown with the administration and the CBC. Rangel (D-NY) and Waters (D-CA) were critical in the press of the crime bill's adoption of three-strikes legislation. As

Representative Rangel said, although there is agreement that violent crimi-
nals should be kept off the streets, "the question is not how many strikes
and you are in [prison], but how do you keep people out?" (Hedges 1994).
Thus, Rangel favored crime prevention legislation, not three strikes. Rangel and others voted against the final bill, but 66 percent of the CBC still
voted in favor of it. Because the measure also authorized new spending
programs for crime prevention, many liberal Democrats were won over.
Black Democrats had also campaigned for a racial justice provision for
the bill, which would permit the use of racial statistics to be used showing strong racial disparities against Blacks in the court's sentencing phase.
However, President Clinton met with the CBC and told members that he
would "order federal prosecutors to consider race in death-penalty cases"
if they voted for his Omnibus Crime Bill lacking the racial justice provision (Hallow 1994). While CBC chairman Mfume urged members to vote
against the bill if it did not contain the racial justice provision, he still voted
for it in the end. The bill also expanded use of the death penalty in sentencing for federal crimes.

Another matter dividing the CBC in 1994 was free trade. The House
strongly adopted the General Agreement on Tariffs and Trade known as
GATT. However, only 46 percent of the Black Democrats in the House
voted for GATT as measured as a "key vote." The Black southern delegation split because of pressure from the president, but members of the old
guard, such as Clay, Rangel, and Dellums, remained opposed.

Once the Republicans took over the House in 1995, divisions within
the CBC disappeared. There were no significant divisions in the CBC on
these issues, outside of the anti-gay Defense of Marriage bill in 1996 and
the crime bill in 1994, which will be discussed later. Under Republican
control, the Black Democrats found little to disagree with in the House.
Party unity scores increased during the 1990s for Black as well as White
lawmakers. Had Republicans not captured control of the House as a result
of the 1994 elections, divisions might have widened between moderate and
liberal members of the CBC. Liberal CBC members might have dissented
more from Clinton's policies, while southern members and newly elected
Blacks might have also failed to back the president as much as they did.

Haiti and the Defense of Marriage Act

The CBC remained active on foreign policy toward Africa. They sought
to meet with the president specifically about the urgent problems in that

region. They discussed African debt relief, American policy regarding Angola, Zaire, and also Haiti. "We have deferred with due respect to the fact that he has not been on the job too long," explained Rep. Kweisi Mfume, a Maryland Democrat and chair of the Congressional Black Caucus. "But the problems are so urgent that we feel it is high time that the Administration hears us. We expect a kind of meeting that we and the President will leave from with some kind of plan of action" (Holmes 1993).

The CBC wanted the Clinton administration to intervene in Haiti where a coup had stripped the popular President Jean-Bertrand Aristide of power. It is a charge they leveled against the Bush administration as well. "It is simply unacceptable that President Aristide remains in exile with no date certain for his return," stated Rep. John Conyers Jr. (Goshko 1993). Conyers wanted substantial American efforts, namely for the United States to freeze the assets in this country of the Haitians who backed the coup, to use American warships to block shipments of oil and consumer goods to Haiti, and to put pressure on Europe to cooperate with this embargo. Clinton, the CBC charged, has made only halfhearted attempts to restore Aristide, who had been ousted from power in 1991 after being democratically elected in 1990 with 67 percent of the vote. In addition, the CBC wanted the United States to stop the forced returns of the Haitian "boat people." Mfume was one of the Black leaders arrested at a protest at the White House about U.S. policy toward the Haitian refugees.

There was also a 27-day hunger strike over U.S. policy on Haiti by Randall Robinson, the director of TransAfrica. In response to this Black protest, President Clinton dismissed his old adviser on Haiti and appointed William Gray, president of the United Negro College Fund and a former Black congressman. In a statement, the president said that there a clear American interest in bolstering the cause of democracy in Haiti and in the Americas (Ifill 1994). Ultimately, the CBC divided over a military solution for Haiti, with some speaking out against a planned invasion in the press. Lewis and Towns were among those totally opposed to a military invasion, while Major Owens was in favor (Taylor 1994b).

In 1996, President Clinton signed into law the Defense of Marriage Act. The law banned federal recognition of gay marriages and authorized states to refuse to recognize same-sex marriages from other states. The House overwhelmingly approved the law, voting 342 in its favor with only 67 votes against it. The law split the CBC, with a majority voting against it. Only 41 percent voted for it. Two members, Owens (D-NY) and Jackson Lee (D-TX) voted "present" only.

Conclusion

Just two months before the unexpected Republican takeover of the House, CBC chairman Mfume told the press that he gave President Clinton a grade of C on the promotion of issues that Blacks care about. "There is a great deal of goodwill and effort," he said, noting the administration's efforts on health care and discrimination in banking (Taylor 1994a). In contrast, some Black lawmakers had clearly failed President Carter for his grade on promoting policies that Blacks want.

Gary Franks, the only Republican member of the Congressional Black Caucus, left the group because "of ideological differences and conflicts with other members" in 1993. Then Franks changed his mind. "As long as I am a member of Congress and black, I will continue to belong to the Congressional Black Caucus," Franks stated at a news conference (Moss 1993). The source of the conflict was over keeping Franks out of private meetings between Democrats, including their canceled meeting with the president over the 1993 budget standoff. Months later, the caucus voted to limit Franks's participation to lunches only; he was barred from Democratic Party planning sessions. Two caucus members, Clay and Mel Reynolds, had asked that Franks be excluded from the Caucus altogether (Puga 1993).

The Clinton presidency helped transform the CBC into a more ideologically fractured group because of his leadership. Black radicals in the CBC were unable to win unanimous solidarity to fight for racial policies, notably the absence of the racial justice provision, in Clinton's 1995 crime bill. The challenge for radicals is that the Republican ascendancy threatened Democrats in Congress into more compliance with their party and president. Party unity increased during this period. The party continued to also liberalize in response to the Republican ascendancy, and as a response to pressures from Blacks and other liberal groups. So Black Democrats responded by voting for legislation that Clinton had crafted that tactically won Republican support, too. In short, they increased the percentage of time they voted with the institutionally moderate-to-conservative House majority.

CHAPTER 5

President Bush and the New Black Moderates

Like it or not, the Congressional Black Caucus and heads of civil rights and labor groups are trusted by Black voters. Republicans should try talking to them.

—*New York Times* editorial on George W. Bush's
2000 election and Blacks[1]

About a dozen Black House members walked out in protest as Vice President Al Gore presided over the certification of the 2000 electoral vote in a joint session of Congress. Federal law requires both a House member and a senator to object to congressional certification. But Black House members could not find a senator to register their objection. The controversy over the disputed 2000 election results was relatively short-lived. September 11, 2001, the day when terrorists attacked the World Trade Center and the Pentagon, however, changed the politics decisively as President Bush moved the country to war in Iraq in 2003. The war in Afghanistan had begun earlier, immediately following September 11, 2001.

As in the Carter administration, Black members of Congress objected to Bush's appointment for attorney general. He was John David Ashcroft, also a southerner, like Carter's attorney general, Griffin Bell. A former governor and senator from Missouri, Ashcroft was controversial because he was considered opposed to civil rights and abortion rights. Nevertheless, like the time when 1978 *Bakke* case was before the Supreme Court during the Carter administration, the Bush administration issued briefs in the 2003 University of Michigan affirmative action case stating that the university's policy was effectively a quota system and illegal.

Most Democrats in the Senate still voted against Ashcroft's appointment; he was confirmed by a vote of 58 to 42. (Opposition to Griffin Bell, in contrast, was less partisan; he was confirmed in 1977 by a Senate vote of 75–21.) Party polarization in the Congress helped bring greater support for the policies of Black House members. They won, in fact, some important victories. Republicans seemed more responsive, too. Senator Trent Lott stepped down in 2002 as majority leader after declaring that the country would be "better off" had segregationist Strom Thurmond won in 1948. His apology for the comment was not accepted in Washington. The 1965 Voting Rights Act was extended in 2006. Some contend that leadership in Washington on racial issues reflected the input of a new generation of White members, but the Republican Party played at both ends of a spectrum on race, supporting civil rights for the most part but exploiting race through race-card politics.

Still, this Bush administration was different than the Reagan and Bush Sr. administrations. President Bush made several significant high-profile appointments of African Americans in his administration who were not as controversial or as conservative as the Black Republicans appointed before then. The significant Bush appointments were General Colin L. Powell as secretary of state, Rod Paige as secretary of education, and Condoleezza Rice as national security adviser. The press reported that the Bush administration was the most ethnically diverse in American history. Bush also pledged to seek Black voters in both 2000 and 2004, which was seen as more sincere since he had not campaigned on racial issues as Reagan and his father had.

Bush proposed a summit with Black religious leaders about his faith-based initiative policy, which earmarked federal funds for religious groups for social services, such as drug prevention counseling. He also proposed that he was for education reform. Bush met early with the CBC in 2001 in spite of the fact that some members had loudly denounced his election as "fraudulent."

In the end, despite these new, but mixed, efforts by President Bush, Black voters remained aloof and pro-Democrat. A few Black members of Congress, however, supported Bush's initiatives, including the constitutional ban on gay marriage and his war in Iraq. Charles Rangel, a cofounder of the CBC, points out that such policy divisions are recent. Furthermore, he contends that they made it more difficult for the CBC to take a joint stand on major issues. He writes, "Quiet as it's been kept, four CBC members voted to give President Bush the authority to wage preemptive war, despite the overwhelming opposition to the war by African Americans as a whole. The point is that there is no official caucus position on Iraq. But when people see our overwhelming individual opposition to the war, they just assume we got together and took a vote" (2007, 201). During the Bush administration of eight years there was an increased number of Black moderates in Washington.

The CBC and Bush's Budgets

Bush's first budget for fiscal year 2002 obeyed the "pay as you go" rules, but it also included tax cuts. The tax cuts were back loaded so that they went into effect in the final years. His budget plan was adopted by a party-line vote. Only three Democrats voted for it, while only two Republicans voted no. The House rejected four alternatives, notably the Blue Dogs' plan calling for tax cuts and higher defense spending, a fiscally conservative Republican plan, the Progressive Caucus budget that combined smaller tax cuts with higher domestic spending, and the Democratic leadership's plan, also combining smaller tax cuts with higher domestic spending. Interesting patterns emerged in analyzing the CBC's 2001 vote on these alternative budgets. The vast majority (89 percent) of Black House Democrats backed the conservative Blue Dogs' plan. Only Jackson (D-IL), Waters (D-CA), Owens (D-NY), and Towns (D-NY) opposed it. The vast majority of Black Democratic legislators voted for the Progressive Caucus's budget alternative. Five Blacks opposed it, and, with the exception of Towns, all were from the South: Bishop (D-GA), Thompson (D-MS), Ford (D-TN), and Scott (D-VA). The Democratic leadership's budget plan won every CBC members' vote except for Towns. Towns voted against all these budget plans including the president's.

In 2002, Bush proposed increases in defense spending for his "War on Terror" while also advocating tax cuts. While the House adopted a budget by a party-line vote, Congress failed to pass a budget resolution in 2002. Fiscal conservatives were concerned, as were liberals who wanted to delay these additional tax cuts. In 2003, the federal deficit became a central concern again. Because of an economic recession and the cost of the war on terror as well as Bush's proposed tax cuts, the president's budget plan increased the size of the federal deficit to $338 billion in fiscal 2004. The House narrowly passed a budget by 215–212 in March that protected Medicare and restored some cuts in discretionary spending. The House rejected four alternatives. The Democratic alternatives were a Democratic House leadership plan, a Blue Dog proposal, and the CBC alternative budget. Ninety-five percent of Black House Democrats voted for the House leadership plan; 87 percent voted for the Blue Dog plan in 2003.

In 2004, Bush also called for a defense budget increase of about 7 percent. No Democrat voted for the president's budget plan, which passed by a margin of 215–212. The Democrats offered three alternatives, including the CBC alternative budget, which every Black Democratic legislator voted for, but which failed by 119-302. As shown in chapter 3's table 1, the CBC alternative budget had won slightly increasing numbers of votes since it was issued in 1981, growing from a low of 56 votes in 1987, and dipping again in 1995 to 56 votes, to a record high of 126 votes in 2008. Few Blacks rejected the defeated Democratic leadership proposal and the defeated Blue Dogs' plan. Barbara Lee (D-CA) did not vote for the Democratic leadership's budget alternative. The Blue Dog plan won less CBC support, with 79 percent of Black Democrats favoring it.

In 2004, Congress again failed to enact a budget resolution. In 2005, President Bush's proposal called for a significant cut in domestic spending—the first proposed since the GOP's 1995 takeover. Bush's plan was adopted without a single Democratic vote. The Blue Dogs did not propose an alternative, but David Obey (D-WI) proposed one that increased domestic spending and the Democratic leadership's plan raised taxes. The CBC alternative budget won all of the Black Democratic House votes. As for other alternatives, only Ford Jr. voted against liberal Obey's budget proposal as a new moderate. And Ford and Lee, on two opposing sides ideologically, voted against the Democratic substitute.

In 2006, Bush's plan asked for defense spending to be increased significantly, with domestic spending cut, while tax cuts set to expire in 2010 would be made permanent. All the Black Democratic legislators supported the CBC alternative budget in 2006, and they all lined up to vote for the Democratic alternative, including Lee. In 2006, however, Congress failed to enact a budget resolution.

In 2007, the Democrats had regained their majority status in Congress. Bush's 2007 plan for fiscal 2008 still called for making his tax cuts that passed in 2001 and 2003 permanent. House Democrats were able to pass their own budget resolution in March by a narrow 216–210 vote. No Republican and about a dozen Democrats, most of them members of the Blue Dog coalition, voted against the plan. One hundred percent of the Black House Democrats backed the plan. The vast majority (87 percent) of Black House legislators voted for the Progressive Caucus's budget proposal. Notably voting "no" were five Black southern males: Artur Davis (AL), Meek (FL), Bishop (GA), David Scott (GA), and Scott (VA). Both Davis and Meek made statewide bids for office in 2010.

Bush's final budget request in 2008 included increases for defense while holding domestic discretionary spending to its existing levels. Democrats in Congress, however, had already agreed to a plan that raised domestic spending. The Democrats' budget resolution projected a $340.4 billion deficit in fiscal 2009, decreasing through 2012 to $21.9 billion. The Congressional Budget Office estimated that Bush's budget plan would result in a $342.3 billion deficit for fiscal 2009 before turning into a balanced budget in 2012 (*CQ Almanac* 2008, 4–7). The House adopted the Democratic-majority plan by 212–207 with 100 percent of the Black House vote. It rejected a Republican alternative, a Progressive Caucus plan proposed by Barbara Lee, and the CBC alternative budget proposed by Carolyn Cheeks Kilpatrick (D-MI). The vast majority (86 percent) of the CBC members voted for the Progressive Caucus budget in 2008, while 100 percent of the members voted for their own budget alternative as well. Voting against the Progressive Caucus budget for a second time were Davis, Bishop, and Scott (VA). Scott (GA) voted for it in 2008, after having rejected it in 2007, while Laura Richardson (D-CA) voted against it. Richardson had been elected in a special 2007 election to fill the open seat resulting from Juanita Millender-McDonald's death. Corrine Brown (D-FL) had previously supported the Progressive Caucus budget proposals but turned against it that year. Having won in the historic elections of 1992, she was considering running for Florida's open U.S. Senate seat in 2010. Kendrick Meek (D-FL) entered the race instead.

Because of the trend favoring party unity, most Black legislators supported Democratic House leadership budget proposals during the Bush presidency. After the group's organized opposition to a Democratic president's budget requests during the Carter administration , by the end of Clinton presidency only a few CBC members still dissented . The years 1996 and 1997 represented the lowest points of Black legislative support for their party's budget resolutions. In 1996, one-third opposed Clinton's budget request, and in 1997 two-thirds did. But after 1997 over 90 percent of Black House legislators supported their party's budget proposals, and in the last three years of the Bush administration, 100 percent did so.

In addition, Black voting patterns on budget resolutions during the Bush presidency revealed the growing moderation of Black legislators. While the fiscally conservative Blue Dog caucus had earned 72 percent of the Black House Democratic vote in 1996, support among Black legislators fell to under 40 percent in 1999 and 2000 under President Clinton. Figure 7 shows the percentage of Black House Democrats' votes for the Blue Dogs' alternative budgets. Beginning in the first year of the Bush administration, support from Black legislators shot up to 89 percent, drop-

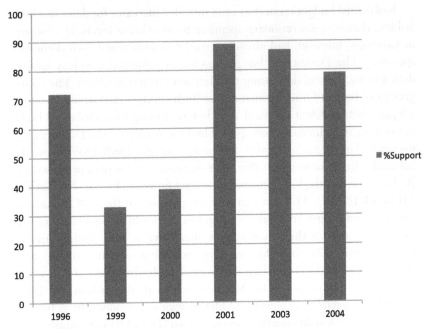

Fig. 7. Percentage of CBC House Democrats' votes for Blue Dogs' alternative budget proposals, 1996–2004

ping slightly to 79 percent in 2004. The picture of Black legislators as fiscal moderates is confusing because an even higher percentage of them support the budget proposals of the Progressive Caucus, which generally asks for higher levels of domestic spending each year. A handful of Blacks, largely from the South, have pointedly refused to vote for the Progressive Caucus budget plans. Artur Davis (D-AL), Sanford Bishop (D-GA), and Scott (D-VA) have sought to define themselves as fiscal conservatives. Other Black legislators from the South, such as Kendrick Meek (D-FL), have voted at times for the Progressive Caucus budgets and at other times have not.

Black Legislators and the War on Terror and against Iraq

The coordinated terrorist attacks on the World Trade Center and the Pentagon on September 11, 2001, transformed the Bush presidency. He had been elected narrowly and only confirmed the winner by a U.S. Supreme Court ruling, *Bush v. Gore*, in 2000. Now, his approval rates soared to over

90 percent in the aftermath of these terrorist attacks. Eight years later, however, his approval rating plummeted to one of the lowest levels for a president, including President Carter's (Norrander and Harper 2010). To do its part in the new realization that America was at war with global terrorists, Congress sent President Bush emergency funds to launch a war on terror on September 14. There was no opposition to H.R. 2888, providing supplemental emergency funds as a response to the terrorist attacks on the United States. That same day Congress also authorized the president to use of U.S. armed forces against those responsible for the recent attacks launched against the United States. There was no opposition in the Senate, but one lone vote against H. J. Res. 64 by African American House legislator Barbara Lee (D-CA). Lee issued a press statement explaining her vote: "I am convinced that military action will not prevent further acts of international terrorism against the United States" (Perlez 2001).

Once the September 11 terrorist attacks were attributed to al Qaeda, the U.S. demanded that the Taliban-led Afghanistan government turn over Osama bin Laden, the head of al Qaeda. When Taliban leaders refused, President Bush sent the U.S. military to bomb Afghanistan in October 2001. After driving the Taliban leaders out, the United States established an interim government in Afghanistan. Afghanistan held its first democratic elections in 2004, but the U.S.-led war in Afghanistan continues, although President Obama has proposed removing all U.S. troops in 2014.

Many Democrats in Congress had opposed President George H. W. Bush's war against Iraq eleven years earlier. One hundred percent of the Black Democrats in the House had opposed the resolution granting President Bush the authorization to wage war two weeks after he had sent troops to the region in 1990. Now his son, George W. Bush, was seeking Congress's approval to wage war against Iraq to remove its dictator, Saddam Hussein, from office in 2002. After the Gulf War in 1991, the UN Security Council required that Iraq rid itself of weapons of mass destruction, but the Bush administration alleged that Hussein was stockpiling these weapons. The move to go to war against Iraq had actually begun shortly after the terrorist attack of September 11, 2001, in the United States, which had left nearly 3,000 dead.

President Bush sought the United Nations' approval, but without it, he proposed acting unilaterally. The congressional resolution granted the president the authority to use force against Iraq at an unspecified time, also requiring him to report to Congress within 48 hours after military action had begun. The House passed the resolution by a vote of 296–133 in October 2002. A total of 81 House Democrats voted to pass it, while 126 were opposed. Nearly 90 percent of the Black House Democrats opposed it. Four Black legislators, however, voted in favor, Bishop (D-GA), Jefferson (D-LA), Wynn (D-MD), and Ford (D-TN). Thus, as the CBC grew in size, a new division emerged over Congress's authorization for war against Iraq this second time. Rep. J. C. Watts, a Black Republican from Oklahoma, who, unlike Black Republican Gary Franks in the past, had not joined the CBC, also voted for the resolution.

Three amendments aiming to change the resolution were defeated. One amendment required the president to obtain a UN Security Council resolution authorizing the use of force. This amendment was defeated by 155–270. Barbara Lee (D-CA) also sponsored an amendment that urged the use of peaceful means to resolve the issue. It failed by a vote of 77–355. Dennis Kucinich (D-OH), a progressive member of Congress, wanted the resolution amended to require the president to report to Congress prior to the use of military force. This amendment garnered 101 votes. The amendment votes show that the vast majority of Black legislators favored Lee's resolution, which did not authorize the use of military force. Ninety-one percent of Black Democratic legislators voted for Lee's amendment. A smaller share (86 percent) voted for Kucinich's amendment requiring congressional notification before the taking of military action. A sizeable minority of Black legislators, such as Barbara Lee, refused to vote for the Democratic amendment, requiring that the president obtain United Nations approval before waging war. Only 72 percent of the Black legislators voted for this amendment. Thus, while there was a new division in the CBC over the Iraq War issue, most Black legislators saw themselves as decidedly against authorizing the president to go to war at any point during the diplomatic standoff between the U.S. and Iraq over weapons inspections.

In March 2003, the United States invaded Iraq. The U.S. military quickly won some decisive victories, including winning control of most of Baghdad in April, and capturing Saddam Hussein in December. American support for the war was high in the beginning, but it began to erode by 2005. There were strong partisan differences, with Republicans remaining far more supportive of the war than Democrats (Jacobson 2007). Furthermore, the Democratic Party in 2004 did not openly oppose the war. Senator John Kerry, the party's presidential nominee in 2004, had voted in 2002 to authorize the war. He said during the campaign he wouldn't have changed his vote in light of growing public dissatisfaction with the war.

By 2006, however, enough Democrats were upset enough that the party began to take steps to force the president to discuss a timetable for withdrawing troops from Iraq. In the 2006 elections, Democrats won majorities in both the House and the Senate. To force a time limit on the deployment of troops in Iraq, in 2007 the House voted on a supplemental spending bill requiring that most troops leave by August 2008. Ironically, four liberal Blacks (Lee, Watson, Waters, and Lewis) voted against giving the military emergency funds even with a timetable, but every other member of the CBC voted for it, including three who had voted to authorize the war in 2002. The Senate passed a version that specified the 2008 date as a goal, not a mandate. Senator Obama voted for it. Thus, to reconcile the House version with the Senate version, the House voted on a bill specifying a withdrawal date goal. This time, Lee, Waters, and Lewis were the only Black legislators objecting to the bill.

President Bush vetoed this 2007 legislation, and the Democratic-controlled Congress backed down, authorizing emergency funds without a timetable for the troops there. The vote on the new emergency spending bill was 280–142 in the House and 80–24 in the Senate. Only 16 percent of the Black legislators voted for this bill, and of those who did, all were from the South (Meek, Bishop, Scott (GA), Thompson, and George Kenneth Butterfield). Senator Obama, also, did not back down either, and voted against the bill. His state colleague, Dick Durbin of Illinois, however, did. Senator Hillary Clinton, who ran for president in 2008, also didn't back down. Her fellow senator, Charles Schumer, failed to record a vote on this bill. During his presidential bid, Obama called for a withdrawal of all U.S. troops within 16 months of taking office. After he won the nomination, however, Obama then told reporters he would ask for his military advisers to prepare a plan for a drawdown of troops.

The 2006 Reauthorization of the Voting Rights Act

President Bush signed a 25-year extension of the 1965 Voting Rights in 2006. It had been set to expire in 2007. Much was made of the Voting Rights Act (VRA) being "permanent" following its 1982 extension, even though major provisions of the law are temporary. In 1982, Section 2, a permanent feature of the law, was amended so that election laws having the result of reducing minority voters' ability to elect candidates of their choice are prohibited under the VRA (Davidson and Grofman 1994). Section 4, Section 5, and Section 203 are major but temporary parts of the VRA that could have expired in 2007. Section 4 provides the basis for identifying which jurisdictions require federal oversight, and Section 5 requires covered jurisdictions to submit election changes to the Justice Department. Section 203 provides language assistance to non-English-speaking minorities.

The CBC directed much of the floor debate on the bill, noting the historic significance of the act and calling it untouchable legislation given its importance to minorities. While some Republicans tried to argue that Blacks and minorities no longer needed federal protection for their voting rights in the light of the record number serving in government since 1982, that argument did not take off. Republicans still sponsored amendments targeting Section 4, Section 203, the bailout provision, and reducing the length of the extension from 25 to 10 years. These amendments got votes ranging from 96 to 185, the latter for lifting the federal mandate on multilanguage election material. Black representatives, notably Charles Rangel of New York, whose district includes a sizeable percentage of Latino voters, were adamant about their support for Section 203. Eliminating language assistance for minorities, Rangel argued, was tantamount to disenfranchising them, and equivalent to the Jim Crow tactics used against Blacks in the South (Rangel and Wynter 2007). Black House member Elijah Cummings referred to them as "poison pill amendments." The House still passed the bill. It won a huge margin of support—390–33. The Senate also passed the bill 98–0.

President Bush's signature on the reauthorized VRA represented his party's acceptance that the nation still needs federal supervision of its electoral process for jurisdictions having a history of racial discrimination. In 2009, a Supreme Court ruling sustained the VRA narrowly, affirming the constitutionality of Section 5. Only African American Supreme Court justice Clarence Thomas objected, calling Section 5 unconstitutional. In 2012, the Supreme Court accepted a challenge to the Voting Rights Act, *Shelby County v. Holder.* It challenges the continued constitutionality of the Voting Rights Act, and seeks to return the map-making process to state governments without federal government oversight, or preclearance of voting changes in states with a historic pattern of the suppressing the voting rights of Blacks and other minorities. At the time of this writing, a decision was to be announced in June 2013.

Sudan, Liberia, the United Nations, and Slavery

Civil war had raged in Sudan since the 1980s between the government-backed Muslims and non-Muslims, mostly Christians, based in the South.

In the late 1970s, oil was discovered in the South, and the Islamic government refused to share the profits with the Christian South and began imposing strict Islamic law. Osama bin Laden had been based in Sudan during the early 1990s. As international peace negotiators descended on the nation in 2000 and 2001, violence erupted in Darfur, a non-Arab area in Sudan and Chad that had experienced some of the worst atrocities (Foerstel 2008). The House and Senate passed bills to condemn the government of Sudan for human rights violations, make $10 million available for nonmilitary aid to Sudan, and direct the U.S. ambassador to the United Nations to seek international support in condemning the violence. The House bill went furthest; it proposed to bar foreign companies from engaging in oil and gas development in Sudan. The bill passed by a 422–2 vote in June 2001. The Bush administration, however, was opposed to sanctions against Sudan, preferring constructive engagement instead. Final passage of compromise legislation was blocked in the Senate by Republican Phil Gramm of Texas, and Congress adjourned.

In June 2004, CBC member Donald Payne (D-NJ) sponsored legislation declaring that the "atrocities unfolding in Darfur, Sudan, are genocide" and urged the Bush administration to refer to such atrocities as "genocide." The resolution passed the House unanimously (422–0). Since international law states that countries must stop and prevent genocide, Secretary of State Colin L. Powell at first avoided using that word. Only after there was pressure from humanitarian and religious groups did the Bush administration label the killings taking place Darfur as representing genocide. In 2007, Barbara Lee (D-CA) sponsored two more resolutions, which were approved by votes of 410–0 and 425–1, in the House calling for China and the Arab states to recognize and stop the genocide taking place in Darfur. In May 2008, the leading three presidential candidates, Barack Obama, Hillary Clinton, and John McCain, promised the U.S. government would intervene if elected (Foerstel 2008). Since then, Obama's UN ambassador, Susan Rice, has proposed a mix of sanctions and incentives as the U.S. policy toward Sudan, not U.S. military intervention. Rice also supports the indictment of Sudanese president Omar al-Bashir for crimes against humanity by the International Criminal Court in The Hague (Lake 2009).

Civil war had erupted in Liberia in 1989 and 1990, and continued under the dictatorship of Charles Taylor, who was elected president in 1997. In 2003, as the fighting spread, U.S. special troops were sent to evacuate those working at the U.S. embassy in Monrovia. In July 2003, the CBC urged the United States to send troops to quell the unrest in Liberia as part of a peacekeeping mission (Hurt 2003). Some commentators found it ironic that the vast majority of the CBC opposed the war in Iraq and yet sought a military solution to oust a dictator in Africa. In 2003, Donald Payne (D-NJ) sponsored a resolution supporting a cease-fire agreement in Liberia. It was not voted on. Rep. Vito Fossella also introduced a resolution recognizing the "dire humanitarian situation in Liberia and efforts to introduce peace and justice to that country," but it also was not voted on. The United Nations sent peacekeeping troops as Taylor left the country. The UN mission there is recognized as a successful one, leading to peaceful elections in 2005.

In 2001, the Republicans released the funds to pay what the United States owed the United Nations in back dues. President Bush explained to Congress that the debt was a block in getting diplomatic support for the war on terror. The United States had refused to pay its dues to the United Nations because of a conflict with the United Nations over its abortion policy and a dispute over the calculation of its actual share in the UN budget (*CQ Almanac* 2001, 11–13). Secretary of State Powell refused to attend the UN World Conference against Racism in 2001, based on U.S. opposition to a conference resolution that equated Israeli Zionism with racism. (Under Obama, the United States did not send high-level attendees to the 2009 UN World Conference against Racism for the same reasons.) In addition, African states were seeking an apology and reparations for slavery. In 2003, President Bush traveled to Africa in a five-day tour of Senegal, South Africa, Botswana, Uganda, and Nigeria. In Senegal, the president denounced slavery as "one of the greatest crimes in history" (Sammon 2003), but the statement stopped short of serving as an apology to the descendents of American slaves. From the 107th to the 110th Congress, House legislators, Black and some Whites, sponsored resolutions on slavery and racism and got some to pass in the House. Tom Lantos (D-CA), a White legislator, sponsored a resolution expressing the sense of the House that the UN Conference on Racism "presents a unique opportunity to address global discrimination." Only three representatives voted against it. In 2003, Danny K. Davis, a Black legislator from Illinois, sponsored a resolution approved by the House commending President Abraham Lincoln's efforts to end slavery. In 2005, Davis, Rangel, and Lee successfully sponsored resolutions on the slave trade, Juneteenth Day (a day commemorating the end of slavery in the U.S.), and the ratification of the Thirteenth Amendment banning slavery in the United States. In the 110th Congress, five House legislators won resolutions about racism and slavery. Notably, Steve Cohen (D-TN), a White legislator who won the seat Harold Ford Jr. had vacated to run for the Senate in 2006, got a resolution (H. Res. 194) passed in the House through a voice vote in 2007 apologizing for the enslavement and racial segregation of African Americans.

Barack Obama sponsored legislation on the end of slavery as well during his four years there. In 2005 and 2006, he won passage of resolutions (S. Con. Res. 42 and S. Res. 516) recognizing Juneteenth Independence Day as historically significant. He was then a cosponsor of fellow Senator Richard Durbin's successful 2007 and 2008 bills that also recognized Juneteenth Independence Day and Senator Robert Menendez's successful resolution recognizing the Black spiritual as a national treasure. These efforts, even though symbolic, establish how much Congress has changed from an institution having few Blacks in the 1950s, when the country had discriminatory laws.

Reparations to the descendants of Black slaves remain a radical part of the Black political agenda. Ronald W. Walters (2008) has made a case for reparations since he believes the impact of slavery on Americans, until it is recognized, will continue to harm the objective of racial healing. However, Black politicians have not made a strong case for reparations, choosing instead to highlight the importance of the end of slavery in American history through symbolic legislation. Liberal and progressive leaders have joined conservatives in dismissing the idea of reparations as "impractical." The U.S. Congress, however, because of Black efforts has many legislative sponsors, and not only Black lawmakers, of symbolic measures recognizing the contributions of African Americans.

Yet efforts by legislators to acknowledge the contributions to America from her Black citizens and apology for slavery have been countered by Republican efforts to recognize "Confederate History Month" in seven southern states. In recent Congresses under the Bush administration, however, the only legislation referencing the Confederacy was sponsored by a former Dixiecrat. These were forts Confederates had taken over at the start of the Civil War; they had become national monuments in the late 1940s and 1960s. Thurmond's bill had no cosponsors and never left committee. Truly, the racial atmosphere in Washington has liberalized some, while the scholarship on Black lawmakers in the South raise questions about the racial transformation of the state governments (e.g., Sullivan and Winburn 2011).

Black Legislative Opposition to Bans on Abortion and Gay Marriage

On social issues, Blacks in the electorate have traditionally been divided (Tate 2010), even as some contend that Blacks should be firmly on the left on social issues given their long history of being discriminated against as a social group in the United States. In 2004, President Bush secured a victory as part of his opposition to abortion rights. Congress and the president enacted a law making it a federal crime to harm the fetus of a pregnant woman. Harming a pregnancy, lawmakers argued, should impose extra punishment. The House had passed similar bills in 1999 and 2001, but they failed to be enacted in the Senate. Abortion rights advocates opposed the legislation, claiming it could undermine the 1973 *Roe v. Wade* decision, which made abortion a legal right for women. Furthermore, the bill also had language defining an "unborn child" as a 'member of the species of homo sapiens, at any stage of development, who is carried in the womb" (*CQ Almanac* 2004, 12–3). The bill passed in the House by 254–163. Only three CBC members voted for it: two from Georgia (Bishop and Scott) and Jefferson of Louisiana. A Democratic alternative was offered that excluded language defining an "unborn child." It was rejected 186–229. One hundred percent of the Black legislators voted for this Democratic alternative.

In 2004 and 2006, both election years in which record numbers of states had initiatives on gay marriage, Congress voted to ban gay marriage through the adoption of a constitutional amendment. In 2003, Massachusetts through its state Supreme Court had legalized the right of same-sex couples to marry. Vermont had earlier, in response to a state Supreme Court ruling, passed a law creating civil unions for same-sex couples. In 1996, President Clinton had signed into law the Defense of Marriage Act, which defines marriage as a legal union between one man and one woman. In 1996, Black legislators were divided in spite of its wide appeal to Republicans and many Democrats, with a majority (59 percent) voting against the antigay law (see chapter 4). Because a constitutional amendment requires a two-thirds vote in both chambers, the president-led effort to ban gay marriage failed. In the House, the constitutional ban won 227 votes to 186, well short of the two-thirds majority. A total of 36 Democrats voted for it, including six Black members of Congress, all from the South: Davis (D-AL), Bishop (D-GA), Scott (D-GA), Ford (D-TN), Jefferson (D-LA), and Thompson (D-MS). In 2006, H.J. Res. 88 failed to reach a two-thirds majority in the House with 236 votes in favor and 187 votes against. The same six Black legislators voted for it again. Only 34 Democrats voted for it.

Surprisingly, a large plurality (40 percent) of Black legislators voted for the 2005 legislation that granted Terry Schiavo's parents the right to continue to litigate in federal court to preserve the brain-damaged woman's feeding tube support. Schiavo had been on life support since 1990. Doctors declared that she was in a vegetative state, and her husband sought to end her life by removing the feeding tube. House Democrats divided on this bill as well, with 47 supporting and 53 opposed. Nearly every Republican voted for it, and President Bush signed it into law. Polls showed that most Americans disapproved of Congress taking action on this matter. And, in fact, nearly half of the CBC, such as the California delegation, failed to vote at all on the matter. Those who favored congressional action for Schiavo to save her life were Meek (but not Hastings) of Florida, Bishop and Scott of Georgia, Cummings and Wynn of Maryland, Jackson Jr. of Illinois, Ford Jr. of Tennessee, Fattah of Pennsylvania, and Green and Jackson Lee of Texas. Those opposed were Lewis and McKinney of Georgia, Carson of Indiana, Thompson of Mississippi, Emmanuel Cleaver and Clay Jr. of Missouri, Payne of New Jersey, Butterfield and Watt of North Carolina, Clyburn of South Carolina, and Scott of Virginia. More Blacks than Whites and other minority groups are opposed to euthanasia or physician-assisted suicide, based on 1999 opinion data. In fact, a solid majority of Blacks (64 percent) oppose physician-assisted suicide (Tate 2010).

Faith-Based Initiatives

Traditionally, religious groups were banned from receiving federal money, unless they created an independent, secular branch. As part of his new agenda, the Bush administration favored new laws opening the door to federal dollars for religious groups to provide social services such as juvenile delinquency prevention, drug treatment, and senior citizen programs. As president, he created a White House Office of Faith-Based and Community Initiatives through an executive order in 2001. Black Republican J. C. Watts (R-OK), in a bipartisan bill, tried to win direct aid for church groups as well as tax incentives for a number of new social programs in 2001. While the proposal passed in the House, it was rejected in the Senate. Many religious leaders, including Black Christian ministers, welcomed the faith-based initiative program. Critics such as the ACLU, however, claimed the initiative was using tax dollars to promote religion.

While Black churches provide a number of social services to their members, some CBC members felt that giving money to churches opened the door to discrimination, especially against gays and lesbians. In the formulating of legislation opening the door to federal funds for religious groups, Robert Scott (D-VA), a member of the House Judiciary Committee, was especially aggressive in seeking amendments to the bill to limit discrimination. Charles Rangel (D-NY) also sought, as the ranking Democrat on the House Ways and Means Committee, to reduce the cost of the bill (*CQ*

Almanac 2001, 17–4). The "Care Act" legislation, which also stated that religious groups did not give up their right under the 1964 Civil Rights Act to hire people who shared their religious beliefs, made religious organizations equally eligible to compete for grants to fund a number of social services, such as job training, after-school programs, and crime prevention. The vote on the bill was 233–198. It won only 15 Democratic votes, and was rejected by 100 percent of the Black House Democrats. Rangel proposed a substitute that banned hiring discrimination under the programs and lowered the cost of the bill through different tax rates. It was rejected 168–261. It was approved by the Senate and signed into law by Bush.

President Bush and Republicans in Congress still sought to expand opportunities for religious groups to win federal grants, allowing their participation in federal grant programs without changing their hiring policies in legislation on AIDS prevention and Head Start programs. Furthermore, when funded by the federal government, religious groups were permitted to opt out of certain methods or policies when they had a religious objection.

No Child Left Behind Legislation (2001–2002)

President Bush campaigned on the theme of reforming federal education policy. It was a popular initiative, winning the sponsorship of bipartisan legislation in Bush's first year in office. Called the No Child Left Behind Act (NCLB), the law increased federal funding to elementary and secondary schools for 2002 and tied federal aid to annual testing in reading and math of schoolchildren. There was a block grant component, and financial aid to hire tutors for students in poor-performing schools. States had to establish academic standards based on these test scores for schools to reach. Although President Bush wanted the federal government to support a voucher program, permitting public-school students to get money to attend private schools, the bill did not support it. Where did the CBC stand on the issue of testing? Furthermore, Republicans also tried to attach funds for school vouchers in this bill. Where were Black legislators on school vouchers? Finally, CBC member Major Owens (D-NY) tried to win more money to fix up schools and hire more teachers. How did Black Democrats vote on Owens's amendment?

NCLB legislation was enormously popular and a significant victory for President Bush. It passed by a margin of 384–45. A large majority (83 percent) of Black legislators voted for NCLB. Only 10 Democrats voted against it, while 34 Republicans rejected it. Blacks, however, were six of the 10 Democrats, and they apparently did not like the testing requirement. Three northern, urban Black legislators opposed NCLB (Waters, Conyers, and Payne), and three southern Blacks (Earl Hilliard, Watt, and Scott of Virginia). There was a bipartisan amendment submitted to the floor to eliminate the annual testing requirement for schools receiving federal aid. While conservatives did not like the imposition of federal standards on states as it was contrary to federalism, more Democrats (119 of them) voted against testing than Republicans (52). The amendment striking testing failed to pass.

Barney Frank (D-MA) was a cosponsor of this amendment because liberal Democrats felt that the standardized tests scores would be used to penalize failing schools rather than help turn them around. A whopping 83 percent of Black Democrats in the House voted to eliminate the annual testing component of NCLB. Black Democrats represented a large component of the opposition to standardized testing. Southern moderates such as Bishop and Ford, for example, were for testing, as were a few Blacks representing northern, urban districts. Democratic Party leaders who opposed annual testing included Richard Gephardt (D-MO), the party's minority leader; minority whip David Bonior (D-MI); and David Obey (D-WI), a ranking member of the Appropriations Committee.

On the issue of school vouchers, there were two amendments. The first provided federal money to let students in poor-performing schools attend private schools, including religious ones. It was rejected 155–273. The second provided $50 million to establish a pilot school-choice program in five districts. It also was rejected 186–241. No Black legislator voted for the school voucher amendments. Only a couple of Democrats voted to provide funds for school voucher programs, in fact. All of the Black Democrats in the House backed Owens's effort to win more money for public education. It failed to pass, however, by a vote of 198–210. Only one Republican favored it.

The bipartisan win for President Bush shows some division among Black legislators over the issue of testing. A minority favored the imposition of testing and standards on public schools, not buying into fears that the data will be used against schools that have large minority populations. Even with their misgivings, most Black legislators voted for NCLB because it meant more federal money for public education. The few who did not represented a radical, inflexible core, coming from the North as well as the South. John Conyers was among the six who had voted against the 2001 NCLB.

Minimum Wage

With a majority in both Houses, the Democrats in 2007 got President Bush to agree to an increase in the minimum wage from $5.15 an hour to $7.25 an hour over two years. The last time the minimum wage had been raised was in 1996. In the previous 109th Congress, Democrats had tried to force a vote on minimum wage legislation. In 2006, the House voted on a bill combining the increase in wages with cuts in the estate tax and other tax breaks. But liberal Senators did not like this combination, and filibustered against it. The Democrats under their new Speaker, Nancy Pelosi, decided to play hardball with the president over the Iraq War issue. Thus, after passing one version under a suspension of rules that prohibited amendments and required a two-thirds vote, Speaker Pelosi decided a few months later to attach the wage increase to a defense appropriations bill. The bill also had a timetable for troop withdrawals from Iraq. Although the Senate adopted the bill, President Bush vetoed it, and Congress was unable to override his veto. The House tried one more time to get Bush to agree to a timetable for Iraq, but then dropped the issue and enacted a bill that, along with the minimum wage hike, contained tax breaks. Bush signed the legislation on May 25, 2007.

Changes and Divisions within the CBC

While George W. Bush began his presidency in 2001 winning slightly higher levels of support from House Democrats than from the CBC, by the end of his first term presidential support levels for House Democrats and the CBC were nearly identical. This is the concordance that was realized over the years, as a result of rising levels of party discipline and increasing Black participation in the party. Black Democrats became important party leaders, and White Democrats have found fewer issues to break party ranks over. One discovery during this time is that the Democratic Party has sought its own legislative agenda, liberalizing on its own in response to Republican presidential leadership. This also has meant that policy effectiveness scores, discussed later, were low under President Bush for both House Democrats and Black House Democrats alike. Both groups rejected the majority party's legislative will more than they did under Presidents Reagan and Bush.

The second critical finding is that Black Democrats find their party's policy agenda more acceptable than they did in the past. This is seen in the dramatically high party unity scores for the CBC. CBC members had party unity scores of as low as 74 under Carter. In 2008, the average CBC score was nearly 100. Party unity scores for the CBC soared during the 2000s. Black Democratic lawmakers backed their party nearly 100 percent of the time by the end of the Bush administration, rising from 92 to 99 percent over eight years. House Democrats' party unity scores increase as well. Democrats in the House earned scores of 83 in 2001, rising to 92 by 2008. Black Democrats show higher levels of support for the party than Democrats overall. Although the gap in party unity between the CBC and the House Democrats narrowed during the Bush years, Black legislators have always been more supportive of their party than Democrats overall in the House.

The CBC's record of voting with the House majority was, on average, lower under united Republican control than under divided government under Clinton (see appendix B for these scores by year). Whereas under Clinton and Republican House rule the score was around .52, it averaged .42 under Bush, including even the odd year of 2004, when the CBC effectiveness score was .70. Thus, the CBC voted on key bills with the House majority about 42 percent of the time.

Whereas under Clinton ideological divisions in the CBC emerged briefly in 1994, and then were suppressed under Republican House rule, under President Bush strange patterns emerged reflecting not only ideological sentiments but the willingness of Black legislators to back Republican agendas. There were divisions on a number of key bills. Consider the 2001 antiterrorism measure and a major bill on defense appropriations. In the aftermath of September 11, 2001, the antiterrorism bill was wildly popular in the House. The vote was 357–66. Only three Republicans voted against it. Thus, the CBC represented a substantial part of the House opposition, since only 33 percent of its members voted for it.

The bill gave the Bush administration greater powers for four years to track communications, including those over the Internet, and secretly search a suspect's home. Those opposing it felt that the powers granted to the federal government under this new law were too broad. Attorney General John Ashcroft defended the bill, arguing that government needed new tools to fight the new breed of terrorists on American soil. The southern delegation of the CBC did not uniformly favor the new antiterrorism law, although southerners represented a large part of the minority of CBC members who voted for it. Three of New York State's four Black House representatives, Charles Rangel, Edolphus Towns, and Gregory Meeks, voted for it. Major Owens, who had succeeded Shirley Chisholm when she had retired, did not. Owens himself retired in 2006. Also, some of these pro-Bush Black lawmakers pursued higher offices later, but lost. One, William Jefferson (D-LA), was indicted and defeated for reelection by a Republican minority candidate, Joseph Cao, in 2008.

In 2002 the Bush administration got the House to hugely support a record increase in the federal government's defense budget. This authorization bill came without deficit reduction policies demanding that social services be slashed in order to increase defense spending. Thus, many Democrats across the ideological spectrum voted for it. The House Democratic vote was 146–56. Only a single Republican voted against it. Blacks split, too. Perhaps because it was an election year, more half of the Black Democratic lawmakers voted for it. Strangely, some liberals, such as Maxine Waters and Bobby Rush, voted for it, but most of the support came from the southern delegation of the CBC, with Brown, Meek, Alcee Hastings, Thompson, and Clyburn favoring the large defense budget increase. Old guard CBC members such as Conyers and Rangel did not, nor did many representatives from northern, urban districts, who likely feared the future consequences of the federal deficit on domestic spending programs.

Unlike many of the fellow Democrats, Black members refused to go along with the Reagan tax cuts in 1981. However, more than twenty years later, there is a significant divide among Black Democrats in the House on the issue of tax cuts. In 2004, the Republicans proposed a new $1,000 per-child tax credit and tax cuts for married couples for four to six years. Charles Rangel immediately backed the Republican plan, as did 57 percent of the CBC. The conference report, measured as a key vote, won 336 votes against 65 opposed. Every Republican voted for it. Then, also in 2004, the Republicans offered a bill that gave corporations $137 billion in tax cuts. It also attached a $10 billion buyout of tobacco farmers, winning bipartisan support from Democrats in the South. Democrats were not as enamored with this legislation as the family tax relief, providing only 73 votes for it against 124 opposed. Rangel did not vote for this measure, but 46 percent of the CBC did. Thus, in two votes 57 percent and 46 percent of the CBC voted in 2004 for key conservative tax measures during the Bush administration. Again, this division rooted in support for Republican presidents (or presidents generally) and new political ambitions appears permanent.

In 2007 and 2008 two more significant issues divided the CBC. In 2007, the House voted to pass a free-trade agreement with Peru. The Bush administration had worked out an agreement with Democrats who had won back their House majority after a long period of serving as a minority party. The agreement was that they agreed to reduce trade tariffs with countries only if those countries also agreed to strengthen their labor and environmental protection standards. The House Democrats split on the vote by a margin of 109–116 as did the CBC. About 45 percent of the CBC voted for the free trade agreement with Peru.

Rangel, Clay, Conyers, and Dellums had opposed GATT, the general free trade agreement that passed in the Clinton administration in 1994. Now, of the two remaining in the House, Rangel was in favor of the Peru free trade agreement, while Conyers remained opposed. Both men were chairs of important House committees in 2007; Rangel was the chair of the important Ways and Means Committee and Conyers headed the Judiciary Committee. Meanwhile, Clay had retired, but his son, William Lacy Clay, voted for the free trade agreement in 2007. Dellums had retired as well, but his successor, Barbara Lee, a former legislative aide, opposed the free trade agreement. Voting against free trade was a mix of southerners and northerners. Lewis and Waters, who might be considered old guard, now split on this issue, with Lewis in favor and Waters opposed. The voting patterns are complicated by a new mix of institutional, political, and ideological pressures on Black lawmakers.

In 2008, the House had to vote on one of several pressing issues at the end of the Bush administration, specifically what to do about the failed mortgage industry. Bush wanted the House to pass a measure that permitted the Treasury Department to purchase mortgage assets that were in "trouble" from financial institutions. To make the buyout palatable for liberals, the program limited the compensation for executives of companies whose assets were purchased. It increased the federal deposit insurance to $250,000 per bank account. It also extended tax provisions and other regulations. The CBC had initially opposed the bailout. Furthermore, the 2008 elections were only weeks away, making this a highly controversial decision for lawmakers. The measure was rejected by a vote of 205–228. Republicans as well as Democrats voted against the president. However, the CBC split their vote, as did other caucuses, the Progressives and New Democrats, the Blue Dogs, and the Hispanic Caucus. Fifty-four percent of the CBC voted for the buyout plan.

After this difficult vote, more CBC members voted in favor of the financial industry several days later in October 2008. Seventy-nine percent voted for HR 1424, which was similar to the rejected measure. The vote switchers said that public opinion wanted the buyout to protect the stock market, which had plunged dramatically after the vote rejecting the measure in September. Lee, Diane Watson, Rush, and Jackson were among the vote switchers. Those ardently opposed to rescuing the financial industry still were predominantly from the South.

The divisions in the CBC reveal that they take less openly ideological stands, but express their support or opposition in the language used by main-stream lawmakers. Rangel no longer votes as an ideologue, while Conyers still does. With new "old guard" members such as Waters and Lewis, who are party leaders, there is a strategic mix in remaining ardently liberal and yet supporting a difficult vote. Then there are clear moderates in the CBC now, in part because of the new opportunities for Black politicians to court White voters. Davis, Bishop, and Ford represented the moderate Black Democrats during the Bush administration, but Brown, Meek, Carson, Watt, and even Clyburn can be considered more moderate than strongly liberal. There is a new generation of Black legislators who are still predominantly liberal, such as Lee and Jackson, but they cannot command the support of the entire CBC on defense spending, tax cuts, free trade, and government subsidies to financial institutions. Furthermore, there is the relentless pressure, because of divided government, on members of the CBC to switch sides in order to accommodate the president or the House majority.

Conclusion

African American lawmakers refused to support President Bush's faith-based initiative plans, and only a few favored his popular No Child Left Behind legislation. However, much of the opposition to the Bush presidency was largely partisan. Barbara Lee's issued a lonely dissent to autho-rizing the U.S. war in Afghanistan in 2001, and failed to win unanimous CBC support for her antiwar efforts. But her efforts, along with those of party leaders Lewis and Waters, helped push the Democratic Party toward a timetable for withdrawal from Iraq. In response to the liberalization of the Democratic Party, more Black legislators supported majority sentiment behind tax cuts, free trade, and, surprisingly, the financial sector bailout.

The Democratic Party's ability to head off dissent from the CBC by forging ahead with a liberal policy agenda of its own is working. Further-more, because the divisions within the CBC under the Bush presidency represented a mix of the ideological and pragmatic, there is less effort to formulate a CBC strategy. Leading the way toward a moderate policy agenda are new Black lawmakers, generally located in the South and arriv-ing with stronger ambitions than their predecessors. Thus while the CBC continues to win solidarity for its alternative budget plan, this racial soli-darity is more symbolic than genuine. The divisions within the CBC can be seen in votes on defense and the alternative budgets proposed by the Blue Dogs and the Progressive Caucus.

CHAPTER 6

President Obama and Black Political Incorporation

It is important that there be a rich political diversity in the Black Caucus because there is a rich diversity in America and within the black community.

—Rep. Robert Scott (D-VA) and CBC member

"The caucus is now of an age in which the policies it is promoting are becoming the law of the land. It takes a minute to reflect on that because for far too long that wasn't the case," said Rep. Chaka Fattah (D-Pa.). "It was more like we had viewpoints, but we weren't always in a position to see them through. We've moved that from the complaint window to the claims window."

—"For the New Black Caucus, New Power and an Urgency in Using It," *Washington Post*, September 26, 2009

The election of Barack Obama as the nation's first Black president represented a watershed event in American race relations. For many African Americans it was an emotional moment; their struggle for the ballot in the South had been bloody and lengthy, and participants in that struggle were living witnesses now to the election of this biracial U.S. senator who considered himself Black. During the 2008 Democratic primary, even as some remained undecided, more CBC members initially supported New York senator and former first lady Hillary Clinton than Obama for the presidential nomination (Murray 2007). Founding CBC member Charles Rangel, a fellow New Yorker, for example, supported Clinton. Civil rights veteran and Black lawmaker John Lewis (D-GA) supported Clinton, as did relative newcomer Kendrick Meek (D-FL). Privately, support was based on electability. Clinton was deemed more electable. That view changed as the nomination contest proceeded. Obama beat Clinton in the Iowa Caucus by a good margin. By Super Tuesday, some CBC members, such as Lewis, had switched from Clinton to Obama. Obama had also won the lion's share of the Black Democratic vote over Clinton. Unexpectedly, Congresswoman Stephanie Tubbs Jones of Ohio, a CBC member who stuck by Clinton until she ended her campaign, died before the November election. Clinton had won Ohio by about 10 percentage points.

Obama entered office with an ambitious agenda in very difficult times. He acknowledged these challenges in his 2008 inaugural address, stating that he would confront them in his administration. The Democratic Party had regained control of the House of Representatives and the Senate in 2006, after having been out of power legislatively during much of the last administration under a Republican president. Obama's extraordinary leadership, Democratic Party control, and strong party discipline all worked to give his administration the highest legislative success record in 2009 since President Lyndon B. Johnson. Over 97 percent of the legislative initiatives that Obama pursued in his first year in office were enacted. This measure of presidential success was the highest ever achieved since 1953, although most presidents generally earn between 80 percent to 89 percent success rates in the first year of their presidencies.

The landmark legislation Obama won included the 2009 stimulus bill and 2010 landmark health care legislation. No Republicans in the House voted for the 2009 stimulus bill in the House, and only three Republicans did so in the Senate. No Republicans in either chamber voted for the health care legislation that mandates that every American have health insurance coverage in 2016. However, the November 2010 midterm represented a stinging rebuke to the Democrats in Congress under Obama. Republicans regained majority control of the House. Democrats were able to maintain control of the Senate, but their party still lacked its supermajority of 60 votes. They had lost this supermajority in December 2009 when a Republican won the special election held to fill the seat of U.S. Senator Ted Kennedy, who had died while in office.

The Clinton and Bush administrations had achieved record levels of diversity, which Obama matched, appointing Eric Holder, a deputy attorney general in the Clinton administration, to become the nation's first Black attorney general. In addition to Holder, Black appointees included Lisa Jackson in the Environmental Protection Agency, Ron Kirk as U.S. trade representative, Susan Rice as ambassador to the United Nations, and Margaret A. Hamburg as commissioner of the Food and Drug Administration.

Latinos were represented by Ken Salazar, secretary of the Interior Department, and Hilda Solis, secretary of the Labor Department. Obama made notable Asian American appointments as well with Steve Chu as head of the Department of Energy and Eric Shinseki in charge of the Department of Veterans Affairs.

Notably, Obama brought in a team of African American women to the White House, including Valerie Jarrett, a senior adviser to the president and director of the Office of Public Liaison and Intergovernmental Affairs; Desiree Rogers, the White House social secretary; Melody Barnes as head of the White House Domestic Policy Council; Mona Sutphen, the president's deputy chief of staff; and Cassandra Butts, deputy White House counsel. In fact, the *Washington Post* reported that seven of about three dozen senior positions were filled by Black women (Thompson 2009). Obama was able to make two Supreme Court appointments during his first two years in office. Both appointments were given to women.

One Black adviser in the White House, Van Jones, was forced to resign in September 2009 after conservatives alleged that he had referred to Republicans using an offensive term in a speech. They also charged that he had signed a petition alleging that the Bush administration had allowed the September 11, 2001, terrorist attack to occur in order to create as a pretext for the Iraq War. (The latter charge was later proven false.) A Yale law school graduate and community organizer, Jones had been a special adviser on the promotion of environmental or green jobs. His politics, a White House spokesperson said, was going to get in the way of Obama's policy agenda. Unlike the significant outcry over Clinton's pulling Black law professor Lani Guinier's nomination to head the Civil Rights Division in the Justice Department, after criticisms of her publications, there was no major media coverage of the CBC or any major Black civil rights group taking issue with Jones's forced resignation. The NAACP gave Jones one of its annual Image Awards in 2010, however.

Also in 2010, the White House became embroiled in the wrongful termination of a Black Department of Agriculture worker, Shirley Sherrod. Sherrod was asked to leave after a tape emerged in the media of her expressing biased views against Whites. The tape had been purposefully edited and cut; the full speech exonerated her. President Obama later called Sherrod to apologize for her termination. The CBC also asked for Sherrod's reinstatement. Sherrod was offered a new position in the Department of Agriculture, but she declined the offer.

There have been early complains that Obama was ducking a policy focus on racial problems in America. Jesse Jackson, who ran in 1984 and

1988 for the Democratic presidential nomination, was quoted as saying that Obama needs "to stop acting like he's White" (*Washington Post* 2007). Jackson was referring to a case in Jena, Louisiana, where six Black teenagers had been accused of the attempted murder of a White teenager. Jackson was upset about the excessive charges brought against the Black teenagers, in light of the extreme sentencing penalties imposed against Blacks accused of violent/murderous acts against Whites. Obama also left his Black church, Trinity United Church of Christ, during his 2008 campaign when it emerged that minister Jeremiah Wright Jr. had made anti-U.S. comments during some of his sermons. Some feel that Obama, as the nation's first Black president, should address the policy grievances of African Americans and challenge America to solve the group's problems. Those who reject complaints about Obama's deracialized approach point out that he was running to be president of all Americans, not just Black Americans.

CBC members have strongly supported President Obama. While some Black lawmakers say that they have pressed him to take a stronger stand on issues minorities care about, such as foreclosure relief from banks (Evans 2009), most CBC members have defended the president. He was publicly applauded by Eddie Bernice Johnson (D-TX) who called the president a "miracle worker" in helping to restore the nation's economy.

Although the debate over whether Obama is "Black enough" hasn't emerged as a prominent theme in Black politics, complaints have nevertheless multiplied that he hasn't done enough for Black people. Given the strong partisan tensions in Washington and the historic nature of his presidency, Obama has won the allegiance of the CBC—a CBC that I argue that became more ideologically diverse during the Bush presidency. Thus, with some exceptions, Black liberals and moderates voted for Obama's defense budget request and for health care reform, and furthermore did so without rancor. He won strong support for the second phase of the $700 billion-dollar Wall Street bailout (the bailout was approved by Congress at the end of the Bush administration), with only a few CBC members, such as old guard members Conyers and Rangel, in opposition. A significant minority of the CBC voted to support the president for the extension of tax breaks for the wealthy in 2010. His party also drove Democratic members, including Black moderates, toward the liberal end of social issues, notably gay rights and immigration. In the end, Black Democrats in the House supported President Obama strongly. Furthermore, Black Democratic lawmakers voted with the House majority on key bills about 90 percent of the time in 2009 and 84 percent in 2010—both representing historic highs for the period under study. Basically, the CBC sacrificed formulating a separate agenda apart from that of the president and the Democratic Party. The problem is that to govern effectively, both the president and the national party must ride a roller coaster of ups (victories) and downs (compromising losses) to win significantly. Finally, although this analysis stops at the end of the 111th Congress, the Republican-controlled House in the 112th Congress will likely drive down the CBC's liberal scores, as members still seek to pass legislation and thus work with conservative political leadership as incorporated members working under divided government.

Extreme Politics under Obama

President Obama positioned himself on the liberal side by calling for tax increase on the wealthiest Americans as part of his budget agenda. He also said he wanted to preserve the Bush tax cuts for the middle and working classes. His budget request for 2010 contained some small spending cuts, but also raised spending, notably by shifting Pell grants from a discretionary to a mandatory expenditure.

Under Obama, liberals outside of Washington complained that the president failed to strongly instruct Congress that government needs to engage in serious spending on job creation, and that his stimulus package was inadequate. Conservatives pointed out the federal deficit was dangerously high. Conservative lawmakers used strikingly strong language. Under Obama's budget plan, the federal deficit would continue to grow through 2014.

House Minority Leader John Boehner (R-OH) referred to Obama's policy agenda as a "move to a big socialist government in Washington'" (*CQ Almanac* 2009, 4–9). No Republican voted for Obama's budget in the House. Twenty Democrats opposed it as well. Because of the high levels of party polarization in Congress, fiscally conservative Blue Dog Democrats kept their objections about the rising deficits largely to themselves until the conference report vote, which was adopted by the same vote as the House budget resolution, 233–193. Democratic Party leaders promised that they would support stronger deficit control measures in the future.

Two liberal alternatives came up for a floor vote. Rejected by 84–348, the Progressive Caucus's budget proposal cut defense and created a universal health care system. Seventy-four percent of the CBC voted for it; 10 CBC members voted against it. Among those who opposed the Progressive Caucus's alternative budget plan were some who were planning statewide bids in the South in 2010: Artur Davis was planning to run for governor of

Alabama, and Kendrick Meek and Corrine Brown had expressed interest in running for the open Senate seat in Florida. Kilpatrick of Michigan and Gregory Meeks of New York were the only Black northerners to oppose the Progressive Caucus budget amendment. Also rejected by 113–318 was the CBC's alternative budget which repealed the 2001 and 2003 tax cuts for the wealthiest, transferring the money to domestic policies such as education and health care. Davis, like Bishop and Gray had done earlier a few times, voted "present." However, the CBC won impressive near unanimity from the Black House members.

Health Care Legislation

Obama's biggest victory was passage of national health care legislation. The passage of the Affordable Care Act came in March 2010, but the victory was spoiled by the ugly politicking that emerged over it. Congress took months to pass it, and the debate became highly partisan. One Republican senator initially signed onto the legislation through her participation on the Senate Finance Committee, but eventually no Republican supported the measure. By a narrow 220–215 margin, in November the House passed a bill that required a ban on any federal funding of abortions through covered plans to win the necessary votes. In December, after much publicized negotiations with senators, Majority Leader Harry Reid obtained the 60 votes necessary to bring the legislation to a vote. On Christmas Eve 2009, the Senate passed its bill.

There still needed to be a second vote on the reconciled bill with the House. However, in January, Democrats in the Senate lost their three-fifths majority after the election of Scott Brown, a Republican from Massachusetts, to fill a vacancy caused by the death of Democratic senator Ted Kennedy. Thus, in March, Senate Majority Leader Reid declared that his party would use a process called "reconciliation" to pass the health care legislation, since they could not find 60 votes now in the Senate. Reconciliation requires only 51 votes to pass, and the Senate approved the reconciled bill. In another cliffhanger moment, the House passed the Senate version of the bill by a vote of 219–212. The Senate version contained a number of disliked provisions, including special deals to senators, that Reid pledged to fix through reconciliation. The legislation was signed into law by President Obama on March 30, 2010.

Democrats had majorities in the beginning of the health care legislative process. Yet the party was unable to pass the measure quietly and effectively. Public opinion about health care polarized in response to the partisan divide in Washington, as Republicans were extremely hostile to Obama's health care plan. Legislation generally requires multiple votes, which Democratic legislators took advantage of. Even CBC members engaged in the politics as some bargained openly for their votes. Marcia Fudge (D-OH), who had voted for the legislation in November, moved to the fence, leaning "yes" until two days before the second vote, when she declared her support. Meanwhile, members of Congress were approached by hecklers. A "Tea Party" movement emerged, and two members of the Congressional Black Caucus, John Lewis (D-GA) and Emanuel Cleaver (D-MO), were verbally attacked with racial slurs and spat upon by participants in a Tea Party rally after it was clear that passage in the House was achievable. The protesters also hurled antigay slurs at Barney Frank (D-MA). There were other acts of violence against members of Congress related to the passage of the 2010 health care legislation.

In the end, only one African American House member, Artur Davis of Alabama, voted against the health insurance plan; Davis was a political moderate planning a gubernatorial bid in a conservative state. He claimed it was "too expensive." Davis later lost his primary race to a White Democrat, and many tied his loss to this vote, which had upset Black and liberal Democrats in the state. Although some CBC members, such as Maxine Waters, stressed that they wanted a public option, or a government-backed health insurance program, it became clear that the Senate was too conservative to pass a program that included a public option. President Obama in response signaled his intention to accept whatever plan Congress passed that mandated health insurance coverage for Americans. For the reasons explained here—divided government and incorporation—Black lawmakers backed the president. John Conyers of Michigan represented the one lone Black radical voice to criticize the president in public regarding his strategy for passing health care legislation. On a radio show he told listeners that "President Barack Obama is 'bowing down' to Republicans and corporate interests on health reform" (O'Brien 2009). He also complained that a single-payer proposal, one where the government provides for health insurance, had been rejected by Democrats from the beginning (Seelye 2009).

In interviews with the press, President Obama directly addressed his liberal critics who felt that health care insurance will still remain out of reach for the adult poor, who, if they work, will suffer an annual fine for failing to carry it. It will still propel many more into health care coverage, the president asserted, and thus it is better legislation "than doing nothing." The president also stated his preference for taxing high-end "Cadillac" insurance plans to help pay for the subsidies for low-income citizens. At one point, some liberal senators floated the idea of permitting those 55 and older to enroll in Medicare in lieu of a public option, but the idea did not get enough traction. Because of Republican opposition, the pressures on Democrats to support the president's initiative were enormous. Rep. Dennis Kucinich (D-OH), a progressive, refused to support the health care legislation because it didn't go far enough, but he ultimately voted in favor of it.

Policy analysts, however, believe that the new policy does not go very far. Jacob Hacker quotes one analyst as saying that the bill itself "incorporates all sorts of Republican ideas" (2010, 867). Why? Hacker contends the United States has a strongly privatized system for social benefits. Second, he points to the nature of the U.S. Congress with its conservative Senate, which grants private interests ways to derail costly public policies through the filibuster rule. The filibuster, he writes, has become a normal tool of minority obstruction. He suggests that liberals could have gotten more, but then the conservative electorate sprang up, threatening to derail the process completely.

In this grand playbook, however, the CBC chose not to engage in direct battle with the president and conservative Democrats over the public option. One could imagine the CBC as a counterpoint to the conservatives on the airways and organizing protests, but that type of strategy was never envisioned. Indeed, after Reagan, even with the continued hardening of conservative policy interests in Washington from Republicans, the CBC no longer radicalized in response to Republican ascendancy. A hardening of the CBC's position didn't emerge because its members increasingly work through their party. Furthermore, although African Americans in surveys are far more likely than Whites to endorse a government-backed health insurance plan, the CBC did not have enough strong liberals left to fight aggressively over this issue. It is doubtful with the composition of the 111th Senate that the CBC could have successfully helped push through a plan with a public option, or a national exchange, or a stronger mandate for employers; had they tried, some might argue, Obama would have lost his health care plan. Still, had the CBC put up a radically liberal posture in this debate, it might have helped put the United States closer politically toward a future that included those elements. Maybe, however, the Democratic Party will continue on this path of a public option without significant pressure from its Black members. Yet a number of Republican-led states immediately filed lawsuits against the new health care law; these states object to the individual mandate to carry health insurance, which they contend the federal government lacks the constitutional authority to impose. The Supreme Court upheld the constitutionality of the individual mandate in a 5–4 decision in July 2012.

Economic Stimulus, Jobs, and Mortgage Assistance

A major victory for Obama one month into his term, which Clinton did not enjoy, was passage of his economic stimulus bill. The economic times demanded it. The spending component of the Economic Recovery and Reinvestment Act gave $575.3 billion to states and localities to assist in emergency assistance and unemployment programs, to spend more on education, the environment, and to create jobs. The legislation also gave $211.8 billion in tax cuts to businesses and individuals for over 11 years. The House passed the final legislation in February 2009 by a vote of 246–163. All the Black Democrats voted for this stimulus bill.

The Democratic-controlled Congress also sought passage of an additional jobs bill in December 2009. After Speaker Pelosi won narrow passage of the $154 billion bill in the House, the Senate refused to take up the matter in light of the activity on the health care bill. Here, CBC chairwoman Barbara Lee attempted to redraft the jobs bill to favor government spending in the poorest areas, where minorities generally reside and where unemployment was over twice the national rate. Unemployment in late 2009 had risen nationally to about 10 percent. Rep. Maxine Waters stated that "we're not paying enough attention to the misery in our community" (Newmyer 2009). The media reported that the CBC organized a walkout on the vote on finance regulatory reforms. However, on the December 11 vote on HR 4173, the financial industry regulation overhaul, all of the CBC members voted "yes." Their votes were needed, because no Republicans in the House voted for this bill and 27 Democrats defected.

In 2009, Congress passed a mortgage assistance bill, helping people remain in their foreclosed homes through a new program to refinance their mortgages and adding more funds to increase the borrowing authority of banks. It also added $2.2 billion to social programs for the homeless. One hundred percent of the CBC voted for this bill. And in the end, it won a sizeable percent of Republican support as well.

Obama agreed to continue to bail out the financial industry in order to stabilize the industry in one of the first acts of his presidency. President Bush had already used federal funds to purchase troubled assets. The Obama bailout was the second half of the $700 billion authorized under the law; all the president had to do was request the funds. Liberal Democrats were upset that federal dollars were going to Wall Street bankers. Republicans were unhappy too. However, even as organized opposition formed in the Congress to deny these additional Toxic Asset Relief Program (TARP) funds to President Obama, the Senate voted for the bailout. The Democratic-controlled House, however, voted twice to bar the release of the second half of the funds, and on another bill to restrict the use of these funds. These measures won strong approval from Democrats. The first one restricting the use of TARP funds passed 260–166, with little Republican support. The second one barring the release of the funds also passed 270–155, with virtually all Republican behind it, and Democrats divided but mostly opposed. A nay vote on the second bill was in support of the president's position. Obama had pledged to veto any legislation barring the release of these TARP funds.

Many CBC members initially had objections to authorizing the second half of TARP money to fund the bailout, but most then took the president's position. Thus, 100 percent of the CBC voted to restrict the use of the funds in HR 384. But only 18 percent voted with the House majority to block release of the additional funds. Those seeking to stop additional TARP funds to Wall Street included, notably, the two remaining founding CBC members, Conyers and Rangel. In addition, some of the CBC members running for higher office in 2010 were opposed.

The Wars in Iraq and Afghanistan

On August 31, 2010, Obama announced that the American combat mission in Iraq had ended and that the Iraqi people now had lead responsibility for security in their nation. In December 2011, all U.S. troops were pulled out. Earlier, toward the end of 2009, however, the president decided to escalate the war in Afghanistan by sending in 30,000 additional troops. The president's decision to send additional troops to fight in Afghanistan did not ignite united liberal opposition in Congress. The House Progressive Caucus issued a statement that it had not taken a stand on the Afghanistan War. The CBC's chairwoman, Barbara Lee, was firmly opposed to this war. In October 2009, Lee introduced HR 3699, "To prohibit any increase in the number of members of the United States Armed Forces serving in Afghanistan." This bill had 33 cosponsors. The CBC cosponsors were Yvette Clarke, Cleaver, Conyers, Donna Edwards, Keith Ellison, Jackson Lee, Lewis, Towns, Waters, and Watson.

In July 2010, Lee sponsored HR 6045, the Responsible End to the War in Afghanistan Act, legislation mandating that funds for the military in Afghanistan shall only be authorized to provide for a safe withdrawal. The bill had 24 cosponsors, eight of whom were CBC members: Conyers, Edwards, Ellison, Jackson Lee, Lewis, Payne, Towns, and Waters. Lee, however, voted for the final defense appropriations bill in 2009, which included funds for the wars in Afghanistan and Iraq. This bill, however, had a liberal rider attached to it, extending hate crime legal protection to other minority groups, including gays and lesbians. Whereas Dellums, during the Reagan-Bush years, had been able to win all of the CBC to his side on his opposition to the defense buildup, Lee, who represents Dellums's old district, was unable to round up all the CBC to support U.S. withdrawal from Afghanistan. There is a serious ideological split in the CBC on such matters, with Black moderates unwilling to take positions that appear to jeopardize America's security interests. In June 2011 the president announced plans to end U.S. troop involvement in Afghanistan by the end of 2014, and return security over to the Afghan government. In 2011, there were 100,000 U.S. troops stationed there.

Gay Rights and Don't Ask, Don't Tell

President Obama used his executive authority to give gay and lesbians new federal benefits. Their partners now can receive long-term health insurance, and child-care subsidies can be used by same-sex couples. Federal workers will be able to take family leaves under the Family and Medical Leave Act to care for gay or lesbian partners. The Census Bureau will also report on the number of American residents in same-sex relationships.

The defense authorization that ultimately passed contained new hate crime legislation, covering sexual orientation, gender, and disability. While the House-passed original bill authorizing funds was popular, the conference report that included this Senate hate crimes amendment had only 44 Republican backers in the House. House Minority Leader John A. Boehner (R-OH) opposed it, saying that he was "offended by it" (*CQ Almanac* 2009, 6–6). All CBC members supported the administration's defense request, which pointedly sought no additional money for the F-22 Raptor.

In 2010, the Senate Democrats attempted to win repeal of Don't Ask, Don't Tell (DADT) as an amendment to a defense appropriations bill. However, even with the president's support, they could not win enough Republican votes to secure the necessary 60-member majority and overcome a minority filibuster. The House vote had been 234–194. Artur Davis was missing on the vote for this amendment. Davis claimed his campaign for governor had crowded out his legislative schedule, but after having suffered defeat in the primary, he voted against the repeal in December. Bishop of Georgia voted against it, along with 25 other House Democrats.

Finally, in its lame duck session of 2010, Congress passed a bill repealing DADT. The December 18 bill won eight Republican votes in the Senate along with all of the Democrats voting yes. In the House vote that had occurred a few days earlier, only 15 Democrats opposed the repeal. Davis of Alabama was the only CBC members to vote against the repeal, as Sanford Bishop changed sides and voted for the repeal. Nevertheless, in the highly partisan atmosphere, only 15 House Republicans had voted to let gays and lesbians openly serve in the military. Republican senator John McCain of Arizona said the legislation was being jammed through before the new Congress with its GOP majority in the House could take over (*CQ Almanac* 2010, 6–8).

The Rights of Terror Suspects and Intelligence

Obama pledged to close the Guantánamo facility in his first year as president, in addition to ending the Bush policy permitting some forms of torture. Later, the president asserted that he needed Congress to passage legislation to close it. In 2009, some effort was made to attach funds to a war supplemental bill in the Senate, as Obama requested $80 million, but this request was not in the final bill. Instead, the supplemental appropriations bill barred any Guantánamo detainees from being released or transferred to the United States. Furthermore, liberal Democrats in the Senate wanted to release photos of the detainees through legislation, but the president asserted that he would block legislation permitting this, and so the matter was dropped. The House was not as engaged as the Senate in this debate on the Guantánamo prison facility.

In May 2010 the House voted for a defense bill that explicitly denied funds to transfer or release prisoners at Guantánamo. HR 5136 split the Democrats, while winning all but one vote from the Republicans. Most the CBC members voted against this bill, which was in support of the president's position. However, 19 percent voted for it—all but one (Richardson of California) from the South: Brown, Meek, Bishop, and Johnson.

The House passed an intelligence bill in February 2010 that gave Congress a stronger oversight role over the government's intelligence agencies, notably the Central Intelligence Agency, Federal Bureau of Investigation, and the National Security Agency. With Democrats in control in the 111th Congress, the matter of when House Speaker Nancy Pelosi had been told that the government had used harsh interrogation methods—specifically waterboarding—eroded efforts toward bipartisanship. Another issue was the 2010 disclosure by the CIA director that the House Intelligence Committee, which provides oversight, had not been told about the secret government plan to kill leaders of al Qaeda (*CQ Almanac* 2010, 6–10). This plan had been in place since 2001. The bill required the president to tell all members of the Intelligence Committee within 180 days of certain intelligence plans.

Only one House Republican voted for HR 2701. To win bipartisanship, Republicans had wanted some Republican measures added to the bill, such as forbidding officials to read terrorism suspects their Miranda rights (*CQ Almanac* 2010, C-13). Meanwhile, only four House Democrats opposed it, and Maxine Waters of California had been one of them. Later, in the House vote on the final measure, nine Democrats opposed it, including Lee and Watson, both of California. Waters, who had been initially opposed, voted for the final measure. On May 2, 2011, President Obama went on television to announce that the military had killed Osama bin Laden, the founder and voice of al Qaeda.

Immigration Reform and the DREAM Act

Immigration reform was part of President Obama's legislative agenda. Briefly, the Congressional Hispanic Caucus threatened to withhold its critical support for health care legislation without a pledge from the president to back immigration reform. Because the Congress quickly became so partisan during Obama's first years in office, Republicans who had also wanted to pass immigration reform dropped the issue.

Just prior to the 2010 midterm elections Senate Majority Leader Harry Reid (D-NV) announced that he was attaching an amendment for the DREAM Act, legislation permitting the legalization of children of undocumented immigrants attending college or enrolled in the military, to a 2010 defense authorization bill. Senator McCain (R-AZ) immediately announced his objection to this amendment. In the lame duck session of Congress, however, the Senate voted on the DREAM Act. This measure grants legal status to adults under 30 brought to the United States illegally as children if they complete two years of college or military service. Only five Democrats in the Senate voted against the DREAM Act, while it won the votes of three Republicans (*CQ Almanac* 2010, 278). But at 55–41, it failed to win the necessary 60 votes to gain passage.

Blacks are in the middle between more conservative Whites on immigration issues, who support making it a felony to be an illegal resident in the United States, and more liberal Latinos, who support amnesty for long-term undocumented residents (Tate 2010). In 1986, Blacks divided their votes on the immigration reform that included new sanctions for businesses employing undocumented immigrants and amnesty for long-term ones. Only 65 percent of the CBC voted for it, and those opposed objected to the sanctions for employers, which could be a basis to discriminate against Latino workers. Now with much of the public favoring new laws denying social services and public benefits to undocumented immigrants, liberals are very likely to support any legislation that provides amnesty to some, even if it combines some conservative elements. Because immigration is a social issue as opposed to a purely economic one, Black lawmakers will likely accept their party's liberal leadership on this matter. President Obama, therefore, pledged support to the DREAM Act. However, with the House under GOP control, a few Black legislators might support conservative measures, such as criminalizing undocumented immigrants. Black lawmakers under the CBC may not be united on immigration matters. Several southwestern and southern states, most notably Arizona, Alabama, and Georgia, have passed tough new anti-immigration measures.

Last-Minute Tax Breaks for the Wealthy

The 111th Congress ended with a bang, notably during its lame duck session. President Obama, after campaigning against extension of the Bush tax cuts for the wealthy, surprised the public with his agreement to a deal to extend them for another two years. In return for this, the president won an extended unemployment benefits package. The House initially passed a bill that only extended the tax cuts for families making less than $200,000 a year. The Senate, thus, adopted the new Obama-Republican plan. The House adopted the Senate plan with a sharply divided Democratic vote of 139–112. House Speaker Pelosi campaigned for an amendment that raised it from 35 to 45 percent; but it was defeated, 194–233 (*CQ Almanac* 2010).

A smaller subset of the CBC backed the tax plan deal with 34 percent voting for it. The expected conservative members of the CBC voted for it, while the liberals, including Black Democratic Party leaders, opposed it. Senator Roland Burris, an African American who had been appointed under controversial circumstances to replace President Obama's vacated seat, had his seat taken by the Republican victor in the open-seat contest in the lame-duck session.

On the original votes for these tax cuts during the Bush presidency, only Scott of Georgia voted for them in 2003. Even his moderate Georgia counterparts had opposed the Bush tax cuts. But now Bishop and Johnson favored their extension as part of the Obama deal. The president backed the deal as a compromise necessary to get the extension of unemployment benefits, which were set to expire at the end of the year for millions of the unemployed. Liberals were incensed by the deal because without the extra revenue from letting the tax cuts expire, pressure to cut federal government social programs intensified.

Presidential and Party Support and Policy Effectiveness Measures

Black Democratic lawmakers had emerged as Clinton's biggest supporters over the typical Democratic House member in the last three years of his presidency. Obama benefited from even tighter party discipline than had Clinton. The House Democratic Party's presidential support score in 2009 was 90, nearly a 20 point increase from the support levels President Clinton had earned in the 1990s. It dropped in 2010 to 84 for House Democrats as some House Democrats blinked when it came to supporting conservative bills largely left over from the Bush presidency.

Data from the *CQ Almanac* show that CBC members are among Obama's strongest supporters. In 2009, Jackson (D-IL), Gwen Moore (D-WI), and Brown (D-FL) had presidential support scores of 99. Hastings (D-FL) and Fudge (D-OH) supported the president's policy positions 98 percent or more of the time. The average presidential support score for the CBC in 2009 was 96 and 86 in 2010. Davis (D-AL), unsurprisingly given his opposition to Obama's health care agenda, earned the lowest presidential support score of 86. Davis was an outlier, for all other CBC members had presidential support scores in the 90s. CBC presidential support for Obama dropped by 10 points in 2010. Liberal Blacks did not support the president on key legislative items in 2010, notably on Afghanistan and the extension of the Bush tax breaks. Still, the CBC did not significantly pull away from the president in 2010. The group followed Obama's leadership in Washington more than they had the last two Democratic presidents. And as the multivariate analysis reported in chapter 7 will show, increased support for Democratic presidents is a main reason why the CBC legislative record is less strongly liberal today.

Party unity is obviously importantly related to Obama's policy success in the House. The average Democratic Party score for party unity in the House in 2009 was 91. It 2010 it was slightly lower at 89. House Democrats had achieved a record high of 92 in 2007, the first year they had been restored to majority party status since 1994. Black lawmakers had moved into the 90s in terms of party support after Bush had won reelection in 2000. Now, House Democrats, enjoying party majority support, entered into the 90s with them. The CBC party unity score was 98 in 2009 and 97 in 2010. They still remain a faction more loyal to the party than House Democrats, a pattern that has been consistent since the Carter administration. CBC party loyalty to the Democratic Party only wavered some relative to House Democrats in the early years of the Reagan administration.

Together with strong presidential and party support, Black policy effectiveness scores calculated from *CQ Quarterly's* "key votes" were the highest ever for 2009, dropping some in 2010. Increased support for the House majority is another reason why the CBC is less liberal. In 2008, a year in which President Bush's approval rating and support in Congress had tanked significantly and the House Democrats had a majority, the CBC's policy effectiveness score was already an astonishing 89, indicating that the CBC members voted with the House majority 89 percent of the time. The CBC is astonishingly in sync with the House Democratic majority under President Obama as well. The policy effectiveness score for House Democrats increased to 90. The only key bill they massively lost on was the so-called Stupak amendment, named for Rep. Bart Stupak (D-MI). His amendment barred the use of federal funds to pay for abortions covered under health insurance plans unless the pregnancy was the result of rape, incest, or endangered the woman's life. Only Sanford Bishop (D-GA) of the CBC voted for it; the rest did not. Stupak's amendment won 64 House Democratic votes, enough to win adoption along with a unanimous Republican vote.

The Republican Party's legislative effectiveness score was lopped in half to its lowest point ever of 23 percent. Most of the key bills the House voted on were uniformly opposed by Republicans. The only measures that divided the Republicans were on less strongly ideological matters, such as tobacco regulation and food safety. Forty-one percent of House Republicans voted with the Democrats to impose new label warnings on tobacco products and to ban new flavor additives except menthol, and 31 percent voted to impose a registration fee for food inspections at facilities other than farms, grocery stores, and restaurants. A third popular measure was the "Cash for Clunkers" program, which gave car buyers a $4,500 voucher for trading in an old vehicle for a new one. Forty-five percent of House Republicans voted for this measure. The rest of the major legislative items in 2009 were staunchly opposed, including not only the health care insurance mandate but increased funding for college students, limiting greenhouse emissions, and increased funding for children health insurance programs. On matters not listed as key votes, Republicans also voted with Democrats to impose new disclosure rules on credit card companies, to extend federal unemployment benefits, and to offer a new homebuyer credit for first-time home owners in 2009 (*CQ Almanac* 2009, 1–7).

The Republican effectiveness scores show that President Obama governed by bypassing the staunch Republican opposition. Black House members' effectiveness score dropped to 71 percent. It dropped for House Democrats as well, to 77 percent, while it increased for House Republicans to 36 percent. Thus, on more than one-third of the key fifteen bills that the House voted on, Republicans voted with the majority. Black House members voted with the House majority more than 70 percent of the time a few times during the Reagan/Bush years when the House was under Democratic control. They also voted with the House majority more than 70 percent of the time in the first two years of the Clinton presidency with, again, a Democratic-controlled House.

The legislative effectiveness scores are especially tied to party control of the House, and not so much as to which party controls the presidency. CBC legislative effectiveness scores are slightly lower than House Democrats' effectiveness scores under Republican majorities in the House. These differences may not be statistically meaningful. As the Democratic Party has improved its effectiveness scores in the House, so has the CBC.

In the Carter administration, I argued that the divisions among the CBC on key bills were not strongly ideological. The CBC initially also dissented from the party during the Reagan/Bush years, but that dissent softened as the party began to place members in leadership positions. The group's will to challenge Clinton as they had challenged Carter had withered as Black House members were emerging as key players within the Democratic establishment by the 1990s. Furthermore, the Republican House takeover in 1995 also meant less CBC opposition to their party's leadership.

In 2010, the CBC broke apart on four issues. The first was over an amendment that cut funding from an F-35 fighter plane that had been funded for 14 years. President Obama was for this amendment, arguing that the funding of the project was unnecessary. Fifty-nine percent of the CBC voted to cut the project's funding, while a surprisingly large percent—41 percent—voted against it, in opposition to the president's position. The amendment failed to pass the House by a vote of 193–231. The 41 percent of Black House members who rejected the amendment were not necessarily southerners or conservatives, but a mix. The division reveals the weak ideological group holding new members together; it once was a no-brainer for liberal Blacks to support cutting out large defense projects.

A second bill that divided Black legislators in the House concerned campaign finance laws; it was also more complicated ideologically. H. R. 5175 tightened disclosure requirements for corporations in response to a Supreme Court ruling (*Citizens United v. the FEC*) that permitted corporations to spend unlimited sums in elections and campaigns as independent groups. The rub for Democrats was that the bill contained a loophole exempting the National Rifle Association from some of the new requirements. President Obama still endorsed the bill and thus earned 67 percent of the votes from the CBC. The defectors, constituting 33 percent of the CBC, were mostly from liberal, urban districts—Waters, Kilpatrick, Edwards, Rush, Clarke, Payne, and Fudge. Butterfield (D-NC) voted against the measure, while Conyers surprisingly voted for it. It narrowly passed 216–206 in June 2010, but failed to win a 60-vote majority in the Senate.

Barbara Lee (D-CA) of the CBC sponsored an amendment to HR 4899 to force a withdrawal of U.S. troops from Afghanistan. In a July 2010 vote it received only 100 House votes. This amendment reveals the new ideological divisions in the group. Sixty-five percent of the CBC voted for it. Those opposed were almost all from the South.

The final key bill that divided Black House members pertained to the extension of the Bush-era tax cuts. It was discussed earlier, but 34 percent of the CBC voted for it in support of the president's position. The Black legislators who favored it were moderates.

The End of the Black Empowerment Era?
Obama and the Push for Black Candidates

It is possible to talk about a "Black empowerment" era, the mobilization of Blacks to help Black candidates win elective office. It generally began with the 1983 mayoral campaign of Harold Washington in Chicago. Blacks wanted to see more Black faces in government and within the party, and they wanted national Democratic leadership to back Congressman Washington over other primary contenders. They responded enthusiastically to Jesse Jackson's two presidential bids in the 1980s, aiming among other things to increase the numbers of Black elected officials through the mobilization of Black voters (Tate 1994; Walters 1989).

In contrast, the Congressional Black Caucus responded lukewarmly to

Jackson's 1984 bid. Yet, the members swung around in 1988 and uniformly backed Jackson's second bid. New York-based activist Al Sharpton and former U.S. senator Carol Moseley Braun ran for the party's presidential nomination in 2004, but got only a fraction of the support that Jackson had obtained in 1984 and 1988. CBC members then divided over Barack Obama's presidential bid in 2008, with some members supporting Hillary Clinton, but decisively moved toward it once Obama had won some firm primary victories. Along with Obama, a dozen members of the CBC, including Lee and Lewis, backed Steve Cohen, a liberal White incumbent who had won Harold Ford Jr.'s open seat, in 2010 over a popular former Black mayor of Memphis. Cohen won the primary, and the election, and is the only White member of the House to represent a majority-Black district.

President Obama noticeably had not made any special effort to back Black Democrats in 2010. He did not intervene to help Roland Burris, the Black Senate appointee to his former Illinois seat, who appeared to have purchased the seat from the indicted Illinois governor. Under pressure from Democrats, Burris agreed not to seek reelection in 2010. Significantly, the Obama White House sent a press report indicating that the administration did not favor a reelection bid by David Paterson, the first Black governor of New York. Paterson became governor when the incumbent governor, Eliot Spitzer, resigned over ethic charges. Paterson was contemplating running for reelection in 2010, but backed out after it became clear that state and national Democrats felt he wasn't popular enough to retain office. Andrew Cuomo, the son of a former New York governor, was considered more electable in the state. In 2010, in fact, Cuomo won.

The White House was also unhappy with the set of Democratic candidates who ran for the open Illinois U.S. Senate seat that was once Obama's. Significantly, Obama chose not to endorse the African American candidate, Cheryle Jackson, who placed third in the Illinois primary race. Although he initially seemed to drag his feet on endorsing Kendrick Meek, another African American candidate running for his party's nomination for the U.S. Senate in 2010, Obama made a critical primary endorsement for him in the Florida Democratic primary. Meek then decisively beat a challenge from Jeff Greene, a White self-financed candidate. Still, in both Illinois and Florida, Republicans won the general elections in 2010. Obama, also, and perhaps less surprisingly, enthusiastically backed his White former political adviser, Rahm Emanuel, for the open-seat Chicago mayoral race in 2010. In spite of some lawsuit trouble over residency, Emanuel won handily over three Black candidates, including former U.S. senator Carol Moseley Braun. Emanuel did very well in Black precincts in Chicago, a feat most attribute to Obama's strong endorsement.

Groups continue to make efforts to win political representation. In considering the two vacancies to the Supreme Court, a number of individuals wanted Obama to pick a Latino, a gay, an Asian, or a woman to the Court. There is the absence of a collective push from Black leaders to increase their numbers. It also complicates the debate over whether minorities need special protection from the federal government to win elections. In June 2011, a Black political journalist wrote an opinion piece for the *Atlanta Journal-Constitution* stating that the Voting Rights Act has packed too many Blacks into a smaller number of districts, "re-segregating the South." All in the all, the absence of an open push for increasing Black and minority representation in Washington is another sign of how Black interests have moderated.

New Issues and Money Politics for the CBC

Because most Black legislators are in districts having Democratic majorities, they remain incredibly safe districts for Democrats to run in. The pattern since the 1970s is that often 100 percent of those Black members are reelected once they win their primaries (Tate 2003, 59). There have been a few defeats, for example the 1992 primary losses of two Black incumbents in Illinois, Charles Hayes and Gus Savage. Rep. Barbara Rose Collins of Michigan was defeated in her primary in 1996 by Carolyn Cheeks Kilpatrick. Kilpatrick, herself, faced strong competition in her primaries, having won in 2008 in a three-way race with only 39 percent of the vote. The scandal and later conviction of her son as mayor of Detroit was made an issue. Kilpatrick as an incumbent was able to outspend her opponents, but she still lost in 2010 to state senator Hansen Clarke, whose mother was African American.

Outside financial support helped Artur Davis (D-AL) defeat CBC incumbent Earl Hilliard in the Democratic primary in 2002. The *Washington Post* endorsed Donna Edwards over CBC incumbent Wynn in 2006, claiming that Wynn's votes have often been "at odds with good government" (Almanac of American Politics 2010). Wynn narrowly won reelection, but Edwards defeated him in 2008 in a rematch. She had made Wynn's support of Iraq War an issue, but had also raised $1 million to spend in that race. Because Wynn suddenly quit the House after his primary defeat, Edwards also had to win a special election, which she did.

Hank Johnson defeated CBC incumbent Cynthia McKinney (D-GA) in 2006. She had become embroiled in more controversy during this time, after having regained her seat in 2004 after having lost as a five-time incumbent in 2002. Bobby Rush (D-IL) had been challenged by Barack Obama, who was then serving in the state legislature, in 2000. Rush, however, was able to defend his seat successfully against Obama, whose record with minority communities appeared weak. David Scott (D-GA) was challenged in 2006 in his primary by an opponent who took 36 percent of the vote. Andre Carson (D-IN), the grandson of Julia Carson (who had died in office), faced stiff competition for the seat in 2008.

Money will be more important in the future for Black legislators. In general, Black legislators spend less on their campaigns than White lawmakers (Tate 2003), but Black incumbents are more vulnerable in a context where no one has a solid lock over the racial representation of interests. Thus, as Wynn's defeat illustrates, a floor vote can make a difference now, whereas in the past outside money and personal scandals were key explanatory variables for a Black incumbent's sudden defeat.

Finally, Sanford Bishop, who was considered one of the most conservative Black members in the House, narrowly won reelection in 2010. He almost became a casualty of the pro-Republican tide that swept the nation in 2010. Virtually every conservative Democrat in the South lost to Republican challengers. Two Black Republicans also won election, notably in the South, in 2010. With Republicans in control of the House in 2011, Bishop voted "present" in the election of the former House Speaker Nancy Pelosi to become House majority leader. Nineteen Democrats chose not to vote for Pelosi.

Conclusion

Black lawmakers as part of the governing majority participated with the House majority 90 percent of the time in 2009—their highest rate of participation ever with the House majority for this period under study. Obama is clearly more liberal than Clinton or Carter. He doggedly pursued health care reform, and won, too, in spite of unified Republican opposition. Notably, other minorities—gays/lesbians and Latinos—have found strong responsiveness from the Obama administration. Obama and Democrats in Congress, however, sacrificed a pro-choice women's agenda to pass health care legislation, which was not as liberal as the most liberal Democrats wanted. Although some Democrats were only weakly onboard for a new social program mandated by the federal government, Obama still managed to keep almost all of their support for this landmark bill.

The tax breaks for the wealthy that Obama agreed to with Republicans in the last weeks of the 111th Congress may have permanently stained his presidency for ardent liberals. Yet, Obama's tax-breaks deal with the Republicans still won the support of 34 percent of the CBC. The legislative pull of the presidency on members of Congress is incredibly strong, and because of this even Black House members have become extremely supportive of presidential legislative initiatives.

The Obama administration, however, is under fire for two reasons. First, the economy has remained weak. Black joblessness has now surpassed the high levels seen in the Carter administration. Blacks and Latinos both lost wealth because of the recession and the housing market collapse, thus widening the existing large gap in wealth between Whites and minority Americans. Furthermore, Obama has not chosen to unveil a "Black agenda," or an agenda for the poor and disadvantaged. King and Smith (2011) contend that Obama has strategically chosen to avoid race-conscious policies. Some, including the CBC head, Barbara Lee, have sought special policies to address Black unemployment, but this talk was not coupled with a legislative strategy to compel the president or the Democratic Party to fight Black unemployment. In addition to rising unemployment rates for Blacks, the Black poverty rate has increased as well because of the long recession.

But, in fact, the talk of a Black policy agenda remains controversial. It is outdated, and reflects the idealism of Black lawmakers who were highly influential and persuasive from the 1970s through the Reagan/Bush years. Through incorporation, however, Obama has been able to benefit from high levels of support for his presidency from the CBC. Black Democratic lawmakers have become more pragmatic, working in a legislative environment that now is highly polarized. While the vast majority of Democrats and Blacks cheered wildly when Barack Obama won in 2008, two years later liberal Black critics have emerged voicing their opinion that, as the nation's first Black president, Obama hasn't done enough for Blacks. What about the CBC? In siding with the liberal governing coalition now, and winning more, has the CBC undermined its mission to represent the disadvantaged Black community? Before addressing whether the CBC can effectively represent Blacks if it is no longer the most liberal faction in Congress (the Progressive Caucus now is), the next chapter turns to the empirical evidence explaining concordance.

CHAPTER 7

The Moderating Effect of Institutional Pressures

Concordance holds that in winning incorporation African American Democratic lawmakers have moved closer to the political mainstream even as they have pushed their party to better represent their group's interests. Incorporation, thus, is a two-sided process. In this chapter, I provide a more stringent analysis of the data to provide further support for my theory of concordance. I present data showing support for one side of this process—the ideological movement of Black Democratic legislators toward their party.

Through multivariate analysis of their Poole-Rosenthal ideological scores, I show that important factors reducing Black ideological liberalism point to the greater inclusion of Black lawmakers in the policymaking process in Washington. Critics of concordance, however, might point out that the policy environment mostly pushed Black lawmakers to the center as Washington became more conservative during the 1980s and 1990s. They might not agree that the institutional components of incorporation changed Black lawmakers ideologically.

Additionally, still others might contend (as I noted in chapter 1), that Black ideological moderation in the House is an artifact, through both the creation of new majority-Black districts in the South and as Black majorities in Black-led districts were whittled down from the 1970s to the 2000s. However, more than expanding Black representation in the South or as a consequence of redistricting nationally, I contend that increasing political opportunities for Black lawmakers to be national leaders and to run for statewide offices have subtly changed the legislative behavior all Black lawmakers.

Incorporation Forces Affecting Black Legislative Behavior

Incorporation compels minorities seeking to influence the political process ultimately to follow institutional leaders. The institutional leaders in Congress are usually seen as the Speaker of the House, the Senate and House Majority Leaders, and the two house minority party leaders. In this analysis, however, the institutional leaders are the president, the party, legislative leaders, and the House majority. Additional forces include political ambition, region, age, and potentially gender. The conservative climate in Washington that emerged in the 1980s is also a potential force causing the ideological scores of Black lawmakers to shift toward the political center.

Presidential Leadership

Because of integration as well as party polarization, Black House legislators are more likely to follow the lead of Democratic presidents than in the group's early years. Black House legislators rejected President Carter's leadership initiative to reduce federal spending, seeking an agenda where government-sponsored projects would become a permanent part of national policy to combat Black unemployment instead. Presidential support scores for Democratic presidents have increased because of stronger efforts by presidents to command the policymaking process in Congress and also because of stricter party discipline. Matthew N. Beckmann (2010) finds that despite constitutional limitations American presidents play an enormous role in the legislative process. Presidents, it is theorized, exert conservative pressures on liberal lawmakers, because they generally craft legislation that appeals widely, across the partisan aisle. Clinton sought triangulation, which was not simply pursuing bipartisan bills but pitching policies that had very liberal and extremely conservative elements. Presidents need lawmakers to straddle the partisan divide, not merely sit closer to the middle. This puts pressure on all Democrats, including liberal ones, to help presidents win the necessary votes for their policy agendas.

Support for presidential policymaking will push ideological scores for Blacks toward the center. As discussed in chapter 4, the CBC's presidential support levels for President Clinton were higher than for President Carter. President Clinton entered the legislative arena gifted with better relations with the CBC than President Carter had. For Carter, CBC presidential support scores ranged from 66 to 73, while for Clinton they ranged from 72 to 83. President Obama won even higher presidential support scores from the CBC—an average of 91 for 2009 and 2010. Obama won impressive presidential support scores from House Democrats as well—the highest achieved for these three Democratic presidents. Scores improved for Obama because of the impressively high party discipline that parties have achieved in Congress. Black House members have traditionally shown slightly higher levels of support for Democratic presidents than House Democrats generally. It remains a remarkable period for institutional leadership in Washington, as presidents have continued to rack up impressive presidential support scores from members of their party—moving them from a high of 70 percent under Clinton to 80 percent in the House for George W. Bush to 80 and 90 percent for Obama. Black House members are aggressive supporters of their president's policy agenda as well.

The conservative turn takes place under Clinton. Clinton supporters among the CBC were generally newly elected Blacks from the South. In fact, after a slew of Black southern members were added to the CBC, the ideological scores of the CBC began to diminish at the start of the 103rd Congress (see figure 1). Still, the data show that reduction in liberal Poole-Rosenthal scores fell critically as well for northern Black legislators during Clinton's first year in office. Furthermore, an amazing split emerged in the CBC over the defense budget. For strong liberals, lean defense budgets are preferable in order to ensure there is revenue for the social spending component of the national budget. Thus, only 41 percent of the CBC opposed cutting the defense budget in 1994. Those wanting a stronger defense were mostly Blacks representing the South.

Thus, Clinton is one reason why an ideological split in the CBC emerged in the 1990s. In general, Black legislators are more liberal than their Democratic colleagues, but less so today than in the 1970s and 1980s. Furthermore, the role of the party and the influence of Democratic presidents have increased under Republican majorities and leadership in the House and the U.S. Congress. Having won the House majority back in the 2006 elections and then the presidency in 2008 and 2012, the Democratic Party and President Obama remain very powerful agents in the legislative process because the parties remain deeply polarized, and nothing will pass without mighty efforts by party leaders. The president and the Democratic Party strongly command allegiance from their members in today's political context. Strikingly, only Conyers and Rangel and a few others defied Obama and the Democratic Party leaders, such as CBC member Clyburn, and voted to deny further federal funds to bail out Wall Street in 2009. The fact that the Democratic Party elevated strong Black liberals to its party leadership positions establishes that a trade-off occurs in concordance. Black legislators back institutional leaders in exchange for the appointment of their most ardently liberal members to key institutional leadership posts.

Party Unity and Seniority

Following Michels (1999), in early work I theorized that ardent party supporters might be more conservative than Blacks who dissent from the party. However, since President Carter, Democratic House members have increasingly endorsed more liberal policies. Furthermore, as members of the CBC began to sort themselves into moderates and liberals, the reality is that dissenting Black lawmakers today are more moderate than those who back the party line. Thus, it is hypothesized that party unity scores will have a liberal effect on Black ideological scores. Nevertheless, the Democratic Party indirectly still exerts a conservative force on Black lawmaking. Black members having access to lines of influence within the party now will challenge the institution's policymaking process less.

Chairmanships, still so heavily influenced by seniority, may be liberal forces as well. The oldest and longest-serving Black members of the House hold chairmanships. In the future, the effect of party chairmanship may not exert much influence as post-1992 and younger Black Democrats are not distinctively as liberal as the 1970s and 1980s generation of Black legislators.

Voting with the House Majority

Black Democrats increasingly vote with the House majority on key bills that are either passed or rejected. The increase reflects a pragmatic response from Black lawmakers who have been less isolated from the policymaking process and are less able to see benefits from dissent. This practice of pragmatism is difficult to spot as a matter of public record. The increase also is due to stricter party control. Cox and McCubbins (2007) contend that whoever controls the House will initiate legislation that consolidates their partisans and divides the opposition. Thus, Democratic Party leadership behind the scenes works very hard to ensure that members of the CBC are on board. Voting with the House majority on key bills makes Democrats, including the CBC, look more harmoniously united. The data show that increasingly under a Republican-controlled House, Black Democrats rarely vote with the House majority. Still, those Black Democrats who vote with the House majority, under Democratic or Republican control, will have lower ideological scores than Black Democrats who do not.

A Conservative Response to Divided Government

Divided government strengthens the leadership role of even Republican presidents and Republican-led Houses. Electoral pressures on the Democratic Party increased in the aftermath of the Republican Party's seizing control of the House after the 1994 elections. While Black Democrats initially viewed themselves as outsiders during the Reagan-Bush presidencies, they felt more protective of the stake they have in the policymaking process. The Republican president or Republican House majority will now work with members of the CBC as well as other factions within the Democratic Party to win their support. As the parties have also continued to polarize, the sentiment that gridlock is too costly has increased. Furthermore, disputes over policy matters are ideally handled less publicly. Black Democrats feel more pressure to work with the Republican Party. The fact that Republican ascendancy did not cause the CBC to reradicalize as a political response is due largely to their political incorporation.

Expanding Black Political Ambitions

The ambitions of Black legislators have grown as the nation's voters have become less racially prejudiced against Black candidates. Others argue that it is not a slackening of racial resentment in the electorate, but that the sorting out of voters and leaders has moved many conservatives to the Republican Party (Lublin et al. 2009). Thus, Blacks running as Democrats now find more voters who will vote for them, even when there are White candidates in the race. Moreover, a transition has been achieved where handing power to Blacks may now be less personally threatening to Whites after having experienced Black political leadership (Hajnal 2007). There is also generational change propelling further change in the politics of the CBC, as a "Black agenda" is less prominent in the agendas of young, post–civil rights African American leaders, although this could be due to the expanded political opportunities that Blacks in Washington now have.

In addition, even Black voters are less liberal than they used to be. For example, Tate (2010) shows that, starting in the mid-1980s, support for minority aid from government and a government jobs program fell among Blacks. Although every CBC member voted against Clinton's 1996 welfare reform bill except Sanford Bishop (D-GA), 60 percent of Blacks favored ending the federal entitlement to welfare through welfare reform. Tate (2010) contends that the moderation of Black lawmakers preceded the moderation of the Black electorate. Still, Black lawmakers building moderate records in Washington in order to run for higher office someday might also believe that liberal Blacks will still back their brand of leadership.

Regional and Other Causes

The influx of new Black elected officials from the South may have caused the ideological moderation of the CBC. The data show that southern members of the CBC were less liberal than their northern counterparts as early as the 95th Congress when only two Blacks were elected from the South (Ford of Tennessee and Jordan of Texas). Region has never exerted a persistently strong political influence on the Black electorate (Tate 1994). The regional divide among Blacks in Washington might be due to the influence of conservative southerners on southern lawmakers. Southern Black members may be more electorally vulnerable than northern Black members, causing them to chart moderate records in Washington. Ford's son, Harold Ford Jr. (2010), writes that his father won, defeating an incumbent Republican in 1974 by about 500 votes, when the district was still majority White. Ford's district from 1972 to 1980 was 47 percent Black and 51 percent Black through 1990. From 1992 through 2010, it became 59 percent Black. In Jordan's district in Texas, similarly, Blacks formed 44 percent of the district in the 1970s, but Latinos represented another 19 percent. Unlike Ford, who won with 50 percent of the vote initially, Jordan got over 80 percent in the general election. Complicating the story is Melvin Watt (D-NC), whose district was only 36 percent Black in 1998. Watt remains fairly liberal.

Gender may also be an ideological force among Black lawmakers. Black women legislators may be more liberal than their male counterparts. As the nation remains at war in Afghanistan and is confronted with issues such as extending amnesty to adults brought to the United States as children by their undocumented-immigrant parents, equal rights for gays and lesbians, and persistent budgetary problems that force unpleasant choices, gender within the CBC may become a persistent division. Gender oppression is a prominent concern of Black feminists. There are divisions in the Black community based on how they think policy decisions will affect the lives of Black women as much as on how they will affect the lives of Black people generally (Simien 2006; Dawson 2001). Thus far, the prominent moderates within the CBC have been male, and all of the Black Republicans elected to Congress, thus far, have also been male. This is not to say that there aren't also prominent Black female conservatives or Republicans, but that they represent a smaller presence in the Black community because feminism is generally linked to liberalism. The literature finds that while the gender gap is small, it is persistent, and women are generally more liberal on social welfare issues than men (Sapiro and Shames 2010).

To examine the influence of these factors (presidential support scores, region, party unity, voting with the House majority, divided government, age) as well as others (seniority, gender, party leadership, committee chairmanships) on the Poole-Rosenthal scores systemically, I constructed a set of regression models. The first regression model calculates the effects of these measures on Poole-Rosenthal scores for Black Democratic legislators for all presidents from 1977 to 2009, controlling additionally for Black legislative behavior under Republican presidents versus Democratic ones. The second and third models estimate these effects specifically under the set of Democratic presidents and Republican presidents during this period.

While one can classify some measures as "political," such as party unity scores and divided government, and others as "social and cultural" such as age, region, and gender, there is some overlap. Furthermore, theoretically separating out what constitutes factors related to incorporation and others linked to a temporal thesis involving the current political context, such as Republican ascendancy, is difficult. In all three models, year is added to see if there are pressures on Black lawmakers to shift toward the center that cannot be explained by the existing set of factors.

Coefficients from an ordinary least squares regression were estimated. Because these are time-series cross-sectional data, checks were also performed to rule out autocorrelation, which could lead to erroneous results when the residual error variances are correlated.[1] The results are shown in table 2.

Clearly, the elections of Black Democrats from the South are importantly linked to the moderation of the CBC. Black Democrats from the South have significantly higher scores, indicating conservatism, than their non-South counterparts. The coefficients range from 3.5 to 4.3 for all three models and are statistically significant. Statistically significant coefficients less than five represent modest effects. Thus, region has a small effect on Black legislative behavior.

In contrast, the minority concentration in districts held by Black Democrats has no effect on their Poole-Rosenthal scores in this analysis. In analyses not shown here, the percentage of Blacks and Latinos estimated separately were also statistically unrelated to the Black Democrats' ideological scores. Thus, despite the popularity of claims that the shrinking size of Black majorities in Black-led districts has made Black Democrats less liberal, it is more likely the result of the new policymaking context realized through incorporation and the new ambitions of Black lawmakers. Thus, the handful of Blacks who have made statewide bids are significantly less liberal than other Black legislators in the full model and in the model estimated for Republican presidents.

Seniority has no direct effect on Black ideological records, while age is statistically significant in all three models. A 20-year age difference between two Black legislators translated into a projected ideological difference of approximately 5 points. As theorized, younger Black legislators are less liberal than older Black legislators because they believe the political world has more potential to support their political ambitions. The age difference is not because young Blacks are strikingly less liberal than older Blacks. Young Blacks are pragmatic politicians. They are more likely to craft less liberal records as a consequence.

Black Democratic legislators have moderated in response to the ascendency of the Republican Party in Congress. As theorized, standing firm

TABLE 2. Regression of Analysis of Poole-Rosenthal Scores for Black House Democrats under Democratic and Republican Presidents, 1977–2009

Model	All Presidents		Democratic Presidents		Republican Presidents	
	B	Std. Error	B	Std. Error	B	Std. Error
Constant	−62.59**	6.10	−68.09***	8.15	−63.62***	8.20
Female	−1.42	0.91	−2.02	1.23	−1.20	1.23
Age	−0.20***	0.04	−0.13*	0.07	−.23***	0.05
South	4.27***	0.83	3.82**	1.14	3.52**	1.13
No. of Terms	−0.07	0.12	−0.01	0.17	−0.10	0.15
Party Leader	−4.77**	1.72	−3.76	2.75	−5.70**	2.06
Comm. Chair	1.20	1.49	−1.96	2.72	3.31*	1.70
Statewide Bid	6.03**	1.91	3.65	3.20	5.23*	2.29
Party Unity Score	−0.20***	0.05	−0.43***	0.12	−0.12	0.08
Pres. Support Score	0.12**	0.04	0.32**	0.11	0.22**	0.06
Republican House Control	8.13***	1.41	9.23***	1.84	10.87***	2.86
Republican President	9.87**	2.33	n/a		n/a	
% Vote with House Majority	0.28***	0.04	0.46**	0.07	0.32***	0.06
% Minorities in District	0.03	0.03	0.07	0.04	0.01	0.03
Year	0.55***	0.14	−0.25	0.21	0.71**	0.23
Total Cases	495		218		276	
R^2	0.40		0.38		0.51	

Source: NOMINATE scores (multiplied by 100); other variables created by author, based on data from the CQ Almanac, various years, and the Almanac of American Politics series.

Note: n/a = not applicable.

***$p < .001$; **$p < .01$; *$p < .05$.

against the reduction of a liberal policy agenda was made more difficult in the aftermath of the 1994 elections when Republicans won control of the House and the Senate. The coefficients for both Republicans presidents and Republican majority control of the House are statistically significant for all three models. Black ideological scores are more conservative by an average of 8 to 11 points when the House is dominated by Republicans. Black ideological scores are also about 9 points more conservative under Republican presidents. The measure of participation in House majority victories is also a conservative force on Black Democrats' ideological scores. It is statistically significant in all three models. Increasing Black participation in voting with the House majority by 10 percent cuts their liberalism by 3 to 5 points. In fact, this new measure—participation in votes with the House majority on key bills—has a major effect on Blacks' ideological scores.

The view that parties are also conservative forces in government was completely repudiated by the analysis. First, strong party backers among Black Democrats were significantly more liberal than weak party backers in both models. The effect of party on Black ideological scores was not huge in the full model; a 10 percent increase in party loyalty increases their liberalism by about 2 points. Under Democratic presidents, the increase in party loyalty among Blacks has a larger effect.

Second, Black party leaders were also significantly more liberal than Black rank-and-file members of Congress in the full model and under Republican presidents, but not under Democratic ones. It seems likely that both parties have intensified the trend of party polarization in Washington by elevating strong ideologues to party leadership positions as a response to divided government. In the end, the analysis also helps explain the liberalization of the Democratic Party because Blacks have not become less liberal through their elevation within the party. In fact, loyalty to the Democratic Party is keeping Blacks staunchly liberal. Thus, it is not party leadership directly but pressures from a fractured policymaking arena in the U.S. government that make minority legislators less liberal over time.

Some of the noninstitutional theories were supported in this analysis. While the size of the Black and Latino population in their district had no direct effect on Black legislative behavior, region did. The increase in the number of Blacks representing southern districts reduced Black congressional liberalism. And while newly elected Black House members were not significantly less liberal than senior members, age was an important force. Younger Blacks are less liberal. Young Blacks are less liberal not simply because they represent a post–civil rights (and less oppositional) generation, but because they are responsive to a new working environment in Washington where Blacks can assume greater leadership positions.

A second set of analyses were performed to determine whether, as theorized, African American House Democrats became more responsive to institutional forces after their political incorporation. Table 3 shows the results of the general regression model from 1977 to 1992 and from 1993 to 2009. The results in table 3 show that notably neither party nor presidential authority altered Black ideological scores in the early era under Presidents Carter, Reagan, and Bush. These factors strongly influenced Blacks' ideological scores in the later era of Clinton, Bush, and Obama. And, indeed, while George W. Bush's presidency from 2001 through 2008 was able to help push the ideological profiles of Black Democrats in the House by 20 points less liberal, Presidents Reagan and George H. W. Bush in the earlier era had no effect. The year, which was statistically significant in table 2, is now no longer statistically significant.

At the same time, in both periods, those Black Democrats who had voted with the House majority on key bills had slightly more conservative

TABLE 3. Regression of Poole-Rosenthal Scores (liberal-conservative) for Black House Democrats under All Presidents by Pre-1992 Elections and Post-1992 Elections

Model	All Presidents, 1977–92		All Presidents, 1993–2009	
	B	Std. Error	B	Std. Error
Constant	−71.35***	9.11	−62.94***	8.05
Female	−0.69	2.09	−2.62**	0.94
Age	−0.25**	0.08	−0.02	0.06
South	5.03*	2.07	2.74**	0.86
No. of Terms	−0.26	0.22	−0.31*	0.14
Party Leader	−1.61	3.53	−7.13***	1.77
Comm. Chair	3.88*	1.91	−2.23	2.4
Statewide Bid	11.28**	4.11	4.80*	2.1
Party Unity Score (weak-strong)	−0.08	0.08	−0.42***	0.07
Pres. Support Score (weak strong)	0.12	0.08	0.22**	0.04
Republican House Control	n/a	n/a	7.69***	1.5
Republican President	6.83	4.63	20.67***	
% Vote with House Majority	0.31***	0.09	0.35***	0.04
% Minorities in District	0.10*	0.05	0.05	0.03
Year	−0.88	0.44	0.42	0.25
Total cases	495		340	
R^2	0.40		0.52	

Source: NOMINATE scores (multiplied by 100), see Voteview.com; other variables created by author, based on data from the CQ Almanac, various years, and the Almanac of American Politics series.

Note: n/a = not applicable.

***$p < .001$; **$p < .01$; *$p < .05$.

ideological scores than those who had not. Furthermore, while committee chairmanships had no ideological effect, those Blacks who chaired committees in the pre-1993 period were 3 percentage points more conservative than rank-and-file Black House members. Ambitious Black members who ran for statewide seats were strongly less liberal than other Black members, by about 11 points. And while gender was not statistically significant in table 2, in the post-1992 era Black female House Democrats were slightly more liberal than Black male House Democrats, by about 3 points (as shown in table 3). Seniority, which was not significant in the first set of models shown in table 2, is relevant as well in the post-1992 atmosphere. Senior Blacks are more liberal than newly elected ones. The estimated effect is small; a difference of three terms yields a difference of about 1 point on a 100-point ideological scale.

Thus, the results suggest that Black roll-call votes were independent of two of three main institutional forces from 1977 to 1992. Presidential leadership and Republican presidents become important forces to Black Democrats in the House after 1992. The model fits as estimated by the R-square statistic of .52 for the model limiting the analysis to 1993 to 2009; in fact, it is better than the model for all years shown in table 2, which is .40. Thus, it is best to think of Black behavior as being different in two distinct periods—in the early years when Blacks were contesting for leadership and policy responsiveness in Washington under Carter, Reagan, and Bush, and in the later years under Clinton, Bush, and Obama.

Institutional forces, thus, represented striking and significant ideological forces in these statistical models of Black legislative behavior. These forces become especially significant after 1992, during a period when the Democratic Party was liberalizing and when divided government also increased the dependence of party members on their presidents. Black House legislators have moderated their policy stands because of presidential leadership and a new stake in voting with the House majority on key bills that they play a role in formulating. Furthermore, divided government and new political ambitions for Black lawmakers have also reduced their liberalism in the post-1992 era. While the Democratic Party has been shown to increase Black ideological liberalism, Black Democrats have not been effective in countering the sway of Republicanism. This is probably because under incorporation Black legislators and conservative interests must compromise to pass legislation. In the earlier period, Black Democrats were prepared to accept a smaller role in government if necessary to prevail against Republicanism, but today's Black lawmakers are less likely to step back from the legislative process to fight the presidents and their party.

The Other, Untested Side of Minority Political Incorporation: Party Liberalization

The Democratic Party eventually also accommodated some of political concerns of Black legislators, but I lack strong data to show this result. Black radical interests are not normally accommodated. This represented an untested area of this study, but I contend through incorporation that some policies that minorities care about won support from the party. Although some congressional scholars believe a critical mass may be necessary to promote policy and institutional change, others strongly contend it just takes one member to ignite change (Mayhew 2000).

Jesse Jackson's rebellion within the party led to the appointment of Ron Brown as the party's first African American chairman in 1989. Brown's appointment suggested to Blacks that their candidacies would win better support from the national party. The party also began to make strategic leadership appointments of Blacks because of Black political pressure from the Jackson bids. The data as gathered by *CQ Almanac* reveal that the number of Blacks in party leadership posts increased over the 1980s and 1990s. Data reported in table 3 show that Black leaders after 1992 were significantly more liberal than Blacks as a group. Thus, the party accommodated Blacks politically by elevating their most liberal members.

Ron Dellums's persistent criticism of the weapons buildup during the Reagan administration is also a good example of how he inspired other Democrats to protest this approach. However, Dellums became chair of the House Armed Services Committee in 1993, after having waged a war just to win an appointment to that committee in 1972–73. One reason why the party accommodated Dellums and other liberal Black legislators is because of the power of the newly organized CBC. Dellums writes frankly that in order to win a seat on the Armed Services Committee, Clay (D-MO) told the House Speaker, "If you don't put Ron on the committee, the CBC will call a press conference and denounce the party and the Congress as racist" (Dellums and Halterman 2000, 103). Dellums's impact on the Democratic Party can be seen in the party's leadership to push for a plan for withdrawal from Iraq. Dellums's demands for a peace approach to U.S. foreign policy are no longer considered illegitimate by party leaders.

On economic issues, the Democratic Party supported minimum wage increases, but not a full employment plan. Some Black members support regressive tax policies. On civil rights, the party remains firmly behind extending voting rights and civil rights protection to minority groups. However, reparations and race-targeted approaches have failed to command the party's backing. President Obama, however, used his authority as president to issue a directive calling for more federal efforts at promoting the education of Black schoolchildren. Pressure by Black legislators in Congress may still push the party and its members further to the political left, even as Black House members have moderated their legislative politics.

Conclusion

Concordance is a process whereby Black lawmakers support more conservative policies in exchange for having greater influence over their party's policy agenda. The party wins support from minority lawmakers because the political system favors majoritarian rule and is highly coercive. Included in the policymaking process, Black lawmakers adopt a stronger identity with their party and the institution. In the review of legislative politics, the Democratic Party continues to liberalize and advance minority lawmakers. Black Democratic lawmakers won higher minimum wages, extended unemployment benefits, and, under President Obama, better protection of Black civil rights. Black lawmakers initially sought a federal jobs program for poor, unemployed Blacks. They wanted better and permanent welfare benefits and social programs for single Black mothers and their children. They also sought new federal protection from racial discrimination in the sentencing process. Thus, even under incorporation, the party can continue to refuse to adopt radical minority policies. And, overall, civil rights advocacy is harder precisely because civil rights groups have won so much from Washington from President Johnson and from later presidents in the extension of the Voting Rights Act.

Because of these changes, I believe that a new CBC exists in Washington. The CBC reinvented itself to maximize its power. Data show, in fact, the Congressional Black Caucus is no longer the most liberal group in the House. The Progressive Caucus is, based on data from the 107th to the 109th Congress. Table 4 shows the Poole-Rosenthal (DW-1) scores for four groups for comparative purposes, the House Democrats as a whole,

TABLE 4. Average Poole-Rosenthal Ideological Scores (dimension 1) for the CBC, House Democrats, Blue Dogs, and Progressive Caucus, 107th–109th Congresses

Congress	CBC	House	Blue Dogs	Progressive
107th	−0.49	−0.39	−0.19	−0.51
108th	−0.46	−0.39	−0.19	−0.51
109th	−0.46	−0.40	−0.21	−0.51

Source: Poole-Rosenthal scores; group scores were calculated by author. See Appendix A for the members of these House caucuses.

the Blue Dogs (a moderate Democratic group), the Progressive Caucus (a liberal Democratic group), and the CBC. The Congressional Progressive Caucus (CPC) has the lowest average DW-1 scores at –0.51, compared to the other two caucuses and House Democrats. The DW-1 scores show that the Congressional Black Caucus is not as liberal as the CPC. However, the CBC remains more distinctively liberal than the House Democrats as a whole. The Blue Dog Coalition is considerably more conservative than House Democrats as a whole. These groups have been strengthened by the rise of new minority groups.

Finally, Blacks are not the only minority group having radical-liberal interests. Radical liberal pressures will emerge from other disadvantaged groups whose presence in government is expanding, such as ethnics and gays and lesbians. Latino Democrats have radical interests as well, including their push for amnesty or a pathway to citizenship for undocumented Latinos. This is an interest generally outside of the ideological spectrum. Many Americans on the political Left and Right do not wish to extend formal rights and benefits to a new group of minority workers working below minimum wage. Radical ethnics will need to push the mainstream Left to absorb this interest. Ethnic lawmakers, as a group, however, have more moderate ideological scores than Blacks, although research finds that Latino House legislators are more liberal than their counterparts (Casellas 2011; see also Barreto 2010; Barreto, Segura, and Woods 2004). So while Black lawmakers became more moderate as a result of concordance, we should expect to see Latinos *move toward the center* in exchange for a pledge to accommodate their more radical leaders in the party and in Congress.

Gays and lesbians also have radical interests, which could bring their lawmakers in Washington closer to the Democratic Party if this political party elevates them and pledges support to their group interests. Congress ultimately responded to Black civil rights goals but under duress. Thus, even in winning incorporation for their communities from the Democratic Party, these groups may not win the policies they want except through judicial rulings and from protest politics. Yet Latino, gay and lesbian, and female Democratic lawmakers may move toward the center through concordance. Concordance under minority incorporation occurs because of the fragmented, conservative nature of the American political system.

CHAPTER 8

The New CBC

On another level, the CBC opposition, mostly from veteran CBC members, was hypocritical because so many of them had been elected to Congress by challenging an unresponsive establishment. Now . . . they had become the establishment.

—Harold Ford Jr., *More Davids Than Goliaths*

The data showing a trend favoring the political center for Black House members may not be welcome news for the CBC, which remains an important advocacy group for the economically and socially disadvantaged. This political moderation of Black elected officials, however, was inevitable for both institutional and organizational reasons. A generational change is taking place for sociological reasons, as well. Young Black lawmakers are less liberal than older ones. Age was a consistent liberal predictor of the Poole-Rosenthal measures for Black legislators in the analysis; younger Black Democrats are significantly less liberal than older Blacks serving in the House. Some assert that we are witnessing the rise of a new generation of Black politicians whose styles are less race-oriented and system-challenging than the previous generation (Gillespie 2010; Smith 1996). Older Blacks were able to win only through the collective mobilization of Blacks, and sought race-specific policies in their representation of these Blacks. New, young Black lawmakers believe that they can achieve more through a race-neutral approach. Black policy moderation reflects both political pragmatism and the new electoral opportunities that Black politicians have today.

Perhaps the most surprising finding in this analysis of Black legislative behavior, described in chapter 7, was that Black House Democrats had less liberal scores under Republican presidents and under Republican House majorities. Thus, rather than radicalize as a response to the rival party when it becomes dominant, Black Democrats in Congress have accommodated some of its conservative interests. The old CBC had formed a strong and united oppositional response to President Reagan's conservative tax policies, but it broke down as Black Democrats began to work within the party-legislative process in Washington. As Republican tax policies became widely popular, some Black lawmakers joined the bipartisan tax reform efforts. Choosing to work with the rival party fits Robert Michels's ([1911] 1999) thesis about how party leaders become oligarchical and adopt insider views and values that may no longer represent their constituents' views. Working with the rival party also helps CBC members to craft new reputations as national leaders.

All in all, the willingness to back Democratic presidents, Democratic House majorities, and work cooperatively under Republican-led government along with generational change has transformed the CBC into a less ardently liberal group. This process has also helped liberalize the Democratic House Party. Still, some might also claim that these changes put the CBC closer in line with the Washington Establishment, beholden more to the privileged and special interests than to ordinary people. Furthermore, some might argue that the CBC's greatest victories have chiefly been symbolic. Thus, the question remains what role will the new CBC play in making the federal government more responsive to the needs of African Americans who still represent a socially disadvantaged group?

The CBC in the Future of Black Politics Debate

Political scientist Michael Dawson (2011) writes that African Americans need to rebuild their movement for racial justice and economic empowerment. While he does not single out Black politicians for failure, his work still implies that not enough is being done by Black elected officials. Since Obama's election as the nation's first African American president in 2008, scholars such as Fredrick C. Harris (2012) have begun to ask whether the elections of Blacks, and notably the election of a Black president, has begun to hurt Blacks politically as they represent symbols of progress that has not taken place.

One scholar, Robert C. Smith (1996, 2009), argues that Black politics has entered into a period of accommodationism. Smith contends that if Black leaders don't systematically challenge the political system, which is built on "an imperfect social contract for Blacks," then they have engaged in accommodationism. Accommodationism refers to a dark chapter in American history when African American leader Booker T. Washington endorsed the White South's efforts to construct laws mandating strict separation of the race. Washington had famously declared that "in all things that are purely social we can be as separate as the fingers [in a hand]" (Harlan 1974). The South also passed laws to disfranchise Blacks. Washington later gave speeches stating that a "cancer" was growing in America, indicating his position that Black rights should be recognized. This talk belied the optimistic and misguided faith he had in America that served as a foundation for his Atlanta Compromise speech; Washington's complex politics have been misremembered (see Bieze and Gasman 2012).

Ronald W. Walters (2003) defines accommodationism as the legitimation of existing social and political arrangements by Black leaders, combined with the promotion of self-help philosophies. He contends that Black conservatives promote accommodationism, especially through their adoption of White ethnic values, goals, and leadership. As discussed in chapter 6, President Obama has made conservative speeches arguing that Blacks need to take more responsibility for their plight, which backs up a racially conservative view of American race relations.

The post-Reconstruction era was harsh for ethnic Blacks, marked by lynchings and a harsh sharecropping system, so as to make an analogy between the two periods grossly inappropriate. Nevertheless, some harsh critics of this era of Black politics still feel strongly that the level of racism against Blacks in America remains the same. Thus, a shift away from racial radicalism represents accommodationism of American racism. Furthermore, for the new critics of Black politics, there remains the problem of institutional racism. Institutional racism, defined by Kwame Ture (Stokely Carmichael) and Charles Hamilton, is defined as the active operation of anti-Black attitudes and practices. It is subtle and difficult to identify, but reinforces racial superiority. Institutional racism also is present in policies and practices that ultimately consign Blacks to a lesser place in society because of residential segregation, unequal educational opportunities, the cumulative effects of race and poverty, and discrimination against Blacks (Smith 1995).

There is a pattern of institutional racism. Statistically, African Americans receive poorer government services than White Americans in terms of schooling, housing subsidies, loans, and contracts. As a consequence, they live in less safe neighborhoods with poorer public services such as parks and fewer businesses. Blacks are disproportionately under correctional supervision and receive harsher sentences upon conviction than Whites. Laws remain on the books that make it difficult for former convicts to reenter society fruitfully, including regaining the right to vote. There is an earnest debate as to whether or not these disparities in socioeconomic and political conditions are rooted in continuing racism. However, surveys show more Blacks than other Americans believe that the problems and conditions Blacks face are rooted in racial discrimination. Black ethnics, therefore, need leaders in government who feel like they do, who are committed to ending discrimination in the provision of public goods and services.

Blacks and Whites still have very different views about the pervasiveness of discrimination in society today (Sigelman and Welch 1991; Schuman, Steeh, and Bobo 1985). In a survey conducted in 2009, 43 percent of Blacks said that there remains a lot of racial discrimination against Blacks. Only 13 percent of Whites said that there is a lot of anti-Black prejudice in the United States today. A large majority of Blacks (81 percent) believe that more changes need to take place in society for Blacks to have equal rights with Whites; only 36 percent of Whites believe further changes are necessary. Yet the view that politicians, including Black politicians, should be less group-oriented today is aggressively promulgated by those on the political Left and Right. A nonracial approach to politics, however, would not fully represent the opinions of African Americans.

Second, Blacks, who generally are poorer and less well educated than Whites, need extragovernmental assistance to remain politically organized. A group-oriented approach to politics has been shown to help mobilize Blacks and affect their politics (Gurin, Hatchett, and Jackson 1989; Dawson 1994; Tate 1994). Blacks who are politically active tend to have strong levels of group consciousness (Tate 1994; Shingles 1981; Verba and Nie 1972). Thus, Blacks need group-oriented political leadership to challenge policies and institutions that perpetuate their collective disadvantage in society. To follow politics in Washington, they may need issues framed by Black lawmakers in Washington as "pro-Black" or "anti-Black." As crude as that may appear to some, an ethnic frame can help Blacks keep up with a complicated world in spite of deficiencies they have rooted in their socioeconomic conditions. An ethnic frame in political issues may increase perceptions that politics is important to the welfare of their group.

The opposing view that a shift away from an ethnic agenda may benefit Blacks starts with several contentions. First, there are those who would argue that Blacks can be mobilized without group-oriented campaigning. Research, in fact, finds that Blacks are empowered politically without ethnic issues being very salient. Viable Black candidacies appear to energize and excite the Black community. Barack Obama's 2008 bid was associated with record turnout rates for Blacks, much like Jesse Jackson's 1984 bid. Other studies have found that the presence of Blacks in elected office remains positively linked to feelings of political efficacy among Blacks (Bobo and Gilliam 1990) and to higher levels of satisfaction with their political representation (Tate 2003). Blacks are more likely to recognize and contact their representatives when that representative is Black (Gay 2002; Tate 2003). Jan Leighley (2001) also shows that Blacks holding the mayor's office mobilize Blacks. Furthermore, she establishes that the size of the minority group matters as the party elites are more likely to target voters the greater the population of the group. Harris, Sinclair-Chapman, and McKenzie (2006) also show the positive effect of Black empowerment on Black rates of political participation.

Although surveys show that Blacks continue to remain concerned about the problem of racial discrimination, their rates of optimism about race relations in the aftermath of Obama's victory have increased significantly. A report issued in 2010 showed that, since 2007, twice as many Blacks as in 2009, 39 percent, said that the "situation of Black people in this country" was better than it had been five years earlier. Furthermore, more than half (53 percent) express optimism about the lives of Blacks in the United States, saying they think life will be better for Blacks in the future. A majority of Blacks in 2009 also felt that Obama's election had improved race relations in America; only one-third of Whites felt similarly, with 45 percent saying that Obama's election has made no difference.

Equally striking is the decline, from the mid-1990s to today, in the percentages of Blacks who think that discrimination is the main reason why Blacks cannot get ahead. A 2009 study shows that 52 percent of Blacks, a majority, feel that Blacks are mostly responsible for their situation in life, while about one-third (34 percent) feel that discrimination is the reason. In 1994, nearly 60 percent felt discrimination explained why Blacks couldn't get ahead, and fewer than 40 percent felt that Blacks were to blame. Since the 1980s, Blacks are less likely to name discrimination as the primary problem confronting Black Americans; in a 1996 national survey, they named crime and employment as more important problems than discrimination. Thus, Black politicians are logically responding to a conservative shift in the Black community, as fewer see Black problems as entirely racial.

A shift away from racial radicalism has the potential to lead to broader coalitions in government to win passage of liberal policies to fight unemployment and poverty. Sociologist William J. Wilson in *The Bridge Over the Racial Divide* (1999) argues that progressives should pursue broad-based, multiethnic coalitions to tackle the problems of poverty, unemployment, and the social problems that low-wage workers face. He writes that cultural bigotry obscures the fact that many Americans suffer from "many common problems" as a result of worsening economic conditions. Income inequality is on the rise, and Blacks and other minorities will benefit from an agenda focusing on job creation, increased health coverage, and improvements in public education and access to college. Wilson argues that, in these harsh economic times, Whites benefit along with minorities:

> Despite being officially race neutral, programs created in response to these concerns—programs that increase employment opportunities and job skills training, improve public education, promote better child and health care, strengthen supports for working lone-parent families, and reduce neighborhood crime and drug abuse—would profoundly benefit the minority poor, but they would also benefit large segments of the remaining population, including the white majority. (1999, 42)

Thus, by avoiding an ethnic approach Black politicians today are attempting to knit together the broad coalitions necessary to win passage of liberal social and economic policies.

In many ways, those arguing against an ethnic-oriented approach to politics and policies are winning the debate. This side, however, was aided by institutional and sociopolitical forces. Blacks organized and protested, eventually leading White leaders to accommodate their interests better and to elevate Black liberal leaders. Nevertheless, as discussed in the chapter on the Obama presidency, Blacks pressing hard for an ethnic agenda have been rejected. While UN ambassador Young was retained for longer than most considered politically expedient by President Carter when he complained about U.S. race relations, Clinton summarily rejected Lani Guinier whose academic writings were considered too radical. Now there is a new generation of Black leaders in Washington to choose from by Democratic presidents and the Democratic Party; these new Black leaders don't often see the strong racism in America that older Blacks continue to see.

Thus, whether the new CBC is good or bad for Black Americans will continue to be debated, but enough changes have taken place to assert that Black interests may no longer need a Black agenda as framed by the CBC. Furthermore, the CBC appears to have already taken a stand in this debate over race and Black people in American politics. Thus, the new CBC supports disadvantaged Black Americans without a specific racial frame. At the same time President Obama in 2012 issued an executive order to improve outcomes and advance educational opportunities specifically for

African Americans. Obama's presidential order was issued without major controversy as it comes with his party's general acceptance of conservative school reform.

Conclusion

In the United States, a fragmented, majoritarian (two-party) system leads to concordance for newly empowered social groups. Although the incorporation of minorities is not automatic, once such groups win incorporation their members shift to accommodate the institution's majority interests; they also push their party to meet their interests. Because of their advancement, Blacks are now in greater agreement with the nation's policy leaders. Blacks are better integrated and now participate in an institution that favors consensus and conformity. Thus, the political system breeds a new concordance between Blacks and the national Democratic Party.

The debate over whether Black political representation in Washington will help them socially and materially will persist, as some fear this loss of Black radicalism will hurt Blacks politically, while others think it is the only realistic course left to take, one that yields, in fact, better outcomes for Blacks. It is unlikely that the CBC will re-radicalize as Black members increasingly work within the existing system. Having become major players in the Democratic Party, Black leaders are less poised to dissent from the majority and pursue an outside radical, ethnic agenda. The national policy environment favors ethnic-neutral approaches in public policymaking as well, although some contend that group-conscious politics will persist (King and Smith 2011).

Still, racial radicals contend that we need to judge American government on its effort to reduce racial disparities and conditions in America that adversely affect Black life chances. Government has a special obligation to help Blacks because of past discrimination. The policies they advocate are whatever it will take to eradicate those inequalities, and so they favor whatever they can get, even conservative policies, such as supporting the push for charter schools (see Bell 2007).

Critics of the new Black empowerment era point to the wealth gap between Blacks and Whites, which expanded under Presidents Bush and Obama. Black unemployment continues to be twice as high as the national unemployment rate, and levels have increased under Obama. Racial segregation and racial disparities in educational outcomes remain very high, even though Blacks are no longer barred from prosperous White areas. Incarceration rates for Blacks are dramatically higher than those for Whites and are not simply rooted in geography or socioeconomic status differences. And Black poverty rates, after years of dropping, are rising again.

Thus, a number of Black activists still feel that their communities, generally young, urban, and poor, even with Black political incorporation, remain ignored by the political establishment. Southern-based activist Kevin Alexander Gray (2008) wonders if Obama really cares about the family. Cathy J. Cohen (2010) argues that Obama, in fact, has only strengthened that public hostility through campaign and presidential speeches criticizing Blacks "for not living responsibly."

The U.S. political system favors majorities. This design of governing limits the ability of minorities to change things through routine politics; furthermore, it also compels minority leaders to concede to majoritarian sentiments as they advance. Some argue that voting for Black officials will not yield genuine change for minorities living at the bottom of the social order. An argument could be made that all minority political incorporation theories are flawed, and that minorities are at best only "partially incorporated" given the conservative design of the American political system. For still others, democratic governments in highly socially stratified societies will never favor the disadvantaged group regardless of how many members of the disadvantaged group are elected.

Black lawmakers see things differently. California Congressman and CBC cofounder Ron Dellums (Dellums and Halterman 2000) writes passionately that he did all that was possible as a liberal legislator given the institutional constraints. Political science research backs Dellums's claims, finding that the government is more responsive to the social problems that Blacks experience when Blacks are politically incorporated. Recent evidence of this can be seen in the Obama administration. The Obama Justice Department in 2012, for example, is pursuing a class-action suit for Blacks discriminated against in the predatory housing loan market. Earlier, it settled the long-standing lawsuit over discrimination in the Department of Agriculture's lending program for farmers. It settled another suit over HUD's discrimination against homeowners devastated by Hurricane Katrina. The Justice Department has also filed suit to stop states from enacting discriminatory voter identification laws. This concern for discrimination by government agencies from the U.S. Justice Department was not so strong in the Carter administration. It might not have emerged had Black political power not expanded. Blacks are more influential today in government than in the past.

Thus, the CBC helped make the U.S. government more responsive to Blacks. For Black elected officials in Washington to do more, however, there would need to be institutional reform. New voting systems, such as cumulative voting, which yields proportional representation and also increases group descriptive representation, would open government's door to the policy interests of disadvantaged groups. Similarly, compulsory voting laws would change the incentive structure for political candidates. They could no longer ignore the citizens unlikely to vote or to enact new laws curtailing voter participation rates. Political reform, however, is hard to achieve even during a crisis. So political reform would possibly help disadvantaged groups, but it is unlikely to happen.

A second approach to empowering Blacks further in this period of concordance is to organize Black interests differently. Blacks need to define their interests less broadly and seek new coalitional partners in a climate favoring multiracialism. A narrow Black policy agenda would serve the interests of specific Black groups or communities, such as elderly living on Social Security, the single parent, the eighth grader, the preschooler, the high school dropout, the working poor, the long-term jobless, the incarcerated, female, gay, or lesbian. A narrow Black policy agenda could help elevate these groups so that their problems are less ignored. A narrow Black policy agenda may be more acceptable to Americans. Blacks today are the second largest ethnic group after Latinos, and thus a narrow Black agenda might work best in coalition with liberal Whites who favor post-ethnic politics as well as with Latinos and Asian Americans who generally support increased public services for their communities (Bowler and Segura 2011).

Finally, advocates for Black economic and political empowerment will need to understand the limitations of the present system that is changing the nature of Black elected leadership. Black elected officials should no longer be romanticized as representing the Far Left and rebellious. However, their increasing role in government should not be ignored; nor should descriptive representation efforts be abandoned. In the end, advocates for Blacks will need to organize and press for changes differently, and that includes taking their concerns directly to Democratic Party leaders and defining their interests narrowly as Black Americans. They will need to continue to use all that is presently available, including ballot box methods, interest group representation, and collective action strategies.

Afterword
Will the CBC Re-Radicalize in the Age of Trump?

The book contends that the style and goals of the Congressional Black Caucus changed after Blacks won incorporation into the Democratic Party. Minority political incorporation is defined as the process of outsiders becoming insiders and joining the dominant governing coalition. In exchange, the dominant governing coalition moves closer to the ideological goals of the outside group. Through turnover and accommodation, however, minority legislators also become more moderate. In a majoritarian system, political parties and presidential politics put pressure on members to join in their centrist agendas. There is concordance between Black Democrats and the Democratic Party from the time when the CBC was founded nearly fifty years ago.

Since the initial publication of this book, two of the longest serving Blacks have left the U.S. Congress—Charles Rangel and John Conyers Jr. Both stepped down amid ethics allegations. In fact, Rangel, after two years of an investigation, was censured by the House and had been stripped of his chairmanship of the powerful Ways and Means Committee. He still ran for reelection until retirement at the end of the 114th Congress (2015–16). Conyers was accused of sexual harassment and left quickly at the close of 2017. In 2019, Conyers passed away at the age of 90. They were the last two founding members of the CBC established in 1971 still serving in Congress.

Additionally, both were members of an age cohort that helped shaped the CBC's strategic approach. Another founding member of the CBC, William L. Clay (D-MO), in his congressional memoir, *Just Permanent Interests* (1992), writes about the combative style of the CBC and how they boycotted President Nixon's State of the Union Address because he had refused to meet with them. The combative style carried over to the presidential administration of Jimmy Carter even though he was member of their own political party. They fought the president over his budget proposals, which were too modest for their agenda to fight Black unemployment. The nation owed to Blacks a special effort to fight unemployment in their community. That CBC agenda is part of a radical agenda. Radical interests are defined as those that lie outside the left-right continuum. These agendas are extreme, and, as I write on page 1 of this book, defy "conventional understandings of what constitute government rights and benefits."

Ron Dellums, another founding member of the CBC, is quoted at the beginning of chapter 1 saying that there is a delicate balance between cooperation and refusing to deal with the governing majority, but that compromising was almost always inevitable. There was even division within the organization over whether to back President Carter's reelection bid. There was radicalism in this approach, but they could not organize their rebellion over Carter as a voting bloc. Ronald Reagan won the election in 1980, and as this book finds, the CBC argued forcefully against the conservative policies of Reagan-Bush. Later, the dominance of Republican presidents and the reality that to pass legislation under conditions of stark party polarization forced CBC members to find their party's policy agenda more acceptable than under Carter, Reagan, and Bush.

The movement away from radical liberalism by members of the CBC occurred during a Black empowerment phase culminating in the election of an African American U.S. president, Barack Obama, in 2008. Using statistical measures called NOMINATE scores that capture the ideological profiles of members, the average CBC ideological score moved from −0.56 in 1977 to −0.48 in 2010 (see appendix B). Negative ideological scores represent ultra-liberalism, while positive ones represent ultra-conservatism. These scores are from Poole-Rosenthal's spatial coding of congressional floor votes. President Obama's first year in office was very successful. He enacted 97 percent of his legislative initiatives—the highest success rate since 1953. Presidents generally earn success rates between 80 to 89 percent in their first year. The Black Caucus presidential support rate for 2009, Obama's first year, was high as well at 96 percent (see table B4). By comparison, the presidential support rate for all House Democrats was 90 percent. Presidential success and presidential support are statistics compiled by *Congressional Quarterly (CQ) Almanac*.

Obama's first year saw very high legislative effectiveness scores for the CBC as well. Legislative effectiveness scores are those that I calculated based on the percentage of time that caucus members voted with the House majority on *CQ Almanac*'s list of "key votes." About a dozen bills each year are considered important or key. In 2009, the CBC average legislative effectiveness score was 0.90 (see table B5) indicating that CBC members voted 90 percent of the time with the House majority on key bills. Although the press covered some criticism of Obama that he wasn't "Black" enough, Obama had the strong allegiance of the CBC. The controversial elements of his presidency, namely the second bail out of Wall Street and the extension of tax breaks for the wealthy, had some opposition from the CBC. Obama's biggest victory, of course, was passage of national health care legislation in 2010. Although some CBC members wanted a government insurance plan offered to Americans alongside the private ones known as a "public option," government was too evenly divided between liberals and conservatives to pass a program that would include a public option provision. A national single-payer program, where health insurance is entirely government run, had been rejected by the Democratic Party. Today, a liberal faction within the Democratic Party is still pursuing a single-payer policy agenda as "Medicare-for-all."

The political context for the CBC today is quite different than under the Obama administration. Obama enjoyed unified government under Democratic control in 2009 and 2010. After the 2010 elections, Obama's party lost control of the U.S. House of Representatives. The Republicans would next win party control of the U.S. Senate with the 2014 elections. In 2016, a Republican would surprisingly win the presidential election in a race that many believed would go to the Democratic Party. Donald Trump elected in 2016 is not like George W. Bush elected in 2000. George W. Bush had not campaigned on racially divisive issues like his predecessors Ronald Reagan and George H. W. Bush. Donald Trump entered the 2016 contest as a leading proponent of Birtherism, the claim that Barack Obama was not born in the United States, and, thus, was unqualified constitutionally to be president. He also campaigned on immigration in racialized terms, claiming that the illegal drug trade is fueled by illegal immigration and calling Mexicans drug dealers. While the Democrats regained a majority in the U.S. House following the 2018 elections, the Senate and the presidency today remain under the control of the Republicans. Although presidential leadership in a party polarized Congress was statistically linked to the CBC's centrist voting behavior, the Trump presidency may cause the CBC to re-radicalize.

As shown in chapter 5, however, the election of a Republican president in 2000 caused moderates, not radicals, to emerge in the CBC. During that presidential administration, a break from the Progressive Caucus's alternative budgets became a fixed pattern for the handful of new Black moderates in the U.S. House even as the CBC commanded full allegiance to its alternative budget bills. Black moderates also broke with members of the CBC over the wars in Afghanistan and Iraq and defense spending. Furthermore, updating the findings since publication, the ideological scores have not liberalized since 2010, dropping from –0.48 in 2010 to –0.46 in 2019 (see table 1). In chapter 7, I find that the CBC's average ideological scores are not as liberal as the Progressive Caucus in table 4 for the 107th to 109th Congresses. Removing two from the Black Caucus and the four from the Progressive Caucus as outliers,[1] the average scores are identical for the CBC and the Progressive Caucus at –0.46 for the NOMINATE data thus far collected for the 116th Congress. Thus, the CBC to date is as liberal as the Progressive Caucus.

The trajectory of the CBC is still one where it is not expected to exceed the Progressive Caucus's liberal voting record. Since the initial publication, there was an increase in the number of Blacks elected in 2018, and increases in number should be associated with ideological diversity. New Black lawmakers entered Congress in an unusual manner of defeating existing incumbents, including Republicans in the general election. For example, Lauren Underwood, a young member of Congress, won an open-seat contest in Illinois' Democratic primary election. Underwood, who has a nursing degree, defeated the GOP opponent (who was first elected in 2006) on the issue of the 2010 Affordable Healthcare Act. Freshman Ayanna Pressley (D-MA) defeated a 10-term incumbent in the Democratic primary and ran unopposed in the general election in Massachusetts. In 2018, Colin Allred defeated a long-time Republican incumbent who had served in Congress over 20 years to represent the 32nd district of Texas. While Allred is not as strongly liberal as Pressley, his ideological score is consistent with the CBC's average score of –0.46, noting that extreme liberals earn NOMINATE scores of –0.56 or so.

Generational replacement is also expected to reduce the radicalism of the CBC because older Black Caucus members tend to be more liberal

Table 5. Average 1st Dimension Nominate (Poole-Rosenthal) Scores for 112th–116th Congresses

Congress	CBC
112th (2011–2012)	–0.47
113th (2013–2014)	–0.49
114th (2015–2016)	–0.46
115th (2017–2018)	–0.45
116th (2019–2020)	–0.44 / –0.46

Source: Voteview data as calculated by author.

than younger ones. The book constructed a regression model of ideological scores predicted by a number of variables such as gender, age, region, committee chairmanships and party leadership, party unity and presidential support scores, and statewide bids, and age turned out to be a significant predictor of member ideology. The percentage of women has increased steadily since the 108th Congress. Black women represented 31 percent the House CBC, including the DC delegate in 2003. That percentage has increased to 44 percent for the 116th. This is a much higher percentage of women for the House CBC delegation than the House as whole where women for the 116th Congress represent about 24 percent of all members (Manning 2019). While women are to the political left of men in surveys generally, the book did not find gender to affect the ideological profile of Black Democrats in the House.

Age, as noted earlier, did predict CBC ideology. Older Blacks have more liberal voting records than younger Blacks. An analysis of age shows, however, that age increased from 2002 to 2017, even deleting Conyers and Rangel—two of the longest serving members of the CBC—from the calculations as outliers. A second pattern detected is that older, veteran lawmakers from state government ran for Congress and won. For example, Alma Adams (D-NC) was elected at 68 in 2014. Adams had served for decades in North Carolina's state government. After serving in state government for more than two decades, Al Lawson (D-FL) was elected at 69 in 2016. Bonnie Watson-Coleman of New Jersey was elected to state government in 1998 and then elected to the U.S. of House of Representatives in her 70s. With the addition of young freshmen elected in 2018, however, the average age dropped from 65 to 63. A Congressional Research Service report finds that the average age for the 116th Congress for the House is 58 (Manning 2019), making the CBC older than the House overall. The older average age of the Black Caucus compared to the House overall helps explain its continued liberal profile.

The Constitution requires House members to be 25 years of age to serve. Today, there are four main age cohorts in the U.S. Congress: (1) Silent Generation, (2) Baby Boomers, (3) Generation X, and (4) Millennials. Silent Generation members are those born between 1928 and 1945; Baby Boomers are those born in the era from World War II to 1964; Generation X members range from 1965 to 1980; and Millennials were born after 1980. Members of the Silent Generation[2] witnessed the transformation of society from Jim Crow to a more racially and ethnically inclusive one. John Lewis (D-GA) was born in 1940 and would be considered a member of the Silent Generation. He demonstrated the combative style of the early CBC when he publicly refused to attend the 2017 inauguration of the Republican president Donald Trump. Trump is considered to have made racially inflammatory remarks during his campaign for president. Lewis is currently the most senior member of the CBC. Silent generation members, it was argued based on the data analysis, were most liberal. Analyzing the data from the 116th Congress and comparing members of the Silent Generation to the four Millennial members[3] who joined as freshmen, their average score of -0.51 was still more liberal than the Millennials' average score of -0.47 (omitting Omar's NOMINATE score as someone, although liberal, voted once with the Republicans). It is argued that the oldest Black House members are extreme liberals because they harbor idealist notions about how much farther the United States can go in eradicating racial inequality. In addition, their age might present barriers to further ambitions to run for the U.S. Senate or president. Political ambition was found to promote centrist views among Black lawmakers in the statistical analysis in this book.

Millennials are still very liberal as political leaders who want to take on the problem of climate change, an issue as difficult to address as racial inequality. Public opinion research on age cohorts finds that millennials are the most liberal and Democratic of all the age cohorts (Pew Research Center 2018). They disapprove of President Trump by a larger margin than Generation Xers, Baby Boomers, and members of the Silent Generation. In 2017, 57 percent of millennials said that they would prefer a bigger government providing more services. Millennials are also more likely to believe that race discrimination is why Blacks can't get ahead compared to the other generations. Among the four age cohorts, a higher percentage of millennials believe that good diplomacy is the best way to achieve peace. Part of their liberal profile is also due to ethnic and racial diversity among millennials.

Certainly, younger Black politicians have been characterized as more centrist and less system-challenging than older ones (Gillespie 2010; Smith 1996). However, millennials could potentially re-radicalize the CBC if young Black politicians are responding to left-leaning ideological pressures on the Democratic Party. The Generation X ideological score omitting Pressley, who also had an outlier vote in 2019, was -0.38, making it the most moderate of the four generation groups. Baby boomers had an ideological score of -0.45, close to the score for millennials. These generational divisions are not only present in the Black Caucus but may be found among other caucuses including the Women's Caucus, Hispanic Caucus, and the Congressional Asian Pacific American Caucus.

The transformation of the political landscape for Blacks even before the election of the country's first Black president has been enormous and may have reshaped agendas and political calculations of members of Congress. Notably, younger minorities may have larger ambitions than older ones because of these transformations. In addition to age, the book found that those who made statewide bids for political office had more centrist records than those who had not made such bids. In the 2018 elections, the newness of winning against established Republican incumbents as Black Democrats created a buzz around some who, the media think, should pursue a seat in the U.S. Senate. Already, one freshman from a Blue or pro-Democratic state, Joe Neguse (D-CO), has joined the Progressive Caucus, while two others, from Red or pro-Republican states, Lucy McBath (D-GA) and Colin Allred (D-TX), have not. In circling for a rematch, Republican rivals are already preparing to accuse McBath of being too liberal to represent her district. McBath's ideological score at –0.24 is less liberal than many of her CBC colleagues.

Region was also a significant predictor of ideological profile. Members from the South in the earlier analysis were more centrist than those outside of the South. Two of the freshmen were elected in the South, and they have lower ideological scores than most. Seniority had no effect contrary to expectations that senior members are more ambitious or independent minded from the ideological pressures from their district. Seniority increased from 2003 to 2015, which the record increase in freshmen decreased in 2019. The average number of years served is 10.0 in 2019, slightly more than for the House as a whole, which is 9 years on average (Manning 2019). Committee chairmanships had no effect. Party unity support and party leadership had contrasting effects. Those who voted party line more were more centrist than those who broke from the party. Party leaders, however, were more liberal than rank-and-file members.

Confronting an administration unlike the past Republican one, will the Caucus re-radicalize? There are some reasons to expect that the newest members of the CBC may be as radical as the senior set. First, the Democratic Party has become more liberal, and there remains continued pressure on it to continue to liberalize from the grassroots political left. In a short period of time, newcomers to the Democratic Caucus support a public option for health care insurance; they also support the impeachment of Republican President Donald Trump over allegation he denied assistance to a foreign country to secure a political favor. Their extremely liberal profiles might not limit their ambition for higher office as two of the top presidential contenders in 2020, Senators Elizabeth Warren and Bernie Sanders, in the Democratic race talk about systemic political change. As a consequence, young Black lawmakers may radicalize of their generation, replacing Silent Generation members who retire, and thus keeping the CBC still generally very liberal. Generational change may not automatically favor centrism as argued in this book.

On the other hand, there remain important ideological divisions within the Caucus that will likely remain in place. Generation X members of the Black Caucus appear to be the most centrist, and in the current context of extreme party polarization, they are more likely to defer to presidential and party leadership to pass bills. Other than the youngest set, many CBC members are pragmatic and not willing to buck leadership to take principled stands. Furthermore, there is a vision of the CBC where it is a social group caucus willing to reflect ideological diversity and not one that seeks to pressure members into conformity. The CBC states on its website its desire to be a bipartisan group. However, members must pay dues to join, and there is little incentive for Republicans to join this overwhelmingly Democratic group. Gary A. Franks (R-CT) who was elected in 1990 joined the Caucus as a voting member but left after reportedly being shut out of some closed-door meetings (Berke 1991). In 2010, Allen B. West (R-FL) pledged to join the Caucus because the group needed competing voices (Steinhauer 2010). West told the press that he considered leaving after a Caucus member criticized the Tea Party movement with which West was aligned (Steinhauer 2011). While one Black House Republican serves in the 116th U.S. Congress, the Black Caucus currently does not have Republican members.

The reality that the CBC has moved toward the center since its founding to accommodate the Democratic Party in a majoritarian system remains. The political atmosphere in Washington is one of stark party polarization. To pass bills, including bipartisan ones, the Democrats need votes from the CBC. There is statistical evidence that members of the CBC remain among the most party loyal among Democrats in the House. Once proud outsiders, members of the CBC are now insiders in Washington whose interests are not radical. The merging of Black and centrist interests, however, is important in explaining how the promotion of Black interests has been enhanced in government. It is argued that there are more opportunities for Blacks' political concerns with the union of Black and centrist interests. However, it also must be noted that a principled radical vision from the new CBC is unlikely given the political context of party polarization and the group's ideological diversity.

List of Black, Hispanic, Blue Dog, and Progressive Caucus Members by Recent Congresses

Black Representatives

116th Congress (2019–2020)

ALABAMA
Terri Sewell

CALIFORNIA
Karen Bass
Barbara Lee
Maxine Waters

COLORADO
Joseph Neguse

CONNECTICUT
Jahana Hayes

DELAWARE
Lisa Blunt Rochester

FLORIDA
Val Butler Demings
Alcee L. Hastings
Al Lawson
Frederica S. Wilson

GEORGIA
Sanford Bishop
Hank Johnson

John Lewis
Lucy McBath
David Scott

ILLINOIS
Danny K. Davis
Robin Kelly
Bobby L. Rush
Lauren Underwood

INDIANA
André Carson

LOUISIANA
Cedric L. Richmond

MARYLAND
Anthony Brown
Elijah E. Cummings

MASSACHUSETTS
Ayanna Pressley

MICHIGAN
Brenda Lawrence

MINNESOTA
Ilhan Omar

MISSISSIPPI
Bennie Thompson
MISSOURI
William Lacy Clay Jr.
Emanuel Cleaver
NEVADA
Steven Horsford
NEW JERSEY
Bonnie Coleman Watson
Donald M. Payne Jr.
NEW YORK
Yvette Clarke
Antonio Delgado
Hakeem Jeffries
Gregory W. Meeks
NORTH CAROLINA
Alma Adams
G. K. Butterfield
OHIO
Joyce Beatty
Marcia L. Fudge
PENNSYLVANIA
Dwight Evans
SOUTH CAROLINA
James E. Clyburn
TEXAS
Colin Allred
Al Green
Will Hurd (Republican)
Sheila Jackson Lee
Eddie Bernice Johnson
Marc Veasey
VIRGINIA
Donald A. McEachin
Robert Scott
WISCONSIN
Gwen Moore
DISTRICT OF COLUMBIA
Eleanor Holmes Norton

SENATORS:
Cory Booker
Kamala Harris

115th Congress (2017–2018)

ALABAMA
Terri Sewell
CALIFORNIA
Karen Bass
Barbara Lee
Maxine Waters
DELAWARE
Lisa Blunt Rochester
FLORIDA
Val Butler Demings
Alcee L. Hastings
Al Lawson
Frederica S. Wilson
GEORGIA
Sanford Bishop
Hank Johnson
John Lewis
David Scott
ILLINOIS
Danny K. Davis
Robin Kelly
Bobby L. Rush
INDIANA
André Carson
LOUISIANA
Cedric L. Richmond
MARYLAND
Anthony Brown
Elijah E. Cummings
MICHIGAN
John Conyers Jr.
Brenda Lawrence
MINNESOTA
Keith Ellison

MISSISSIPPI
Bennie Thompson
MISSOURI
William Lacy Clay Jr.
Emanuel Cleaver
NEW JERSEY
Bonnie Coleman Watson
Donald M. Payne Jr.
NEW YORK
Yvette D. Clarke
Hakeem Jeffries
Gregory W. Meeks
NORTH CAROLINA
Alma Adams
G. K. Butterfield
OHIO
Joyce Beatty
Marcia Fudge
PENNSYLVANIA
Dwight Evans
SOUTH CAROLINA
James E. Clyburn
TEXAS
Al Green
Will Hurd (Republican)
Sheila Jackson Lee
Eddie Bernice Johnson
Marc Veasey
UTAH
Mia Love (Republican)
VIRGINIA
Donald A. McEachin
Robert Scott
WISCONSIN
Gwen Moore
DISTRICT OF COLUMBIA
Eleanor Holmes Norton
SENATORS:
Cory Booker
Kamala Harris

114th Congress (2015–2016)

ALABAMA
Terri Sewell
CALIFORNIA
Karen Bass
Barbara Lee
Maxine Waters
FLORIDA
Corrine Brown
Alcee L. Hastings
Frederica S. Wilson
GEORGIA
Sanford Bishop
Hank Johnson
John Lewis
David Scott
ILLINOIS
Danny K. Davis
Robin Kelly
Bobby Rush
INDIANA
André Carson
LOUISIANA
Cedric L. Richmond
MARYLAND
Elijah E. Cummings
Donna Edwards
MICHIGAN
John Conyers Jr.
Brenda Lawrence
MINNESOTA
Keith Ellison
MISSISSIPPI
Bennie Thompson
MISSOURI
William Lacy Clay Jr.
Emanuel Cleaver
NEW JERSEY
Bonnie Coleman Watson

Donald M. Payne Jr.
NEW YORK
Yvette D. Clarke
Hakeem Jeffries
Gregory W. Meeks
Charles B. Rangel
NORTH CAROLINA
Alma Adams
G. K. Butterfield
OHIO
Joyce Beatty
Marcia L. Fudge
PENNSYLVANIA
Dwight Evans/Chaka Fattah
SOUTH CAROLINA
James E. Clyburn
TEXAS
Al Green
Will Hurd (Republican)
Sheila Jackson Lee
Eddie Bernice Johnson
Marc Veasey
UTAH
Mia Love (Republican)
VIRGINIA
Robert Scott
WISCONSIN
Gwen Moore
DISTRICT OF COLUMBIA
Eleanor Holmes Norton
SENATOR:
Cory Booker

113th Congress (2013–2014)

ALABAMA
Terri Sewell
CALIFORNIA
Karen Bass
Barbara Lee
Maxine Waters

FLORIDA
Corrine Brown
Alcee L. Hastings
Frederica S. Wilson
GEORGIA
Sanford Bishop
John Lewis
Hank Johnson
David Scott
ILLINOIS
Danny K. Davis
Robin Kelly
Bobby Rush
INDIANA
André Carson
LOUISIANA
Cedric L. Richmond
MARYLAND
Elijah E. Cummings
Donna Edwards
MICHIGAN
John Conyers Jr.
MINNESOTA
Keith Ellison
MISSISSIPPI
Bennie Thompson
MISSOURI
William Lacy Clay Jr.
Emanuel Cleaver
NEVADA
Steven Horsford
NEW JERSEY
Donald M. Payne Jr.
NEW YORK
Yvette D. Clarke
Hakeem Jeffries
Gregory W. Meeks
Charles B. Rangel
NORTH CAROLINA
Alma Adams/Melvin Watt
G. K. Butterfield

OHIO
Joyce Beatty
Marcia L. Fudge
PENNSYLVANIA
Chaka Fattah
SOUTH CAROLINA
James E. Clyburn
TEXAS
Al Green
Sheila Jackson Lee
Eddie Bernice Johnson
Marc Veasey
VIRGINIA
Robert Scott
WISCONSIN
Gwen Moore
DISTRICT OF COLUMBIA
Eleanor Holmes Norton
SENATOR:
Cory Booker

112th Congress (2011–2012)

ALABAMA
Terri Sewell
CALIFORNIA
Karen Bass
Barbara Lee
Laura Richardson
Maxine Waters
FLORIDA
Corrine Brown
Alcee Hastings
Frederica Wilson
Allen West (Republican)
GEORGIA
Sanford Bishop
Hank Johnson
John Lewis
David Scott
ILLINOIS
Bobby Rush

Danny Davis
Jesse Jackson Jr.
INDIANA
Andre Carson
LOUISIANA
Cedric Richmond
MARYLAND
Elijah Cummings
Donna Edwards
MICHIGAN
John Conyers
Hansen Clark
MINNESOTA
Keith Ellison
MISSISSIPPI
Bennie Thompson
MISSOURI
Emanuel Cleaver
William Lacy Clay
NEW JERSEY
Donald Payne
NEW YORK
Yvette Clarke
Gregory Meeks
Charles Rangel
Edolphus Towns
NORTH CAROLINA
G. K. Butterfield
Melvin Watt
OHIO
Marcia Fudge
PENNSYLVANIA
Chaka Fattah
SOUTH CAROLINA
James Clyburn
Tim Scott (Republican)
TEXAS
Al Green
Sheila Jackson Lee
Eddie Bernie Johnson

VIRGINIA
Robert Scott
WISCONSIN
Gwen Moore
DISTRICT OF COLUMBIA
Eleanor Holmes Norton

111th Congress (2009–2010)

ALABAMA
Artur Davis
CALIFORNIA
Diane Watson
Barbara Lee
Laura Richardson
Maxine Waters
FLORIDA
Corrine Brown
Alcee Hastings
Kendrick Meek
GEORGIA
Sanford Bishop
Hank Johnson
John Lewis
David Scott
ILLINOIS
Bobby Rush
Danny Davis
Jesse Jackson Jr.
INDIANA
Andre Carson
MARYLAND
Elijah Cummings
Donna Edwards
MICHIGAN
John Conyers
Carolyn Cheeks Kilpatrick
MINNESOTA
Keith Ellison

MISSISSIPPI
Bennie Thompson
MISSOURI
Emanuel Cleaver
William Lacy Clay
NEW JERSEY
Donald Payne
NEW YORK
Yvette Clarke
Gregory Meeks
Charles Rangel
Edolphus Towns
NORTH CAROLINA
G. K. Butterfield
Melvin Watt
OHIO
Marcia Fudge
PENNSYLVANIA
Chaka Fattah
SOUTH CAROLINA
James Clyburn
TEXAS
Al Green
Sheila Jackson Lee
Eddie Bernie Johnson
VIRGINIA
Robert Scott
WISCONSIN
Gwen Moore
DISTRICT OF COLUMBIA
Eleanor Holmes Norton
SENATOR: ROLAND BURRIS

110th Congress (2007–2008)

ALABAMA
Artur Davis
CALIFORNIA
Diane Watson
Barbara Lee

Laura Richardson
Maxine Waters
FLORIDA
Corrine Brown
Alcee Hastings
Kendrick Meek
GEORGIA
Sanford Bishop
Hank Johnson
John Lewis
David Scott
ILLINOIS
Bobby Rush
Danny Davis
Jesse Jackson Jr.
INDIANA
Julia Carson
LOUISIANA
William Jefferson
MARYLAND
Elijah Cummings
Albert Wynn
MICHIGAN
John Conyers
Carolyn Cheeks Kilpatrick
MINNESOTA
Keith Ellison
MISSISSIPPI
Bennie Thompson
MISSOURI
Emanuel Cleaver
William Lacy Clay
NEW JERSEY
Donald Payne
NEW YORK
Yvette Clarke
Gregory Meeks
Charles Rangel
Edolphus Towns

NORTH CAROLINA
G. K. Butterfield
Melvin Watt
OHIO
Stephanie Tubbs Jones
PENNSYLVANIA
Chaka Fattah
SOUTH CAROLINA
James Clyburn
TEXAS
Al Green
Sheila Jackson Lee
Eddie Bernie Johnson
VIRGINIA
Robert Scott
WISCONSIN
Gwen Moore
DISTRICT OF COLUMBIA
Eleanor Holmes Norton
SENATOR: BARACK OBAMA

109th Congress (2005–2006)

ALABAMA
Artur Davis
CALIFORNIA
Diane Watson
Barbara Lee
Juanita Millender-McDonald
Maxine Waters
FLORIDA
Corrine Brown
Alcee Hastings
Kendrick Meek
GEORGIA
Sanford Bishop
Cynthia McKinney
John Lewis
David Scott

ILLINOIS
Bobby Rush
Danny Davis
Jesse Jackson Jr.
INDIANA
Julia Carson
LOUISIANA
William Jefferson
MARYLAND
Elijah Cummings
Albert Wynn
MICHIGAN
John Conyers
Carolyn Cheeks Kilpatrick
MISSISSIPPI
Bennie Thompson
MISSOURI
Emanuel Cleaver
William Lacy Clay
NEW JERSEY
Donald Payne
NEW YORK
Major Owens
Gregory Meeks
Charles Rangel
Edolphus Towns
NORTH CAROLINA
G. K. Butterfield
Melvin Watt
OHIO
Stephanie Tubbs Jones
PENNSYLVANIA
Chaka Fattah
SOUTH CAROLINA
James Clyburn
TENNESSEE
Harold Ford Jr.
TEXAS
Al Green
Sheila Jackson Lee

Eddie Bernie Johnson
VIRGINIA
Robert Scott
WISCONSIN
Gwen Moore
DISTRICT OF COLUMBIA
Eleanor Holmes Norton
SENATOR: BARACK OBAMA

108th Congress (2003–2004)

ALABAMA
Artur Davis
CALIFORNIA
Diane Watson
Barbara Lee
Juanita McMillender-McDonald
Maxine Waters
FLORIDA
Corrine Brown
Alcee Hastings
Kendrick Meek
GEORGIA
Sanford Bishop
Denise Majette
John Lewis
David Scott
ILLINOIS
Bobby Rush
Danny Davis
Jesse Jackson Jr.
INDIANA
Julia Carson
LOUISIANA
William Jefferson
MARYLAND
Elijah Cummings
Albert Wynn
MICHIGAN
John Conyers

Carolyn Cheeks Kilpatrick
MISSISSIPPI
Bennie Thompson
MISSOURI
William Lacy Clay
NEW JERSEY
Donald Payne
NEW YORK
Major Owens
Gregory Meeks
Charles Rangel
Edolphus Towns
NORTH CAROLINA
Frank W. Ballance
Melvin Watt
OHIO
Stephanie Tubbs Jones

PENNSYLVANIA
Chaka Fattah
SOUTH CAROLINA
James Clyburn
TENNESSEE
Harold Ford Jr.
TEXAS
Sheila Jackson Lee
Eddie Bernie Johnson
VIRGINIA
Robert Scott
DISTRICT OF COLUMBIA
Eleanor Holmes Norton

*95th–107th Congresses, see
Tate's Black Faces in the
Mirror, appendix B (Princeton
University Press, 2003)*

Hispanic Caucus

109th Congress (2005–2006)

ARIZONA
Raúl Grijalva
Ed Pastor
CALIFORNIA
Joe Baca
Xavier Becerra
Graciela Flores Napolitano
Lucille Roybal-Allard
Linda Sanchez
Loretta Sanchez
Hilda Solis
COLORADO
John Salazar
FLORIDA
Lincoln Diaz-Balart
Mario Diaz-Balart

Ileana Ros-Lehtinen
ILLINOIS
Luis V. Gutiérrez
NEW JERSEY
Robert Menendez
NEW YORK
José E. Serrano
Nydia Velázquez
TEXAS
Henry Bonilla
Henry Cuellar
Charlie Gonzalez
Ruben Hinojosa
Solomon P. Ortiz
Silvestre Reyes

108th Congress (2004–2005)

ARIZONA
Raúl Grijalva
Ed Pastor
CALIFORNIA
Joe Baca
Xavier Becerra
Graciela Flores Napolitano
Lucille Roybal-Allard
Linda Sanchez
Loretta Sanchez
Hilda Solis
FLORIDA
Lincoln Diaz-Balart
Mario Diaz-Balart
Ileana Ros-Lehtinen
ILLINOIS
Luis V. Gutiérrez
NEW JERSEY
Robert Menendez
NEW YORK
José E. Serrano
Nydia Velázquez
TEXAS
Henry Bonilla
Charlie Gonzalez
Ruben Hinojosa
Solomon P. Ortiz
Silvestre Reyes
Ciro D. Rodriguez

108th Congress (2003–2004)

ARIZONA
Raúl Grijalva
Ed Pastor
CALIFORNIA
Joe Baca
Xavier Becerra
Graciela Flores Napolitano
Lucille Roybal-Allard
Linda Sanchez
Loretta Sanchez
Hilda Solis
FLORIDA
Lincoln Diaz-Balart
Mario Diaz-Balart
Ileana Ros-Lehtinen
ILLINOIS
Luis V. Gutiérrez
NEW JERSEY
Robert Menendez
NEW YORK
José E. Serrano
Nydia Velázquez
TEXAS
Henry Bonilla
Charlie Gonzalez
Ruben Hinojosa
Solomon P. Ortiz
Silvestre Reyes
Ciro D. Rodriguez

107th Congress (2002–2003)

ARIZONA
Ed Pastor
CALIFORNIA
Joe Baca
Xavier Becerra
Graciela Flores Napolitano
Lucille Roybal-Allard
Loretta Sanchez
Hilda Solis
FLORIDA
Lincoln Diaz-Balart
Ileana Ros-Lehtinen
NEW JERSEY
Robert Menendez

NEW YORK
José E. Serrano
Nydia Velázquez
TEXAS
Henry Bonilla
Charlie Gonzalez
Ruben Hinojosa
Solomon P. Ortiz
Silvestre Reyes
Ciro D. Rodriguez

107th Congress (2001–2002)

ARIZONA
Ed Pastor
CALIFORNIA
Joe Baca
Xavier Becerra
Graciela Flores Napolitano
Lucille Roybal-Allard
Loretta Sanchez
Hilda Solis
FLORIDA
Lincoln Diaz-Balart
Ileana Ros-Lehtinen
ILLINOIS
Luis V. Gutiérrez
NEW JERSEY
Robert Menendez
NEW YORK
José E. Serrano
Nydia Velázquez
TEXAS
Henry Bonilla
Charlie Gonzalez
Ruben Hinojosa
Solomon P. Ortiz
Silvestre Reyes
Ciro D. Rodriguez

106th Congress (2000–2001)

ARIZONA
Ed Pastor
CALIFORNIA
Joe Baca
Xavier Becerra
Matthew G. Martinez
Graciela Flores Napolitano
Lucille Roybal-Allard
Loretta Sanchez
FLORIDA
Lincoln Diaz-Balart
Ileana Ros-Lehtinen
ILLINOIS
Luis V. Gutiérrez
NEW JERSEY
Robert Menendez
NEW YORK
José E. Serrano
Nydia Velázquez
TEXAS
Henry Bonilla
Charlie Gonzalez
Ruben Hinojosa
Solomon P. Ortiz
Silvestre Reyes
Ciro D. Rodriguez

105th Congress (1997–1998)

ARIZONA
Ed Pastor
CALIFORNIA
Xavier Becerra
Matthew G. Martinez
Lucille Roybal-Allard
Loretta Sanchez
Esteban E. Torres
FLORIDA
Lincoln Diaz-Balart

Ileana Ros-Lehtinen
ILLINOIS
Luis V. Gutiérrez
NEW JERSEY
Robert Menendez
NEW YORK
José E. Serrano
Nydia Velázquez
TEXAS
Henry Bonilla
Henry B. Gonzalez
Ruben Hinojosa
Solomon P. Ortiz
Silvestre Reyes
Ciro D. Rodriguez

104th Congress (1996–1997)

ARIZONA
Ed Pastor
CALIFORNIA
Xavier Becerra

Matthew G. Martinez
Lucille Roybal-Allard
Esteban E. Torres
FLORIDA
Lincoln Diaz-Balart
Ileana Ros-Lehtinen
ILLINOIS
Luis V. Gutiérrez
NEW JERSEY
Robert Menendez
NEW MEXICO
Bill Richardson
NEW YORK
José E. Serrano
Nydia Velázquez
TEXAS
Henry Bonilla
E. "Kika" De la Garza
Henry B. Gonzalez
Solomon P. Ortiz
Frank Tejeda

Blue Dog Caucus Members

109th Congress (2005–2006)

Baca, Joe
Barrow, John
Berry, Marion
Bishop, Sanford D., Jr.
Boren, Dan
Boswell, Leonard L.
Boyd, Allen
Cardoza, Dennis
Case, Ed
Chandler, Ben
Cooper, Jim
Costa, Jim
Cramer, Robert E.

Davis, Lincoln
Ford, Harold E., Jr.
Harman, Jane
Herseth, Stephanie
Holden, Tim
Israel, Steve
Matheson, Jim
McIntyre, Mike
Melancon, Charlie
Michaud, Michael H.
Moore, Dennis
Peterson, Collin C.
Pomeroy, Earl
Ross, Mike

Salazar, John
Sanchez, Loretta
Schiff, Adam B.
Scott, David
Tanner, John
Tauscher, Ellen O.
Taylor, Gene
Thompson, Mike

108th Congress (2003–2004)

Alexander, Rodney
Baca, Joe
Berry, Marion
Bishop, Sanford D., Jr.
Boswell, Leonard L.
Boyd, Allen
Cardoza, Dennis
Carson, Brad
Cramer, Robert E.
Davis, Lincoln
Ford, Harold E., Jr.
Hall, Ralph M.
Hill, Baron P.
Harman, Jane
Holden, Tim
Israel, Steve
John, Chris
Lipinski, William O.
Lucas, Ken
Matheson, Jim
McIntyre, Mike
Michaud, Michael H.
Moore, Dennis
Peterson, Collin C.
Pomeroy, Earl
Ross, Mike
Sanchez, Loretta
Sandlin, Max
Schiff, Adam B.
Scott, David

Stenholm, Charles W.
Tanner, John
Tauscher, Ellen O.
Taylor, Gene
Thompson, Mike
Turner, Jim

107th Congress (2001–2002)

Baca, Joe
Berry, Marion
Bishop, Sanford D., Jr.
Boswell, Leonard L.
Boyd, Allen
Carson, Brad
Condit, Gary A.
Cramer, Robert E.
Ford, Harold E., Jr.
Hall, Ralph M.
Harman, Jane
Hill, Baron P.
Holden, Tim
John, Chris
Lipinski, William O.
Lucas, Ken
Matheson, Jim
McIntyre, Mike
Moore, Dennis
Peterson, Collin C.
Phelps, David
Ross, Mike
Sanchez, Loretta
Sandlin, Max
Schiff, Adam B.
Shows, Ronnie
Stenholm, Charles W.
Tanner, John
Tauscher, Ellen O.
Taylor, Gene
Thompson, Mike
Turner, Jim

Progressive Caucus Members

116th Congress (2019–2020)

Alma Adams
Nanette Barragán
Karen Bass
Eddie Bernice Johnson
Don Beyer
Earl Blumenauer
Lisa Blunt Rochester
Suzanne Bonamici
Brendan Boyle
André Carson
Matt Cartwright
Judy Chu
David Cicilline
Gil Cisneros
Katherine Clark
Yvette Clarke
William Lacy Clary Jr.
Steven Cohen
Angie Craig
Madeleine Dean
Peter DeFazio
Rosa DeLauro
Mark DeSaulnier
Debbie Dingall
Lloyd Doggett
Adriano Espaillat
Veronica Escobar
Dwight Evans
Lois Frankel
Marcia Fudge
Tulsi Gabbard
Ruben Gallego
Jesus "Chuy" Garcia
Sylvia Garcia
Raúl Grijalva
Jimmy Gomez

Deb Haaland
Eleanor Holmes Norton
Steven Horsford
Jared Huffman
Sheila Jackson Lee
Pramila Jayapal
Hakeem Jeffries
Hank Johnson
Joe Kennedy III
Ro Khanna
Dan Kildee
Andy Kim
Brenda Lawrence
Barbara Lee
Andy Levin
Grace Meng
Mike Levin
John Lewis
Ted Lieu
David Loebsack
Zoe Lofgren
Alan Lowenthal
Carolyn Maloney
James McGovern
Gwen Moore
Joe Morelle
Debbie Murcarsel-Powell
Jerrold Nadler
Grace Napolitano
Joe Neguse
Donald Norcross
Alexandria Ocasio-Cortez
Ilhan Omar
Frank Pallone
Jimmy Panetta
Chellie Pingree
Mark Pocan
Katie Porter

Ayanna Pressley
Jamie Raskin
Lucille Roybal-Allard
Linda Sanchez
Mary Gay Scanlon
Jan Schakowsky
José Serrano
Brad Sherman
Adam Smith
Darren Soto
Mark Takano
Rashida Tlaib
Bennie Thompson
Lori Trahan
Juan Vargas
Nydia Velázquez
Maxine Waters
Bonnie Watson Coleman
Peter Welch
Frederica Wilson
John Yarmuth

109th Congress (2005–2006)

Abercrombie, Neil
Baldwin, Tammy
Becerra, Xavier
Brown, Corrine
Brown, Sherrod
Capuano, Michael E.
Carson, Julia
Clay, William Lacy
Conyers, John, Jr.
Davis, Danny K.
DeFazio, Peter A.
DeLauro, Rosa
Evans, Lane
Farr, Sam
Fattah, Chaka
Filner, Bob

Frank, Barney
Grijalva, Raúl M.
Gutiérrez, Luis V.
Hinchey, Maurice D.
Jackson Lee, Sheila
Jackson, Jesse L., Jr.
Jones, Stephanie Tubbs
Kaptur, Marcy
Kucinich, Dennis J.
Lantos, Tom
Lee, Barbara
Lewis, John
Markey, Edward J.
McDermott, Jim
McGovern, Jim
Miller, George
Moore, Gwen
Nadler, Jerrold
Olver, John W.
Owens, Major R.
Pastor, Ed
Payne, Donald M.
Pelosi, Nancy
Rush, Bobby L.
Sanders, Bernard
Schakowsky, Jan
Serrano, José E.
Solis, Hilda L.
Stark, Pete
Thompson, Bennie
Tierney, John F.
Udall, Tom
Velázquez, Nydia M.
Waters, Maxine
Watson, Diane
Watt, Melvin
Waxman, Henry A.
Woolsey, Lynn

108th Congress (2003–2004)

Abercrombie, Neil
Baldwin, Tammy
Becerra, Xavier
Brown, Corrine
Brown, Sherrod
Capuano, Michael E.
Carson, Julia
Clay, William Lacy
Conyers, John, Jr.
Davis, Danny K.
DeFazio, Peter A.
DeLauro, Rosa
Evans, Lane
Farr, Sam
Fattah, Chaka
Filner, Bob
Frank, Barney
Grijalva, Raúl M.
Gutiérrez, Luis V.
Hinchey, Maurice D.
Jackson Lee, Sheila
Jackson, Jesse L., Jr.
Jones, Stephanie Tubbs
Kaptur, Marcy
Kucinich, Dennis J.
Lantos, Tom
Lee, Barbara
Lewis, John
McDermott, Jim
McGovern, Jim
Miller, George
Nadler, Jerrold
Olver, John W.
Owens, Major R.
Pastor, Ed
Payne, Donald M.
Pelosi, Nancy
Rush, Bobby

Sanders, Bernard
Schakowsky, Jan
Serrano, José E.
Solis, Hilda
Stark, Pete
Thompson, Bennie
Tierney, John F.
Udall, Tom
Velázquez, Nydia M.
Waters, Maxine
Watson, Diane
Watt, Melvin
Waxman, Henry A.
Woolsey, Lynn

107th Congress (2001–2002)

Abercrombie, Neil
Baldwin, Tammy
Becerra, Xavier
Bonior, David E.
Brown, Corrine
Brown, Sherrod
Capuano, Michael E.
Carson, Julia
Conyers, John, Jr.
Davis, Danny K.
DeFazio, Peter A.
DeLauro, Rosa
Evans, Lane
Farr, Sam
Fattah, Chaka
Filner, Bob
Frank, Barney
Gutiérrez, Luis V.
Hilliard, Earl F.
Hinchey, Maurice D.
Jackson, Jesse L., Jr.
Jones, Stephanie Tubbs
Kaptur, Marcy

Kucinich, Dennis J.
Lantos, Tom
Lee, Barbara
Lewis, John
McDermott, Jim
McGovern, Jim
McKinney, Cynthia A.
Meek, Carrie P.
Miller, George
Mink, Patsy T.
Nadler, Jerrold
Olver, John W.
Owens, Major R.
Pastor, Ed

Payne, Donald M.
Pelosi, Nancy
Sanders, Bernard
Schakowsky, Jan
Serrano, José E.
Stark, Pete
Thompson, Bennie
Tierney, John F.
Udall, Tom
Velázquez, Nydia M.
Waters, Maxine
Watt, Melvin
Waxman, Henry A.
Woolsey, Lynn

Tables of NOMINATE, Party Unity, Presidential Support, and Legislative Effectiveness Scores for the CBC and Other House Caucuses

TABLE B1. Average 1st Dimension Poole-Rosenthal Scores for CBC and House Democrats, 95th–111th Congresses (std. deviations in parentheses), and Regression Coefficient for Year

	CBC	All House Democrats	House Democrats Minus Blacks
95th	−0.56 (.07)	−0.29 (.20)	−0.27 (.19)
96th	−0.56 (.07)	−0.29 (.20)	−0.27 (.20)
97th	−0.56 (.07)	−0.29 (.20)	−0.27 (.20)
98th	−0.57 (.07)	−0.30 (.19)	−0.27 (.18)
99th	−0.57 (.07)	−0.31 (.17)	−0.29 (.17)
100th	−0.56 (.09)	−0.31 (.17)	−0.29 (.16)
101st	−0.56 (.10)	−0.32 (.17)	−0.29 (.16)
102nd	−0.58 (.11)	−0.32 (.17)	−0.30 (.16)
103rd	−0.54 (.09)	−0.34 (.17)	−0.31 (.15)
104th	−0.53 (.08)	−0.37 (.16)	−0.33 (.16)
105th	−0.52 (.09)	−0.38 (.15)	−0.35 (.14)
106th	−0.51 (.09)	−0.38 (.15)	−0.35 (.15)
107th	−0.51 (.09)	−0.39 (.14)	−0.36 (.14)
108th	−0.48 (.11)	−0.39 (.14)	−0.37 (.14)
109th	−0.48 (.11)	−0.40 (.13)	−0.38 (.13)
110th	−0.47 (.10)	−0.38 (.15)	−0.36 (.15)
111th	−0.48 (.11)	−0.36 (.16)	−0.34 (.16)
B coefficient for year	.007** (.001)	−.007** (.001)	−.007** (.001)

Source: Poole-Rosenthal nominate scores, first dimension, and as calculated for Black House legislators and House Democrats.

**T-statistic probability value < .001

TABLE B2. Average 2nd Dimension Poole-Rosenthal Scores for CBC and House Democrats (std. deviations in parentheses), and Regression Coefficient for Year

	CBC	All House Democrats	House Democrats Minus Blacks
95th	0.16	0.16	0.18
96th	0.15	0.15	0.17
97th	0.12	0.12	0.16
98th	0.10	0.10	0.14
99th	0.11	0.11	0.15
100th	0.13	0.13	0.17
101st	0.12	0.12	0.16
102nd	0.13	0.13	0.17
103rd	0.11	0.11	0.14
104th	0.09	0.09	0.13
105th	0.05	0.05	0.09
106th	0.08	0.08	0.12
107th	0.07	0.07	0.11
108th	0.08	0.08	0.12
109th	0.07	0.07	0.12
110th	0.13	0.13	0.19
111th	0.18	0.18	0.24
B coefficient for year	0.016** (0.003)	−0.002 (0.001)	0.000 (0.001)

Source: Poole-Rosenthal nominate scores, second dimension, and as calculated for Black House legislators and House Democrats.

**T-statistic probability value < .001

TABLE B3. Average CQ *Almanac* Party Unity Scores for CBC House Democrats and House Democrats, 1977–2010 (std. deviations in parentheses)

Year	CBC House Democrats	House Democrats
1977	81 (7.4)	68
1978	74 (13.8)	63
1979	80 (14.0)	69
1980	75 (5.1)	69
1981	79 (9.3)	69
1982	77 (9.8)	72
1983	84.5 (5.9)	76
1984	83 (7.6)	74
1985	83 (8.8)	80
1986	82 (8.2)	79
1987	85 (7.7)	81
1988	81 (7.4)	80
1989	84 (10.0)	81
1990	n/a	81
1991	87 (6.9)	81
1992	83 (11.0)	79
1993	90 (7.4)	85
1994	87 (7.7)	83
1995	88 (7.1)	80
1996	88 (7.3)	80
1997	88 (5.5)	82
1998	88 (5.7)	82
1999	94 (4.4)	83
2000	94 (5.6)	82
2001	92 (5.4)	83
2002	95 (3.8)	86
2003	95 (5.0)	87
2004	94.5 (5.1)	86
2005	94 (5.3)	88
2006	93 (5.7)	86
2007	98 (1.1)	92
2008	99 (0.7)	92
2009	98 (1.4)	91
2010	97 (1.9)	89

Source: Calculated for CBC House Democrats by author and as reported in *CQ Almanac,* various years, for House Democrats.

Note: n/a = not applicable.

TABLE B4. Average *CQ Almanac* Presidential Support Scores for CBC House Democrats and House Democrats, 1977–2010 (std. deviations in parentheses)

	CBC House Democrats	House Democrats	Gap
1977	66 (8.7)	62	4
1978	65 (12.2)	62	3
1979	70 (12.8)	64	6
1980	62 (4.6)	61	1
1981	28 (5.8)	42	−14
1982	23 (5.9)	36	−13
1983	11 (4.1)	28	−17
1984	20 (3.6)	34	−14
1985	15.5 (2.1)	30	−14.5
1986	13 (2.6)	25	−12
1987	12 (2.9)	24	−12
1988	15 (2.8)	25	−10
1989	25 (5.2)	36	−11
1990	n/a	25	n/a
1991	24 (2.8)	34	−10
1992	11 (2.8)	25	−14
1993	78 (7.9)	77	1
1994	72 (12.0)	75	0
1995	80 (9.3)	75	1
1996	77 (6.8)	74	1
1997	74 (5.8)	71	2
1998	79 (6.4)	74	5
1999	83 (4.8)	73	10
2000	83.5 (7.6)	73	10.5
2001	22 (9.3)	31	−9
2002	26 (7.6)	32	−6
2003	20 (8.6)	26	−6
2004	26 (11.2)	30	−4
2005	20.5 (9.9)	24	−3.5
2006	28 (13.4)	31	−3
2007	5 (2.6)	7	−2
2008	15 (3.9)	16	−1
2009	96 (2.4)	90	6
2010	86 (5.3)	84	2

Source: Calculated for CBC House Democrats by author and as reported in *CQ Almanac,* various years, for House Democrats.

Note: n/a = not applicable.

TABLE B5. Average Legislative Effectiveness Scores for the CBC (Democrats only), House Democrats, House Republicans, and Other Caucuses, 1977–2010

	CBC	House Democrats	House Republicans	Blue Dogs Caucus	Progressive Caucus	Hispanic Caucus
1977	0.63	0.51	0.47			
1978	0.55	0.57	0.46			
1979	0.61	0.64	0.55			
1980	0.42	0.57	0.73			
1981	0.44	0.56	0.67			
1982	0.77	0.67	0.45			
1983	0.60	0.62	0.46			
1984	0.55	0.6	0.49			
1985	0.55	0.52	0.62			
1986	0.56	0.64	0.54			
1987	0.78	0.77	0.34			
1988	0.65	0.73	0.52			
1989	0.57	0.66	0.62			
1990	0.78	0.71	0.42			
1991	0.56	0.63	0.6			
1992	0.75	0.7	0.54			
1993	0.71	0.7	0.37			
1994	0.69	0.65	0.54			
1995	0.34	0.41	0.8			
1996	0.56	0.63	0.75			0.61
1997	0.46	0.54	0.7			0.55
1998	0.55	0.61	0.69			0.57
1999	0.52	0.55	0.68			0.56
2000	0.70	0.73	0.74			
2001	0.32	0.39	0.78			0.45
2002	0.37	0.41	0.75			0.45
2003	0.31	0.36	0.8			0.39
2004	0.67	0.73	0.61			0.67
2005	0.57	0.56	0.72			0.55
2006	0.27	0.3	0.87			
2007	0.78	0.71	0.49	0.73	0.69	
2008	0.89	0.88	0.48	0.86	0.87	
2009	0.9	0.86	0.23			
2010	0.72	0.77	0.36			

Source: Average legislative effectiveness scores were based on the percentage of time that caucus members voted with the majority on the *CQ Almanac* (various years) list of "key votes" bills. These scores for caucuses were calculated by the author. House party scores were calculated using aggregate reported votes by parties on key bills as reported in *CQ Almanac.*

Notes

Chapter 1

1. The Poole-Rosenthal or NOMINATE measures have won almost universal acceptance in congressional studies. Lee (2009) is a critic of the NOMINATE methodology, contending that it measures not ideology but "team party cooperation." The NOMINATE methodology includes the universe of all bills, but Lee points out that some bills are nonideological, reflecting a spoils system rather than intrinsic policy preferences. She advocates classifying bills by ideological content, which she did for about 40 percent of all roll-call votes from 1981 to 2004. Her data are limited to the U.S. Senate. I agree that additional coding work needs to be done to support my broad claims. Yet even if NOMINATE scores measure only "team support," it seems clear that Black Democratic House members have moved closer to their team. This shift, I contend, is rooted in their political incorporation. Furthermore, my analysis in chapter 7 introduces party unity measures, which are not identical to the NOMINATE scores but also predict, as expected, more liberal scores.

2. In appendix B, I report the average scores of the second dimension for Black House Democrats from 1977 to 2010. The gap for average second dimension scores between CBC members and the House Democrats is very small relative to the gap for the first dimension. After the 1980s, these second dimension scores no longer meaningfully predict the voting behavior of members; therefore, I chose not to analyze the second dimension scores of Black Democrats in the House.

Chapter 2

1. Quoted in Trescott 1977a.

2. See the October 5, 2011, publication on TED for these data, http://www.bls.gov/opub/ted/2011/ted_20111005_data.htm.

Chapter 5

1. "Can Bush Mend His Party's Rift with Black America?" *New York Times,* December 17, 2000, section 4, 17.

Chapter 7

1. In the case of autocorrelation, all the key or statistically significant findings are most likely wrong (see King 2001). To test for autocorrelation, dummy variables for all the years as "fixed effects" were constructed and included to see whether results emerging from the multivariate analysis were different from the first model.

Afterword

1. The 116th Congress shows two scores, as two members' scores were dropped from the calculations which would have lowered the CBC's average score to –0.44. Because these two CBC members (out of four women of color, known as the "Squad") refused to vote for emergency immigration funds and voted along with the Republicans (Lewis 2019), this lowered the CBC score for the 116th Congress. Removed, the average score is –0.46. All four Squad members are members of the Progressive Caucus.

2. In addition to John Lewis, the other members of the Silent Generation are Jim Clyburn, Bonnie Watson Coleman, Maxine Waters, Eleanor Holmes Norton, Alcee Hastings, Eddie Bernice Johnson, Danny K. Davis, David Scott, Emanual Cleaver, and Frederica Wilson. Birth dates were collected from bioguide.congress.gov

3. The millennials include Underwood born 1986, Omar born 1982, Neguse born 1984, and Allred born 1983.

References

Abramson, Paul R., John H. Aldrich, and David W. Rohde. 1982. *Change and Continuity in the 1980 Elections.* Washington, DC: Congressional Quarterly Press.

Aldrich, John H. 2011. *Why Parties? A Second Look.* Chicago: University of Chicago Press.

Alpern, David M., Elaine Shannon, and James Doyle. 1977. "All Hands on Board Ship." *Newsweek*, January 3, 57.

Ayres, B. Drummond, Jr. 1992. "The 1992 Campaign: Democrats, Buoyed Clinton Goes on the Offensive." *New York Times*, July 1, A15.

Barker, Lucius J., Mack H. Jones, and Katherine Tate. 1999. *African Americans and the American Political System.* 4th ed. Upper Saddle River, NJ: Prentice Hall.

Barreto, Matt A. 2010. *Ethnic Cues: The Role of Shared Ethnicity in Latino Political Participation.* Ann Arbor: University of Michigan Press.

Barreto, Matt A., Gary M. Segura, and Nathan D. Woods. 2004. "The Mobilizing Effect of Majority-Minority Districts on Latino Turnout." *American Political Science Review* 98 (1): 65–75.

Beckmann, Matthew N. 2010. *Pushing the Agenda: Presidential Leadership in U.S. Lawmaking, 1953–2004.* New York: Cambridge University Press.

Bell, Derrick. 2007. *Silent Covenants: Brown v. Board of Education and the Unfulfilled Hopes for Racial Reform.* New York: Oxford University Press.

Berke, Richard L. 1991. "Black Caucus Votes to Oppose Thomas for High Court Seat." *New York Times*, July 12, A1.

Bieze, Michael Scott, and Marybeth Gasman, eds. 2012. *Booker T. Washington Rediscovered.* Baltimore: Johns Hopkins University Press.

Binder, Sarah A. 2003. *Stalemate: Causes and Consequences of Legislative Gridlock.* Washington, DC: Brookings Institution Press.

Bobo, Lawrence. 1983. "Whites' Opposition to Busing: Symbolic Racism or Realistic Group Conflict?" *Journal of Personality and Social Psychology* 45 (6): 1196–1210.

Bobo, Lawrence, and Franklin D. Gilliam Jr. 1990. "Race, Sociopolitical Participation, and Black Empowerment." *American Political Science Review* 84 (2): 377–93.

Bowler, Shaun, and Gary M. Segura. 2012. *The Future Is Ours: Minority Politics, Political Behavior, and the Multiracial Era of American Politics.* Thousand Oaks, CA: CQ Press/Sage.

Brady, David W., and Craig Volden. 2006. *Evolving Gridlock: Politics and Policy from Jimmy Carter to George W. Bush.* 2nd ed. Boulder: Westview Press.

Brown, Warren. 1979. "Black Caucus Critical of Carter, Wary of Kennedy." *Washington Post,* September 22, A7.

Browning, Rufus P., Dale Rogers Marshall, and David H. Tabb. 1984. *Protest Is Not Enough: The Struggle of Blacks and Hispanics for Equality in Urban Politics.* Berkeley: University of California Press.

Brunell, Thomas L., Bernard Grofman, and Samuel Merrill III. 2010. "Replacement Effects and the Slow Cycle of Ideological Polarization in the U.S. House, 1856–2006." Paper presented at the Annual Meeting of the Public Choice Society, Monterey, CA, March 8–12.

Bruno, Hal. 1977. "Democrats in Distress." *Newsweek,* December 19.

Canon, David T. 1995. "Redistricting and the Congressional Black Caucus." *American Politics Quarterly* 23 (2): 149–89.

Canon, David T. 1999. *Race, Redistricting, and Representation.* Chicago: University of Chicago Press.

Casellas, Jason. 2011. *Latino Representation in State Houses and Congress.* New York: Cambridge University Press.

Champagne, Richard, and Leroy N. Rieselbach. 1995. "The Evolving Congressional Black Caucus: The Reagan-Bush Years." In *Blacks and the American Political System,* ed. Huey L. Perry and Wayne Parent. Gainesville: University of Florida Press.

Christopher, Maurine. 1971. *Black Americans in Congress.* New York: Thomas Y. Crowell.

Clay, William L. 1992. *Just Permanent Interests: Black Americans in Congress, 1870–1991.* New York: Amistad Press.

Clymer, Adam. 1993. "Black Caucus Threatens Revolt on Clinton Budget." *New York Times,* June 10, A22.

Cohen, Cathy J. 2010. *Democracy Remixed.* New York: Oxford University Press.

Cox, Gary W., and Mathew D. McCubbins. 2007. *Legislative Leviathan: Party Government in the House.* 2nd ed. New York: Cambridge University Press.

Davidson, Chandler, and Bernard Grofman, eds. 1994. *Quiet Revolution in the South: The Impact of the Voting Rights Act, 1965–1990.* Princeton: Princeton University Press.

Dawson, Michael C. 1994. *Behind the Mule: Race and Class in African-American Politics.* Princeton: Princeton University Press.

Dawson, Michael C. 2001. *Black Visions: The Roots of Contemporary African-American Political Ideologies.* Chicago: University of Chicago Press.

Dawson, Michael C. 2011. *Not in Our Lifetimes: The Future of Black Politics.* Chicago: University of Chicago Press.

DeBose, Brian. 2005. "Black Caucus Shows Constituent Changes." *Washington Times,* May 6, A1.

Dellums, Ronald V., and H. Lee Halterman. 2000. *Lying Down with the Lions: A Public Life from the Streets of Oakland to the Halls of Power.* Boston: Beacon Press.

DeVries, Hilary. 1981. "Black Caucus Raps Foreign Policy." *Christian Science Monitor,* March 27, 2.

Devroy, Ann. 1989. "Hill Caucus Nudges Bush on Black Policy Agenda." *Washington Post,* May 24, A6.

Economist. 1978. "Congress: Marco Polo's Homecoming." April 1, 78.

Eisinger, Peter K. 1982. "Black Empowerment in Municipal Jobs: The Impact of Black Political Power." *American Political Science Review* 76:380–92.

Evans, Ben. 2009. "Black Caucus Presses Obama." *New York Newsday,* December 11, A42.

Fiorina, Morris P. 1992. "An Era of Divided Government." *Political Science Quarterly* 107 (3): 387–410.

Fleisher, Richard, and Jon R. Bond. 2000. "Partisanship and the President's Quest for Votes." In *Polarized Politics: Congress and the President in a Partisan Era,* ed. Jon R. Bond and Richard Fleisher. Washington, DC: CQ Press.

Foerstel, Karen. 2008. "Crisis in Darfur: Is There Any Hope for Peace?" *CQ Global Researcher* 2 (9).

Ford, Harold, Jr. 2010. *More Davids Than Goliaths: A Political Education.* New York: Crown.

Frymer, Paul. 1999. *Uneasy Alliances: Race and Party Competition in America.* Princeton: Princeton University Press.

Gamble, Katrina L. 2007. "Black Political Representation: An Examination of Legislative Activity within U.S. House Committees." *Legislative Studies Quarterly* 32 (3): 421–47.

Garcia Bedolla, Lisa, Katherine Tate, and Janelle Wong. 2005. "Indelible Effects: The Impact of Women of Color in the U.S. Congress." In *Women and Elective Office: Past, Present, and Future,* ed. Sue Thomas and Clyde Wilcox. 2nd ed. New York: Oxford University Press.

Garrett, Major. 1991. "House Shows Support of War Effort in Gulf." *Washington Times,* January 19, A4.

Garrett, Major. 1993. "Left-Right Standoff Snags Clinton Economic Program." *Washington Times,* March 18, A5.

Gay, Claudine. 2002. "Spirals of Trust? The Effect of Descriptive Representation on the Relationship between Citizens and Their Government." *American Journal of Political Science* 46 (4): 717–32.

Gillespie, Andra, ed. 2010. *Whose Black Politics? Cases in Post-Racial Black Leadership.* New York: Routledge.

Goshko, John M. 1993. "Administration Aides Defend Haiti Policy: Gradual, Step-by-Step Approach Described As Best Chance for Restoring Democracy." *Washington Post,* May 21, A30.

Gray, Kevin Alexander. 2008. *Waiting for Lightning to Strike: The Fundamentals of Black Politics.* Oakland, CA: Counterpunch and AK Press.

Griffin, John D., and Brian Newman. 2008. *Minority Report: Evaluating Political Equality in America.* Chicago: University of Chicago Press.

Grose, Christian. 2011. *Congress in Black and White: Race and Representation in Washington and at Home.* New York: Cambridge University Press.

Guinier, Lani. 1994. *Tyranny of the Majority.* New York: Free Press.

Guinier, Lani, and Gerald Torres. 2012. "Don't Go It Alone." *Boston Review,* January/February. http://www.bostonreview.net/BR37.1/ndf_lani_guinier_gerald_torres_black_politics.php.

Gurin, Patricia, Shirley Hatchett, and James S. Jackson. 1989. *Hope and Independence: Blacks' Response to Electoral and Party Politics.* New York: Russell Sage Foundation.

Hacker, Jacob. 2010. "The Road to Somewhere: Why Health Reform Happened." *Perspective on Politics* 8 (3): 861–76.

Hajnal, Zoltan. 2007. *Changing White Attitudes toward Black Political Leadership.* New York: Cambridge University Press.

Hallow, Ralph Z. 1994. "Clinton Offers Deal on 'Racial Justice': Seeks Black Votes for Crime Measure." *Washington Times,* July 27, A1.

Hamilton, Charles V. 1991. *Adam Clayton Powell, Jr.: The Political Biography of an American Dilemma.* New York: Atheneum.

Hammond, Susan Webb. 1998. *Congressional Caucuses in National Policy Making.* Baltimore: Johns Hopkins University Press.

Harlan, Louis R., ed. 1974. *The Booker T. Washington Papers.* Vol. 3. Urbana: University of Illinois Press.

Harris, Fredrick C. 2012. *The Price of the Ticket: Barack Obama and the Rise and Decline of Black Politics.* New York: Oxford University Press.

Harris, Fredrick C., Valeria Sinclair-Chapman, and Brian D. McKenzie. 2006. *Countervailing Forces in African-American Civic Activism, 1973–1994.* New York: Cambridge University Press.

Hawkeworth, Mary. 2003. "Congressional Enactments of Race-Gender: Toward a Theory of Raced-Gendered Institutions." *American Political Science Review* 97 (4): 529–50.

Haynie, Kerry. 2001. *African American Legislators in the American States.* New York: Columbia University Press.

Haynie, Kerry. 2005. "African Americans and the New Politics of Inclusion: A Representational Dilemma?" In *Congress Reconsidered,* ed. Lawrence C. Dodd and Bruce I. Oppenheimer. 8th ed. Washington, DC: CQ Press.

Hedges, Michael. 1994. "Black Caucus Members Rip President's Crime Proposals." *Washington Times,* February 23, A3.

Heflin, Jay. 2010. "DNC Chairman Laments Rangel Stealing Spotlight from State-Aid Bill." *The Hill,* www.thehill.com, August 11.

Hero, Rodney. 1992. *Latinos and the U.S. Political System: Two-Tiered Pluralism.* Philadelphia: Temple University Press.

Holmes, Steven A. 1993. "Administration Seeks Ways to Ease Africa's Wars and Debt Burden." *New York Times,* May 18, A9.

Hood, M. V., Quentin Kidd, and Irwin L. Morris. 1999. "Byrd[s] and Bumpers: Using Democratic Senators to Analyze Political Change in the South, 1960–1995." *American Journal of Political Science* 43 (2): 465–87.

Hood, M. V., Quentin Kidd, and Irwin L. Morris. 2001. "The Key Issue: Constituency Effects and Southern Senators' Roll-Call Voting on Civil Rights." *Legislative Studies Quarterly* 26 (4): 599–621.

Hornblower, Margot. 1980. "Haitians Facing Eviction; Quick Asylum Is Sought for Haitian Refugees." *Washington Post,* May 8, A1.

Huckfeldt, R. Robert, and Carol Weitzel Kohfeld. 1989. *Race and the Decline of Class in American Politics.* Urbana: University of Illinois Press.

Hurt, Charles. 2003. "Powell Sees 'Limited' Role in Liberia: Black Caucus Urges Bush to Send Troops." *Washington Times,* July 11, A1.

Ifill, Gwen. 1994. "President Names Black Democrat Adviser on Haiti." *New York Times,* May 9, A1.

Ifill, Gwen. 2009. *The Breakthrough: Politics and Race in the Age of Obama*. New York: Doubleday.

Jacobson, Gary C. 2007. *A Divider, Not a Uniter: George W. Bush and the American People*. New York: Pearson Longman.

Karnig, Albert K., and Susan Welch. 1980. *Black Representation and Urban Policy*. Chicago: University of Chicago Press.

Katznelson, Ira. 2005. *When Affirmative Action Was White: An Untold History of Racial Inequality in Twentieth Century America*. New York: W. W. Norton.

Kinder, Donald R., and Lynn M. Sanders. 1990. "Mimicking Political Debate with Survey Questions: The Case of White Opinion on Affirmative Action for Blacks." *Social Cognition* 8:73–103.

Kinder, Donald R., and Lynn M. Sanders. 1996. *Divided by Color: Racial Politics and Democratic Ideals*. Chicago: University of Chicago Press.

King, Desmond S., and Rogers M. Smith. 2011. *Still a House Divided: Race and Politics in Obama's America*. Princeton: Princeton University Press.

King, Gary. 2001. "Proper Nouns and Methodological Propriety: Pooling Dyads in International Relations Data." *International Organization* 55:497–501.

Knowles, Louis L., and Kenneth Prewitt, Eds. 1970. *Institutional Racism in America*. Englewood Cliffs, NJ: Prentice-Hall.

Lake, Eli. 2009. "Two Obama Aides Clash over Policy for Sudan; Envoy Reluctant to Take Hard Line." *Washington Times*, July 31, A1.

Lanoue, David J. 1989. "The 'Teflon Factor': Ronald Reagan and Comparative Presidential Popularity." *Polity* 21 (3): 481–501.

Lebo, Matthew, Adam J. McGlynn, and Gregory Koger. 2007. "Strategic Party Government: Party Influence in Congress, 1789–2000." *American Journal of Political Science* 51 (3): 464–81.

Lee, Frances E. 2009. *Beyond Ideology: Politics, Principles, and Partisanship in the U.S. Senate*. Chicago: University of Chicago Press.

Lee, Frances E., and Bruce Oppenheimer. 1999. *Sizing Up the Senate: The Unequal Consequences of Equal Representation*. Chicago: University of Chicago Press.

Lee, Jennifer. 1993. "Senate Newcomer Gets Last Laugh." *USA Today*, August 6, 6A.

Leighley, Jan. 2001. *Strength in Numbers? The Political Mobilization of Racial and Ethnic Minorities*. Princeton: Princeton University Press.

Lewis, Jeff. 2019. "Why Are Ocasio-Cortez, Omar, Pressley and Tlaib Estimated to Be Moderates by NOMINATE?" Blog post, Voteview.com. August 5.

Lewis, Neil A. 1993. "Clinton Abandons His Nominee for Rights Post amid Opposition." *New York Times*, June 4, A1.

Lorber, Janie. 2009. "Black Caucus Studies Racial Makeup of House Committee Staffs." *New York Times*, July 9.

Lowry, William R., and Charles R. Shipan. 2002. "Party Differentiation in Congress." *Legislative Studies Quarterly* 27 (1): 33–60.

Lublin, David, Thomas L. Brunell, Bernard Grofman, and Lisa Handley. 2009. "Has the Voting Rights Act Outlived Its Usefulness? In a Word, 'No.'" *Legislative Studies Quarterly* 34 (4): 525–53.

Mann, Thomas E., and Norman J. Ornstein. 2012. *It's Even Worse Than It Looks: How the American Constitutional System Collided with the New Politics of Extremism*. New York: Basic Books.

Manning, Jennifer E. 2019. "Membership of the 116th Congress: A Profile." Congressional Research Service, November 4, R45583. https://crsreports.congress.gov/product/pdf/R/R45583

Marable, Manning. 1991. *Race, Reform, and Rebellion: The Second Reconstruction in Black America, 1945–1990.* Jackson: University Press of Mississippi.

Marschall, Melissa J., and Anirudh V. S. Ruhil. 2007. "Substantive Symbols: The Attitudinal Dimension of Black Political Incorporation in Local Government." *American Journal of Political Science* 51 (1): 17–33.

Mayhew, David. 1966. *Party Loyalty among Congressmen: The Difference between Democrats and Republicans, 1947–1962.* Cambridge, MA: Harvard University Press.

Mayhew, David R. 1991. *Divided We Govern: Party Control, Lawmaking, and Investigations, 1946–1990.* New Haven: Yale University Press.

Mayhew, David R. 2000. *America's Congress: Actions in the Public Sphere, James Madison through Newt Gingrich.* New Haven: Yale University Press.

McBee, Susanna. 1977. "House Censures 'Repressive' South African Tactics." *Washington Post*, November 1, A13.

McCarty, Nolan M., Keith T. Poole, and Howard Rosenthal. 2006. *Polarized America: The Dance of Ideology and Unequal Riches.* Boston: MIT Press.

McCarty, Nolan, Keith T. Poole, and Howard Rosenthal. 2009. "Does Gerrymandering Cause Polarization?" *American Journal of Political Science* 53 (3): 666–80.

McClain, Paula D., and Joseph Stewart Jr. 2010. *Can We All Get Along: Racial and Ethnic Minorities in American Politics.* Boulder: Westview Press.

McIlwain, Charlton D., and Stephen M. Caliendo. 2011. *Race Appeal: How Candidates Invoke Race in U.S. Political Campaigns.* Philadelphia: Temple University Press.

Meier, Kenneth J., Eric Gonzalez Juenke, Robert Wrinkle, and J. L. Polinard. 2005. "Structural Choices and Representational Biases: The Post-Election Color of Representation." *American Journal of Political Science* 49 (4): 758–68.

Meier, Kenneth J., and Joseph Stewart Jr. 1991. *The Politics of Hispanic Education.* Albany: State University of New York Press.

Mendelberg, Tali. 2001. *The Race Card, Campaign Strategy, Implicit Messages, and the Norm of Equality.* Princeton: Princeton University Press.

Michels, Robert. 1999. *Political Parties: A Sociological Study of the Oligarchical Tendencies of Modern Democracy.* Introduction by Seymour Martin Lipset, translated by Eden and Cedar Paul. New Brunswick, NJ: Transaction Publishers.

Miler, Kristina C. 2011. "The Constituency Motivations of Caucus Membership." *American Politics Research*, online publication, June 28.

Miller, Lisa Lynn. 2008. *The Perils of Federalism: Race, Poverty, and the Politics of Crime Control.* New York: Oxford University Press.

Minta, Michael D. 2009. "Legislative Oversight and the Substantive Representation of Black and Latino Interests in Congress." *Legislative Studies Quarterly* 34 (2): 193–218.

Minta, Michael D. 2011. *Oversight: Representing the Interests of Blacks and Latinos in Congress.* Princeton: Princeton University Press.

Moss, J. Jennings. 1993. "Franks to Remain in Black Caucus." *Washington Times*, June 15, A4.

Murray, Shailagh. 2007. "Black Leaders Torn over Endorsement: For Many, the Focus Is Electability." *Washington Post*, December 1, A6.

Naughtie, James. 1981. "Black Caucus Calls Veto on S. Africa 'All-Time Low.'" *Washington Post*, September 2, A20.

Newmyer, Tory. 2009. "CBC Outlines Wish List for Jobs Package." *Roll Call*, December 11.

New York Times. 1981. "Black Legislators Urge Dismissal of Mrs. Kirkpatrick." March 27, A8.

New York Times. 1993. "Stop Flogging Franks." Editorial, June 20, E16.

Norrander, Barbara, and Tiffany Harper. 2010. "The Rise and Fall of George W. Bush: Popular Support for the President." *Understanding Public Opinion*, 3rd ed., ed. Barbara Norrander and Clyde Wilcox. Washington, DC: CQ Press.

Ochs, Holona Leanne. 2011. "The Politics of Inclusion: Black Political Incorporation and the Use of Lethal Force." *Journal of Ethnicity in Criminal Justice* 9 (3): 238–65.

Parker, Frank R. 1990. *Black Votes Count: Political Empowerment in Mississippi after 1965*. Chapel Hill: University of North Carolina Press.

Perlez, Jane. 2001. "After the Attacks: The Overview; U.S. Demands Arab Countries 'Choose Sides.'" *New York Times*, September 15, A1.

Peterson, Bill. 1977. "Proposed Justice Dept. Brief Draws Fire of Rights Groups." *Washington Post*, September 9, A2.

Peterson, Paul. 1981. *City Limits*. Chicago: University of Chicago Press.

Pew Research Center. 2018. "The Generation Gap in American Politics." March 1. https://www.people-press.org/2018/03/01/the-generation-gap-in-american-politics/

Pianin, Eric. 1987. "Black Caucus Members Face Dilemma of Hill Loyalties: Tensions Grow as Group Comes of Age." *Washington Post*, September 23, A1.

Pine, Art, and Jane Seaberry. 1979. "Set-Aside Restored by Carter: White House Gives In on Minority Trade Plan." *Washington Post*, March 23, F1.

Poole, Keith T., and Howard Rosenthal. 2007. *Ideology and Congress*. New Brunswick, NJ: Transaction Publishers.

Preuhs, Robert R. 2006. "The Conditional Effects of Minority Descriptive Representation: Black Legislators and Policy Influence in the American States." *Journal of Politics* 68 (3): 585–99.

Preuhs, Robert R. 2007. "Descriptive Representation as a Mechanism to Mitigate Policy Backlash: Latino Incorporation and Welfare Policy in the American States." *Political Research Quarterly* 60 (2): 277–92.

Puga, Ana. 1993. "Black Caucus Fights to Oust Republican." *Boston Globe*, August 1, 17.

Rangel, Charles B., and Leon E. Wynter. 2007. *And I Haven't Had a Bad Day Since: From the Streets of Harlem to the Halls of Congress*. New York: Thomas Dunne Books/St. Martin's Press.

Reed, Adolph Jr. 1986. *The Jesse Jackson Phenomenon: The Crisis of Purpose in Afro-American Politics*. New Haven: Yale University Press.

Remnick, David. 1985. "Randall Robinson, from Boyhood Pain to a Crusade against Apartheid." *Washington Post*, February 5, E1.

Rich, Wilbur C. 2007. "Presidential Leadership and the Politics of Race: Stereotypes, Symbols, and Scholarship." In *African American Perspectives on Political Science*, ed. Wilbur C. Rich. Philadelphia: Temple University Press.

Rocca, Michael S., Garbiel R. Sanchez, and Ron Nikora. 2009. "The Role of Personal Attributes in African American Roll-Call Voting Behavior in Congress." *Political Research Quarterly* 62 (2): 408–14.

Rohde, David W. 1991. *Parties and Leaders in the Postreform House*. Chicago: University of Chicago Press.

Rule, Sheila. 1980. "Blacks, Reacting to Vote, Seek Way to Keep Gains." *New York Times*, November 8, A8.

Russell, Mary. 1979. "Budget Resolution Heads for Fracas on the House Floor." *Washington Post*, April 29, A6.

Russell, Mary, and Robert G. Kaiser. 1978. "Move to Impeach Young Killed: House Tables Move to Impeach U.N. Envoy Young." *Washington Post*, July 14, A1.

Safford, John L. 1995. "John C. Calhoun, Lani Guinier, and Minority Rights." *PS: Political Science and Politics* 28 (2): 211–16.

Sammon, Bill. 2003. "In Senegal, Bush Denounces Legacy of Slavery: President Says U.S. Problems Have Roots in 'One of the Greatest Crimes.'" *Washington Times*, July 9, A16.

Sapiro, Virginia, and Shauna L. Shames. 2010. "The Gender Basis of Public Opinion." In *Understanding Public Opinion*, ed. Barbara Norrander and Clyde Wilcox. 3rd ed. Washington, DC: CQ Press.

Schickler, Eric. 2001. *Disjointed Pluralism: Institutional Innovation and the Development of the U.S. Congress*. Princeton: Princeton University Press.

Schuman, Howard, Charlotte Steeh, and Lawrence Bobo. 1985. *Racial Attitudes in America: Trends and Interpretations*. Cambridge: Harvard University Press.

Seelye, Katharine Q. 2009. "Conyers Derides White House Strategy on Health Care." *New York Times*, November 11. http://prescriptions.blog.nytimes.com.

Seper, Jerry. 1993. "Guinier Laments Her Withdrawal: Blacks, Women Blast Clinton." *Washington Times*, June 5, A1.

Shefter, Martin. 1994. *Political Parties and the State: The American Historical Experience*. Princeton: Princeton University Press.

Shepsle, Kenneth, and Barry Weingast. 1995. "Positive Theories of Congressional Institutions." In *Positive Theories of Congressional Institutions*, ed. Kenneth Shepsle and Barry Weingast. Ann Arbor: University of Michigan Press.

Shingles, Richard D. 1981. "Black Consciousness and Political Participation: The Missing Link." *American Political Science Review* 75 (1): 76–91.

Sigelman, Lee, and Susan Welch. 1991. *Black Americans' Views of Racial Inequality: The Dream Deferred*. New York: Cambridge University Press.

Simien, Evelyn M. 2006. *Black Feminist Voices in Politics*. Albany: State University of New York Press.

Sinclair, Barbara. 1983. *Majority Leadership in the U.S. House*. Baltimore: Johns Hopkins University Press.

Sinclair, Barbara. 2006. *Party Wars: Polarization and the Politics of National Policy Making*. Norman: University of Oklahoma Press.

Singh, Robert. 1998. *The Congressional Black Caucus: Racial Politics in the U.S. Congress*. Thousand Oaks, CA: Sage Publications.

Smith, Robert C. 1995. *Racism in the Post–Civil Rights Era: Now You See It, Now You Don't*. Albany: State University of New York Press.

Smith, Robert C. 1996. *We Have No Leaders: African-Americans in the Post–Civil Rights Era*. Albany: State University of New York Press.

Smith, Robert C. 2009. "System Values and African American Leadership." In *Barack Obama and African American Empowerment*, ed. Manning Marable and Kristen Clarke. New York: Palgrave MacMillan.

Smith, Steven S. 2007. *Party Influence in Congress*. New York: Cambridge University Press.

Steinhauer, Jennifer. 2010. "The 2010 Elections: Black and Republican and Back in Congress 2 House Members Will Be the First Since '03." *New York Times*, November 6, A14.

Steinhauer, Jennifer. 2011. "Taking Issue with Criticism." *New York Times*, September 1, A18.

Stephens, David. 1983–84. "President Carter, the Congress, and NEA: Creating the Department of Education." *Political Science Quarterly* 98 (4): 641–63.

Sullivan, Jas M., and Jonathan Winbun. 2011. *The Louisiana Legislative Black Caucus: Race and Representation in the Pelican State*. Baton Rouge: Louisiana State University Press.

Tate, Katherine. 1994. *From Protest to Politics: The New Black Voters in American Elections*. Cambridge, MA: Harvard University Press and the Russell Sage Foundation.

Tate, Katherine. 2003. *Black Faces in the Mirror: African Americans and Their Representatives in the U.S. Congress*. Princeton: Princeton University Press.

Tate, Katherine. 2004. "Political Incorporation and Critical Transformations of Black Public Opinion." *Du Bois Review: Social Science Research on Race* 1 (2): 345–59.

Tate, Katherine. 2010. *What's Going On? Political Incorporation and the Transformation of Black Public Opinion*. Washington, DC: Georgetown University Press.

Tate, Katherine, Kevin L. Lyles, and Lucius J. Barker. 2007. "A Critical Review of American Political Institutions: Reading Race into the Constitutional 'Silence' on Race." In *African American Perspectives on Political Science*, ed. Wilbur C. Rich. Philadelphia: Temple University Press.

Taylor, Ronald A. 1994a. "Hill Caucus Leader Gives Clinton a C on Black Issues." *Washington Times*, September 15, A4.

Taylor, Ronald A. 1994b. "Black Caucus Split on Haiti." *Washington Times*, September 16, A17.

Tesler, Michael, and David O. Sears. 2010. *Obama's Race: The 2008 Election and the Dream of a Post-Racial America*. Chicago: University of Chicago Press.

Thernstrom, Abigail M. 1987. *Whose Votes Count? Affirmative Action and Minority Voting Rights*. Cambridge, MA: Harvard University Press.

Thompson, Krissah. 2009a. "The Ties that Align: Administration's Black Women Form a Strong Sisterhood." *Washington Post*, March 18, C1.

Thompson, Krissah. 2009b. "For the New Black Caucus, New Power and an Urgency in Using It." *Washington Post*, September 26, A9.

Tillery, Alvin B. 2011. *Between Homeland and Motherland: Africa, U.S. Foreign Policy, and Black Leadership in America*. Ithaca: Cornell University Press.

Tolchin, Martin. 1983. "Congress: For Blacks, Racism and Progress Mix." *New York Times*, March 11, A20.

Trescott, Jacqueline. 1977a. "The Caucus and the Comic: The Congressional Black Caucus and the Comic." *Washington Post*, September 26, B1.

Trescott, Jacqueline. 1977b. "'One of God's Angry Men'; He's Parren Mitchell, Black Caucus Chief." *Washington Post*, September 23, C1.

Trescott, Jacqueline. 1979a. "The Survival of Andrew Young: Thirty Months on a Tightrope." *Washington Post*, August 8, E1.

Trescott, Jacqueline. 1979b. "The Coming Out of Cardiss Collins." *Washington Post*, September 21, C1.

Tucker, Cynthia. 2011. "Voting Rights Act: I Was Wrong about Racial Gerrymandering." *Atlanta Journal-Constitution*, June 1. http://blogs.ajc.com.

Valelly, Richard. 2004. *The Two Reconstructions.* Chicago: University of Chicago Press.

Verba, Sidney, and Norman H. Nie. 1972. *Participation in America: Political Democracy and Social Equality.* New York: Harper & Row.

Walsh, Edward. 1979. "Black Caucus Warns of Fight for Funds." *Washington Post*, March 1, A9.

Walsh, Edward. 1980. "Miami Blacks Boo, Throw Bottles at Carter Motorcade." *Washington Post*, June 10, A1.

Walsh, Edward, and Mary Russell. 1978. "Humphrey-Hawkins Provokes Confrontation; Rep. Conyers Angered by White House in Humphrey-Hawkins Bill Dispute; Conyers Stalks Out of White House Meeting." *Washington Post*, September 27, A1.

Walters, Ronald. 1988. *Black Presidential Politics in America: A Strategic Approach.* Albany: State University of New York Press.

Walters, Ronald W. 2003. *White Nationalism, Black Interests: Conservative Public Policy and the Black Community.* Detroit: Wayne State University Press.

Walters, Ronald W. 2008. *The Price of Racial Reconciliation.* Ann Arbor: University of Michigan Press.

Walzer, Michael. 1970. *Obligations: Essays on Disobedience, War, and Citizenship.* Cambridge, MA: Harvard University Press.

Washington Post. 1979. "Group Decries Rhodesia Elections, Urges Sanctions." March 21, A17.

Washington Post. 2007. "Democrats Weigh In on Jena 6." September 20, A4.

Weir, Margaret. 1992. *Politics and Jobs: The Boundaries of Employment Policy in the United States.* Princeton: Princeton University Press.

Welch, William M. 1994. "Ford 'Ready' to Redo Welfare." *USA Today*, January 27, 5A.

Whitby, Kenny J. 1997. *The Color of Representation: Congressional Behavior and Black Interests.* Ann Arbor: University of Michigan Press.

Whitby, Kenny J. 2007. "Dimensions of Representation and the Congressional Black Caucus." In *African American Perspectives on Political Science*, ed. Wilbur C. Rich. Philadelphia: Temple University Press.

Whitby, Kenny J., and Franklin D. Gilliam, Jr. 1991. "A Longitudinal Analysis of Competing Explanations for the Transformation of Southern Congressional Politics." *Journal of Politics* 53:504–18.

Williams, Dennis A., Mary Lord, and Susan Agrest. 1980. "Worry Time for Blacks." *Newsweek*, December 1, 39.

Williams, Linda F. 2003. *The Constraint of Race: Legacies of White Skin Privilege in America.* University Park: Pennsylvania State University Press.

Wills, Garry. 2003. *"Negro President": Jefferson and the Slave Power.* Boston: Houghton Mifflin.

Wilson, William Julius. 1987. *The Truly Disadvantaged: The Inner City, the Underclass, and Public Policy.* Chicago: University of Chicago Press.

Wilson, William Julius. 1996. *When Work Disappears: The World of the New Urban Poor.* New York: Knopf.

Wilson, William Julius. 1999. *The Bridge Over the Racial Divide: Rising Inequality and Coalition Politics.* Berkeley: University of California Press.

Index

Printed and bound by CPI Group (UK) Ltd, Croydon, CR0 4YY

13/04/2025